SHADOW WAR

SHADOW WAR

The Untold Story of Jihad in Kashmir

ARIF JAMAL

MELVILLEHOUSE
BROOKLYN, NEW YORK

To Nadia

and Vali

whose time I stole to write this book

SHADOW WAR

© 2009 Arif Jamal

Melville House Publishing
145 Plymouth Street
Brooklyn, NY 11201

www.mhpbooks.com

ISBN: 978-1-933633-59-6

First Melville House Printing: April 2009

Map courtesy of the UN Department of Peacekeeping Operations, Cartographic Section: Map No. 3953 Rev. 3, October 2005.

Book design: Kelly Blair

Library of Congress Control Number: 2009925116

TABLE OF CONTENTS

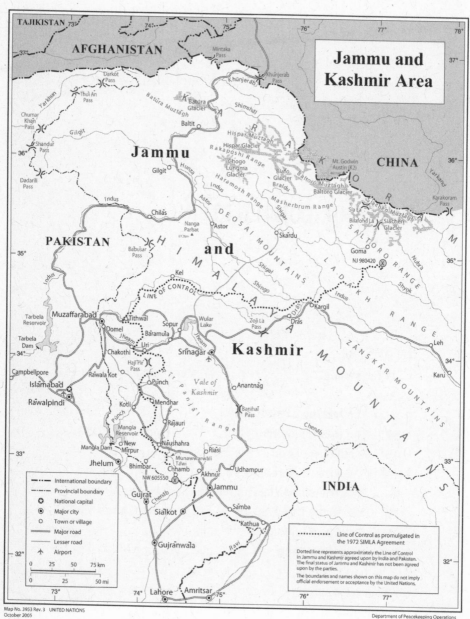

Jammu and Kashmir Area

TAJIKISTAN

AFGHANISTAN

CHINA

PAKISTAN

Jammu

and

Kashmir

INDIA

HIMALAYA MOUNTAINS

KARAKORAM RANGE

LADAKH RANGE

ZANSKAR MOUNTAINS

SALTORO RANGE

Islamabad
Rawalpindi
Muzaffarabad
Srinagar
Gilgit
Skardu
Leh
Jammu
Jhelum
Sialkot
Gujranwala
Lahore
Amritsar

International boundary
Provincial boundary
National capital
Major city
Town or village
Major road
Lesser road
Airport

0   25   50   75 km
0   25   50 mi

Line of Control as promulgated in
the 1972 SIMLA Agreement

Dotted line represents approximately the Line of Control
in Jammu and Kashmir agreed upon by India and Pakistan.
The final status of Jammu and Kashmir has not been agreed
upon by the parties.

The boundaries and names shown on this map do not imply
official endorsement or acceptance by the United Nations.

Map No. 3953 Rev. 3   UNITED NATIONS
October 2005

Department of Peacekeeping Operations
Cartographic Section

PRINCIPAL CHARACTERS

IN KASHMIR

FAROOQ ABDULLAH, chief minister of Jammu and Kashmir, 1982–1984; 1986–1990; 1996–2002.

SHAIKH MOHAMMAD ABDULLAH, the "lion of Kashmir," and arguably the most important political figure in modern Kashmiri history. Early member of the Reading Room Party, the All India Kashmir Muslim Conference, and the Jammu and Kashmir National Conference. Later head of the Emergency Administration, prime minister, and chief minister of Jammu and Kashmir.

ASIYA ANDRABI, leader of Dukhtaran-i-Millat.

MAULANA ABDUL BARI, founding amir of Jamat-i-Islami of Azad Jammu and Kashmir.

HILAL AHMED BEG, the head of Jammu and Kashmir Students Liberation Front, the JKSLF.

MAQBOOL BHAT, an early Kashmiri fighter with the JKLF.

AHSAN DAR, an early militant who founded Hizbul Mujahideen.

ABDUL MAJEED DAR, chief operational commander of Hizbul Mujahideen.

SA'ADUD DIN, the founding amir of the Jamat-i-Islami of Indian-controlled Kashmir.

MIRWAIZ UMAR FAROOQ, a moderate leader of the Hurryyat Conference.

SYED ALI SHAH GEELANI, an important Jamat-i-Islami member and the undisputed secessionist leader in Jammu and Kashmir.

DR. FAROOQ HAIDER, vice president of the JKLF and the NLF.

AMANULLAH KHAN, leader of Plebiscite Front (for Azad Kashmir and Pakistan) and the founder of the JKLF.

ABDUL GHANI LONE, a moderate leader of the Hurryyat Conference.

YASIN MALIK, a JKLF fighter and chief of his own faction of the JKLF.

HILAL AHMED MIR, founder of Ansarul Islam.

HAKEEM GHULAM NABI, appointed amir of Jamat-i-Islami of Indian-controlled Kashmir in 1988; retired in 1995.

GHULAM NABI NOWSHEHRI, vice amir of the Jamat-i-Islami of Indian-controlled Kashmir.

MASOOD SARFRAZ, an early Jamat-i-Islami member and a founder of Hizbul Mujahideen.

YUSUF SHAH, alias Syed Salahuddin, amir and then supreme commander of Hizbul Mujahideen.

HARI SINGH, the last ruling maharaja of the princely state of Jammu and Kashmir.

GHULAB SINGH, acquired the Valley of Kashmir from the British in 1846, adding it to his other territories, which included Ladakh, Jammu, and Gilgit-Baltistan.

ABDUR RASHID TURABIB, amir of the Jamat-i-Islami of Pakistani-controlled Kashmir.

IN PAKISTAN

BENAZIR BHUTTO, prime minister, 1988–1990 and 1993–1996.

ZULFIKAR ALI BHUTTO, foreign minister, 1963–1966; prime minister, 1963–1966; and president, 1971–1973.

ZAFARULLAH KHAN JAMALI, prime minister, 2002–2004.

MOHAMMAD ALI JINNAH, first governor-general of Pakistan, 1947–1948.

COLONEL AKBAR KHAN, later a major general, architect of the 1947 jihad under his nom de guerre of "General Tariq." His plans for jihad in Kashmir are still used by the ISI.

AYUB KHAN, commander in chief of the Pakistan Army, 1951–1958; prime minister October 1958; and president, 1958–1969.

LIAQUAT ALI KHAN, the first prime minister of Pakistan, 1947–1951.

YAHYA KHAN, commander in chief of the Pakistan Army and president, 1969–1971.

PERVEZ MUSHARRAF, chief of the army staff 1998–2007; chief executive 1999–2002; president 2001–2008.

NAWAZ SHARIF, prime minister, November 1980–April 1993; May–June 1993; and February 1997–October 1999.

MOHAMMAD ZIA-UL-HAQ, chief of the army staff, 1976–1988; president 1978–1988.

IN INDIA

JAWAHARLAL NEHRU, the first prime minister of India, 1947–1964.

LAL BAHADUR SHASTRI, prime minister, 1964–1966.

V.P. SINGH, prime minister, 1989–1990.

ATAL BIHARI VAJPAYEE, prime minister of India, May 1996–June 1996; March 1998–May 2004.

PREFACE

On the evening of November 26, 2008, dinghies carrying at least ten men landed in Mumbai, India. The men were carrying large backpacks, each stuffed with dried fruit, grenades, an AK-47 rifle, some 200 rounds of ammunition, and a satellite phone. Four days earlier, the group had departed from the harbor of Karachi, the largest city in Pakistan. Two of them, Mohammad Amir Ajmal Qasab and Ismail Khan, the leader of the group, landed in the Budhwar Park neighborhood of Mumbai. They calmly walked past a crowd of fisherman, but few noticed them—everyone was busy watching a cricket match. There, the men hailed a cab and traveled to central Mumbai, to the VT rail station, where they arrived at approximately 9:20 p.m. Once inside the rail station, they opened fire, aiming precisely but shooting randomly, killing fifty-eight people and injuring more than one hundred.

Qasab and Khan then left the station, in search of hostages and other targets. They entered the Cama and Albless Hospital, but, finding no hostages, quickly left. As they were leaving, they encountered a police car containing three senior police officials. Shots were fired, and Qasab was wounded in the hand. But Khan shot and killed the three officers, and the two took off inside the police car. Sometime later, they were stopped at a police checkpoint. Khan was killed in a shootout that followed, but Indian police apprehended Qasab.

The two were part of a sophisticated series of attacks: Their group had struck eleven targets throughout Mumbai, including the Taj and Oberoi hotels. Members of the group held the hotels hostage for nearly sixty hours, eventually setting them on fire. In all, they killed 183 people, including twenty-two foreigners, in one of the worst terrorist attacks in Indian history.

All the known attackers were killed in the fighting except for Qasab, the captured gunman. He later told Indian interrogators that he and the other fighters in his group were recruited and trained by Lashkar-i-Taiba (Army of the Good), a Pakistani jihadi group that fights in the divided state of Kashmir. The group had recruited Qasab in Rawalpindi and sent him to a Lahore-based Salafi school, the Markaz-al-Dawa wal-Irshad (Center for Call and Instruction). There he was indoctrinated with the group's jihadi message and later sent to a militant training camp in Kashmir. According to Qasab's statement, "We were taken in a vehicle to a place called Mansehra [in the Pakistani North-West Frontier province, where] we were given training of all weapons for twenty-one days.... Handling of hand grenade, rocket launchers and mortars, Uzi gun, pistol [and] revolver." From Mansehra, Qasab was transferred to another training camp just outside Muzaffarabad, the capital of Pakistani-controlled Kashmir. There, according to his statement, he was chosen for the Mumbai mission.

Lashkar-i-Taiba was founded in the early 1990s as an armed wing of the Markaz-al-Dawa wal-Irshad. It is one of many groups that were and perhaps remain directly supported by the ISI, Pakistan's largest and most important intelligence agency, which recruited jihadi groups to infiltrate and destabilize Indian-controlled Kashmir.

The Lashkar-i-Taiba camps where Qasab trained are only one node in a vast network of jihadi military infrastructure that has been developed by the ISI over the last sixty years. The network stretches from Kashmir, to Afghanistan, to Pakistan, and to the rest of world, passing through Nepal and Saudi Arabia. Since they were established in 1980 in the Pakistani tribal areas to train fighters for the Afghan war against the Soviets, jihadi camps have trained half a million militants, nearly 200,000 from Lashkar-i-Taiba. Since the first ISI camps were constructed, the jihad in Kashmir has been privatized and jihadis allowed to establish their own training camps. This infrastructure has spread so much, it seems, that even the ISI has lost track of its scale. (This has been apparent from continuous and repeated attacks on Pakistani defense forces and installations since September 11, 2001.)

The Mumbai terrorist attacks are only one result of this larger infrastructure, although the dramatic and deadly attacks also point to a coming chaos. They show that jihadis once active only in Kashmir are now looking for global targets. The meticulously planned attack was also revealing: The gunmen targeted Hindus, but they also took precise aim at Christians and Jews and particularly Americans. Increasingly, Lashkar-i-Taiba is being considered an emerging threat more powerful and dangerous than al-Qaeda.

Shadow War is the story of the origins of the jihad in Kashmir from its inception in 1947 to the present day. The book focuses narrowly on Pakistan's efforts to use jihadi fighters as an element of defense and foreign policy. It shows how relatively junior officers in the Pakistani Army under the leadership of Colonel Akbar Khan conceived a jihad in Kashmir in 1947–48 and determined the future of the region, and, arguably, that of the rest of the world. It also focuses on early Pakistani links with the Jamat-i-Islami of Indian-controlled Jammu and Kashmir and the JKLF, two of the most important early militant groups. These unholy alliances have caused the deaths of some 50,000 Kashmiris, if we accept official Indian sources, or more than 100,000, if jihadi sources are to be believed. I have focused, in particular, on the rise of Hizbul Mujahideen, the largest and most powerful jihadi group active in Kashmir. I have not focused on Pakistani jihadis like Lashkar-i-Taiba and the Jaish-i-Mohammad. Although they are mentioned throughout the book and can be considered offshoots of the Kashmir jihad, they have a global agenda in which Kashmir is no more than a training ground.

This book is woven around hundreds of small episodes that have been narrated to me by Kashmiri militants over hundreds of hours of interviews during the last eleven years. I have tried to check each and every detail using at least two sources who were directly involved in the particular event under discussion. In writing the book, I have also relied on a wealth of secondary sources in confirming my information. I have used news articles and secondary sources to continue the story uninterrupted or where first-person accounts are not available, and I took great pains in selecting the secondary sources as well.

Militants active in Kashmir talk with great candor, though their information is sometimes of questionable value. I have been amazed to confirm that most militants I spoke with have told the truth, knowing full well it could do them harm. Having compared numerous accounts of the various incidents under discussion, I believe that what is written here is accurate. Since September 11, reporting on this topic has become more difficult. While Kashmiri groups have to a certain extent remained forthcoming, most Pakistani jihadis, like Lashkar-i-Taiba, have not. Although many fighters agreed to speak on the record, most fighters asked to remain anonymous. Because this book is about one of the most sensitive subjects in the world today, I have been particularly cautious with identifying sources. It should be said, however, that some of the former fighters who were disillusioned with the jihad and the role of the

ISI went out of their way to talk. There were very few who refused to be interviewed.

Ghulam Nabi Nowshehri, the Islamabad-based vice president of the Jamat-i-Islami of Indian-controlled Jammu and Kashmir, and Abdur Rashid Turabi, former President of the Jamat-i-Islami of Pakistani-controlled Jammu and Kashmir, refused on-the-record interviews. Nowshehri refused to speak when I met him in 2001, saying he and his party had no role in the jihad. When I asked him why he was based in Pakistan, he relented and confirmed some of the events I insisted on talking about over the next hour-and-a-half. Abdur Rashid Turabi insisted on responding only to written questions, which I of course sent, though I never received any reply. He has also not returned any of my inquiries since we met in his office in Rawalpindi in 2001. I later learned that he also asked his party staff to refuse my interview requests.

I regret that I did not have the opportunity to interview Syed Salahuddin, the supreme commander of Hizbul Mujahideen. I met him and his press secretaries at public rallies and press conferences, but I was never granted an exclusive interview. On many occasions I was promised as much, but he turned down my repeated requests for interviews between 2000 and 2005, when I abandoned the idea of interviewing him.

There are several shortcomings in this book worth mentioning. For one, I have not discussed the precise funding structure of the jihad in Kashmir, in part because no militant was willing to talk about the subject on the record. There is also no reliable documentary evidence of the jihad's finances. This isn't to say the topic isn't important, but my sense is that an ISI insider will have to come forward for significant information to come into the public record, much as Brigadier Yusuf did with his remarkable book about Afghanistan, *The Bear Trap*. Unfortunately, this is unlikely. The Pakistani military considers the Afghan jihad a great success while the Kashmir jihad is considered a failure, and there is no tradition of accepting failure in Pakistan.

Though I reported extensively from India, Pakistan, and Pakistani-controlled Kashmir, I also regret that I never had the opportunity to report from Indian-controlled Jammu and Kashmir. India has discouraged Pakistani journalists and writers from visiting the area since 1988, and I was denied a visa on several occasions during my research. Since 2005, India has selectively allowed some Pakistani journalists visas, but I have not undertaken these supervised trips, partially because of the excessive limits placed on reporting from the region.

I have been careful throughout to accurately portray the roles of jihadi forces and the ISI in this story, and to not overstate what's known about either. In some cases, the record up until now has been inaccurate. In my chapter on the Kargil war, for instance, I show that the involvement of jihadis in that operation has been much overstated. In the concluding chapters on the peace process inaugurated in 2000, I have told three interrelated stories: of the jihadis, of the Pakistani and Indian governments, and of the political groups in Indian-controlled Kashmir. Though the three stories appear to be disconnected, I have tried to show how each overlaps with the other. What becomes clear is that Pakistan has long been playing a "double game" in Kashmir: On the one had, Pakistani leaders vow to be fighting the militant movements active in the state, while elements of the government, particularly the ISI and the Pakistani military, support and expand the jihadi groups.

I have been encouraged by a large number of friends and readers during my research. I particularly owe my thanks to Beena Sarwar, former editor of *The News on Sunday*, who encouraged me in the late 1990s to write on this sensitive topic when few understood its importance. I also want to thank Ashar Rehman, who succeeded Beena Sarwar at *The News on Sunday* and is currently the resident editor of *Dawn*, for understanding the importance of what I was doing and for keeping me writing. David Rohde and Carlotta Gall, Pakistan correspondents of the *New York Times* were also a great source of encouragement.

I have also received encouragement from many outside Pakistan. I owe my thanks to Sarah Sewall and Samantha Power, the former directors of the Carr Center for Human Rights Policy at the Kennedy School of Government at Harvard University, for providing me a fellowship to continue my research. I am also grateful to Bruce Jones, director of the Center on International Cooperation at New York University, and Barnett Rubin, director of studies and senior fellow at the center, who offered me another fellowship to continue my work. Elizabeth Rubin, Edward R. Murrow fellow at the Council on Foreign Relations and a contributing writer to *The New York Times Magazine*, has helped and encouraged me in different ways since 2002, when we first met in Pakistan.

I particularly owe my thanks to Dennis Loy Johnson of Melville House for agreeing to publish this book when few in America understood the importance of this conflict. I also thank my editor, Kelly Burdick, for giving the book its present shape.

CHAPTER ONE

"CHRONICLE OF KINGS"
THE MAKING OF A DISPUTE

To look at a map of the Valley of Kashmir today is to look at a divided land: Roughly the southern two-thirds of the valley is marked as Indian Jammu and Kashmir, India's northernmost state, which shares borders with Tibet and China. Unlike the other Indian states, Jammu and Kashmir is relatively autonomous; its legislature must ratify any national law for it to take effect, though the national government of India is responsible for matters of law and security. To the west and north of Indian Jammu and

Kashmir sits a territory demarcated as Azad Kashmir, or free Kashmir—a self-governing state under Pakistani control, though not constitutionally part of Pakistan. The territory extends north to the Northern Areas, which border Afghanistan and China, and west to the vast North-West Frontier Province of Pakistan. Both Jammu and Kashmir and Azad Kashmir elect their own governments and legislatures, and they have their own flags.

Both Pakistan and India lay absolute claim to the entire territory of what was called Jammu and Kashmir at the time of Pakistani and Indian independence, August 14, 1947. To reflect this dispute, Pakistan calls the Indian-controlled part of Jammu and Kashmir "Indian-held Jammu and Kashmir," while India calls Azad Kashmir "Pakistan-occupied Kashmir" or PoK. Pakistan and China resolved a border dispute in 1963, when Pakistan theoretically ceded a small piece of territory, Aksai Chin, to China. Aksai Chin was shown as a part of the state of Jammu and Kashmir on British maps but was always held by China, as it is inaccessible by land from Pakistan. China handed over another slice of territory, the Shaksam Valley, which was accessible by land, to Pakistan. India, however, still lays claim to Aksai Chin. Despite the ongoing dispute, neither India or Pakistan has ever been able to control the region fully. For the past sixty years, it has sat divided and contested.

Some one hundred years before the formation of modern India and Pakistan, the state of Jammu and Kashmir had been cobbled together by the Hindu Dogra ruler Ghulab Singh, who acquired the Valley of Kashmir from the British in 1846, adding it to his other territories, which included Ladakh, Jammu, and Gilgit-Baltistan. In creating the greater territory of Jammu and Kashmir, Singh created an ethnically and religiously diverse state, ruled by a religious minority. (Before this merger, the term "Kashmir" demarcated only the valley.) According to a 1941 census, the Valley of Kashmir had a population of 1,728,600, and nearly 90 percent of the inhabitants were Muslim. The total population of Jammu was 1,561,580, with the majority of the population Hindu Dogra and Sikh. Almost the entire population of Ladakh was Buddhist. Gilgit-Baltistan had a population of 160,000; its majority was Shia Muslim. The total population of the two other states of Baltistan totalled nearly 100,000; they were also mostly Muslim.

Ghulab Singh's great-grandson kept the princely state of Jammu and Kashmir intact and independent until October 1947, when, confronted with a military invasion from Pakistan, he chose to join the state with India. The move was immediately controversial and contested by Pakistan because the majority of the population in Kashmir was Muslim. War between India and Pakistan continued until 1949, when the newly founded United Nations halted the conflict and sent its Military Observer Group to monitor the region. War broke out again in 1965, prompted by Pakistan's Operation Gibraltar, a failed Pakistani attempt to reoccupy the region. India and Pakistan went to war again in 1971, this time over East Pakistan, now Bangladesh. And in 1999, in what is known as the Kargil War, the two countries battled over Kashmir once more, prompting U.S. political intervention and another cease-fire. The Kashmir conflict still lurks today, unresolved. Informal lines have been drawn on a map, but rhetoric on both sides keeps those lines from being formally recognized or becoming permanent. The working border between the two countries was established in 1949 as a cease-fire line. Following the

Bangladesh War, the 1972 Simla Agreement between India and Pakistan renamed the border the "Line of Control," or LoC. For nearly forty years, the Line of Control has been the de facto border, with each state building institutions on its side. The border has also become heavily militarized, with infantry and artillery forces on both sides.

The Valley of Kashmir is just eighty-four miles long and about twenty-five miles wide. It is a small piece, about 10 percent, of erstwhile Jammu and Kashmir, which at its largest included some 84,000 square miles, though more than half of the population was concentrated in the valley. The historic Silk Road lies to its north, linking central Asia with China by way of Tibet. To the east is the Ladakh route, from Leh in Ladakh to Sinkiang in China, passing through the Karakoram Pass. To the west is the Gilgit route, which links Gilgit to Sinkiang, passing through Hunza and the Khunjerab Pass.

The valley is surrounded by stunning mountains: the Great Himalayan Range to the east, the North Kashmir Range to the north, and the Pir Panjal Range to the south. The northern frontiers of the former state run along the Karakoram Range and its affiliated ranges. They are a watershed between the Tarim basin, which is now part of Sinkiang, and the Indus river system. In the west, mountains lead up to the Pamirs in Tajikistan and to the Hindukush of Afghanistan. In the east, they lead to the western edge of the Tibetan plateau.

Though Kashmir appears to be completely surrounded by mountains, there are twenty passes used for passage in and out of the valley. Three are particularly important: One is an opening from the west, passing through Balakot in the North-West Frontier Province or Rawalpindi in Pakistani Punjab and through Muzaffarabad, the capital of Pakistani-controlled Kashmir, Baramula, and Uri, and leading to Srinagar, the most important city in the valley. The second route connects Srinagar to Punjab and passes through Shopian and Bhimber and over the Pir Panjal pass. The third runs over the Banihal Pass and connects the Valley of Kashmir to Jammu.

There is also an intricate system of waterworks. Flowing from its source in western Tibet to its mouth in Sindh in Pakistan, the River Indus cuts across Jammu and Kashmir. One of its major tributaries, the River Jhelum, has its source in Kashmir. Another major tributary, Chenab, has its source in Lahul in India but passes along the extreme southern corner of Pakistan.

The amalgamation of formally separate states that make up Jammu and Kashmir are stunning in their diversity: Through a geographic lens, the landscape is strikingly beautiful and breathtaking in its scale. It has been a tourist destination since ancient times. There is great cultural diversity, not only in religion—which has often been a source of conflict—but also in the language of Kashmir, which is different from the Hindi and Urdu spoken elsewhere, and in customs. Scholars of the region have often remarked on its strong cultural identity and pride, their *Kashmiriyat*. Indeed the region, the product of thousands of years of amalgamation and conquest, inherits much from this diversity.

If we follow historian Pandit Kalhana, who lived during the first half of the twelfth century, the conflict in the Valley of Kashmir dates back more than 4,000 years. Kalhana's *Raj Tarangini* ("Chronicle of Kings") is perhaps the first-somewhat authentic history of the region, though the text is woven around much myth and hearsay. Written in Sanskrit, *Raj Tarangini* records the lives of hundreds of kings belonging to twenty-one dynasties. Ruins across the Valley of Kashmir, at Martand, Avantipura, Pattan, and Wangat, show that these early kings were sophisticated builders, and cultured and learned in many areas. Until the fourteenth century, the Valley of Kashmir was ruled exclusively by Hindu kings, legendary for their dedication to arts and philosophy. One, Premier Pandit Koka, wrote an ancient text on sex, the *Koka Shastra*. Another, King Vasunand, wrote the *Kamashastra*, a fourteenth-century book on the art of love.

These kings practiced their own form of Hinduism, called Trika or Kashmiri Shaivism, a monotheistic form of Hinduism.[1] The Hindu era gave way to the Muslim sultans at the beginning of the fourteenth century when Shah Mir, an outsider from the Valley of Swat, in what is now Pakistani tribal region, converted the Buddhist prince Rinchin to Islam. Rinchin came to power by killing a chief minister and potential rival and marrying his daughter. (Some speculate that the region's monotheistic form of Hinduism made the conversion to Islam easier.) Rinchin died in 1322, and Hindu rule was briefly restored. But Shah Mir eventually succeeded in founding a Muslim dynasty that would last more than two and a half centuries.

This first period of Muslim rule saw the rapid conversion of the kingdom to Islam, often by barbaric means. The Muslim sultans expanded the territory by annexing a number of principalities. But the kingdom's status as an independent state came to an end in 1586, when it became part of Mughal India. The Mughals had used Kashmir as a holiday resort, and the historical record documents this use—and their enjoyment of the land—as the Mughals' chief motivation for conquest. Much of the romanticism about the valley dates back to the Mughals, who described it throughout their literature as a paradise on earth. But their rule was short-lived: Soldiers rebelled during a salary dispute. And the Afghan ruler Ahmed Shah Durrani, who had his eyes on all of India, decided to annex it. An Afghan general, Abdullah Aqasi, led a 1,500-strong army into the Valley of Kashmir—and proved to be victorious, ending Mughal rule in the valley. Afghan rule lasted well into the nineteenth century, though the state became independently controlled after the death of Ahmed Shah Durrani in 1772.

The Afghans were succeeded by Sikh rulers from Punjab: Owing to a powerful agreement with the British, Punjab's legendary Maharaja Ranjit Singh, had the opportunity to conquer Kashmir in 1819. Singh's agreement with the British, known as the Treaty of Amity and Concord, was signed in 1809 and clarified territorial borders in Punjab enough to give Singh supremacy in the region.[2] In July 1819, Singh's army entered Srinagar and won a military victory. He ruled Kashmir through a succession of governors, as the Mughals and Afghans had before him, though he never actually visited Kashmir.

Ranjit Singh next set his eyes on expansion of Sikh authority into Jammu, where he launched a military campaign in 1808. There he encountered resistance from a six-

teen-year old, Ghulab Singh, a Hindu Dogra from Jammu.
Ghulab Singh was defeated in Jammu, but he resurfaced in
1809 as a member of Ranjit Singh's army. He later participated in a successful campaign in 1819, when Ranjit Singh's
army captured the Valley of Kashmir. Ghulab Singh was
also again victorious in Jammu, where he quelled a rebellion. As a reward for service, Ranjit Singh granted Ghulab
Singh the right to collect taxes in Jammu. In 1822, he was
given hereditary rights and the title of Raja. Ghulab Singh's
younger brother was also granted the district of Pooncch as
a *jagir*, or fief. Ghulab Singh was ambitious and next moved
to consolidate his rule in Jammu and to extend it to the
adjoining principalities. In 1834, he sent an army of 10,000
under the command of the powerful general Zorawar Singh
to invade Ladakh and succeeded in turning it into a vassal
kingdom of Jammu. Four years later, Ghulab Singh sent
General Zorawar to conquer Baltistan with an army of
Dogras and Ladakhis. There the Baltis army destroyed the
only bridge the invading army could use to cross the Indus, but General Zorawar's army crossed the river where it
was frozen, overwhelmed the Baltis, and installed a vassal
prince. Raja Ghulab Singh also revived an ancient Ladakhi
claim on Tibet. There, his army met little resistance and
would likely have proved victorious if the British East India
Company had not interceded, worried that the move would
interfere with their trading activities in Tibet. Under pressure from both the British and the Punjab ruler Sher Singh,
who had assumed power in Punjab after the death of Ranjit
Singh, Ghulab Singh asked Zorawar Singh to withdraw.
The long military expedition in Tibet decimated Ghulab
Singh's army.

After recovering from the Tibet expedition, Ghulab Singh turned his attention to the Valley of Kashmir. His influence in the valley continued to rise as the hold of the Punjab rulers and their feudatories dwindled in the face of the rising British colonial power. An opportunity arose when a Sikh battalion in the Valley of Kashmir rebelled in 1841: Ghulab Singh responded by sending a combined army from Punjab and Jammu, which crushed the mutiny and proved his dominance in the region. Though he did not take possession of the valley, his influence there was greatly enhanced, and he installed a Muslim governor, Shaikh Ghulam Mohiud Deen.

In a long series of negotiations, military campaigns, and agreements, Ghulab Singh aligned himself with the British, assisting in a campaign in the first Afghan war, and eventually joining the British in a fight against the Sikh army—all the while appearing to support the Sikhs. On March 9, 1846, the British ratified a peace treaty, the Treaty of Amritsar, between the Sikh Maharaja Dileep Singh and the East India Company. A key stipulation was that the Valley of Kashmir would be sold to Ghulab Singh for 10 million rupees—thus establishing the first Hindu Maharaja in Kashmir.

The British waived one-fourth of the purchase price on the condition they be allowed to retain Kulu and Mandi across the River Beas. Although the area of Hazara also went over to Maharaja Ghulab Singh, he soon exchanged this area for Mandir, Dhadi, Kathua, and Suchetgarh.[3] The British were to help the Maharaja protect against external aggression, while the Maharaja was to acknowledge the supremacy of the British under the treaty. In token of such supremacy, the Maharaja agreed to present one horse, twelve perfect shawl goats, and three pairs of Kashmiri shawls to the British every year. The treaty, however, forbade the Maharaja to change the territories of his state, though the Maharaja would annex several other principalities in the decades to come. When assembled with his other territories, this is how the erstwhile princely state of Jammu and Kashmir came into being in 1846.

The Treaty of Amritsar did not include any articles concerning the internal administration of the state. Maharaja Singh was to be sovereign, and that was the only stipulation. Later, the British regretted not including provisions on internal administration—and worked to reverse themselves. They had not seen the state at the time of the treaty's signing and would only slowly realize its military importance. Soon after the Second Sikh War of 1848, in which the British defeated the combined Sikh forces and paved the way for the annexation of Punjab, the British government asked Maharaja Singh to let the East India Company have a say in the internal administration of the state. The idea was to appoint a permanent British Resident in Kashmir. The Maharaja resisted, but the British again raised this issue in 1851 and the Maharaja agreed to a compromise: the appointment of a seasonal British officer to look after the welfare of the European visitors.

The British government once again raised this question with Maharaja Ranbir Singh, who had become maharaja after the death of his father. Ranbir Singh also refused to concede a greater British role in Jammu and Kashmir. But the British finally succeeded in appointing a political resident for Jammu and Kashmir in 1885, just a few days before Maharaja Pratap Singh took over power after the death of his father, Ranbir Singh. The British interference in state affairs increased, slowly depriving Maharaja Pratap Singh of his powers, with the British political resident becoming the virtual ruler of Kashmir.

The British focused in particular on pacifying the district of Gilgit, an area that was part of what is now the Pakistani Northern Areas. Gilgit had expelled Dogra rule in 1852, although it had later been reestablished. The British army sent troops and stationed them in the district, believing that gaining command of Gilgit would allow them to control the entire Indus Valley.

In 1877, the British posted a permanent political agent in Gilgit to watch imperial interests in the frontier. The British resident soon gained significant control over the entirety of the district, which came directly under the control of the British Indian government. The British, realizing Jammu and Kashmir's military importance—that it could serve as a buffer against China, Russia, and Afghanistan— developed a policy to control the Maharaja and use his army to protect British India. The Dogra state of Jammu and Kashmir eventually became, in the words of historian Victoria Schofield, "an English Fortress."[4]

The Maharaja system, however, remained intact and sovereign, and supreme in internal matters. Maharaja Pratap Singh remained in power until his death in 1925, when the position transferred to a nephew, Maharaja Hari Singh.

Under the Dogra rulers, Muslims in the Valley of Kashmir suffered greatly; they were deprived of opportunity while other communities made rapid progress.[5] In the valley, Kashmiri Hindus, called Pandits, acquired education and jobs, especially as clerks. The Hindus of Jammu, known as Dogras, also found the doors of opportunity open—especially in the army, where they formed an absolute majority. Over time, Punjabis, both Hindu and Sikh, came to occupy senior bureaucratic positions, though they were a small minority within the larger population.

Protest against the ruling order was difficult. The Dogra rulers allowed only one quasi-political organization, the Dogra Sabha in Jammu, to operate. All other political activity was effectively banned, and the Dogra Sabha actually did little more than safeguard the rights and privileges of the upper-class Dogras.

Things started changing by 1930, as a number of young educated but unemployed Muslims came back to the Valley of Kashmir having received schooling in British India. Since political parties were banned in Jammu and Kashmir, they set up a "Reading Room" in Srinagar. The group later came to be known as the Reading Room Party. They discussed such current topics as politics and the problem of unemployment. One of these young Muslims was Shaikh Mohammad Abdullah, who was poised to determine the direction of politics in Kashmir for the next half-century.

Abdullah, born on the outskirts of Srinagar, was one of five children, whose father, Shaikh Mohammad Ibrahim, a middle-class trader, died before he was born. He grew up poor and considered himself an orphan. As a child, he worked in a family workshop, embroidering shawls, and as a sales boy in a grocery. Through the intervention of the family barber, he was encouraged to go to college.

He studied at the Islamia College in Lahore and at Aligarh Muslim University. At university he came into contact with an exploding movement of progressive ideas. On his return to Kashmir, he involved himself in the Reading Room movement.

Muslim Kashmiri expatriates also formed a semi political party named the All India Kashmir Muslim Conference in Lahore. Its main function was to help poor Muslim students in Kashmir raise money for training in various technical and vocational institutions outside Kashmir. It advanced loans, to be repaid after the students were educated and established. Shaikh Abdullah was elected president of the organization in October 1932.

Although the Pandits had significantly better access to employment, they also had grievances against the political system and frequently spoke out. But there was little association between the Pandits and the Muslim activists. A great communal divide then reigned—with Muslims and Hindus having little communication. The two groups struggled separately, with the Pandits largely restricting themselves to lodging formal complaints and occasionally printing propaganda.

Muslim activism in the valley, on the contrary, had a long history. Muslim communalists and Islamists in Punjab had worked for many years to restore Muslim rule in Jammu and Kashmir. Two communalist parties, the Majlis-i-Ahrar and the Ahmadia, were particularly active. The Majlis-i-Ahrar was mostly confined to Punjab and some parts of the United Provinces. It was a radical group of nationalist Islamists.[6] The group, however, favored constitutional means for restoring Muslim rule, even working with the Indian National Congress to oust the British, although it kept its distance from the Civil Disobedience Movement. The Ahmadia community intended to push Muslims against the Hindu prince, and they were open about following communal policies and being pro-British.[7] They wanted to win recognition from mainstream Muslim sects by helping Muslims in the valley, and they hoped such collaboration might eventually lead to a rebellion. The two parties did not see eye to eye. After the creation of Pakistan in 1947, the Majlis-i-Ahrar and other like-minded Islamists ran a sustained campaign and had the Ahmadia constitutionally designated a heretic religion in 1974.

The members of the Reading Room Party faced difficulties in propagating their ideas among the Kashmiri Muslim population because of the ban on politics, but there was much effort spent in trying to spread their message. They wrote articles for *Syyasat* and *Muslim Outlook*, two Muslim dailies published in Lahore. Soon these papers were regularly imported into the state, and in large quantities. Kashmiri Muslims circulated them widely. The papers' impact was so intense that the Maharaja government had them banned. Kashmiri Muslims simply started writing in another Urdu daily, *Inquilab*, with the same results. They also had fiery pamphlets printed in Lahore and secretly imported them to Kashmir for distribution.

The Reading Room Party believed that it was not possible to form a mass Muslim movement without enlisting the support of the two *Mirwaizes*, or chief priests, of Kashmir: the Mirwaiz of Jama Masjid, the principal mosque in Srinagar, and the Mirwaiz of Khanqah-i-Mualla, a shrine just outside Srinagar. The two Mirwaizes, however, were rivals with differing goals, and winning the support of both seemed impossible—a fact that was commonly thought to be restraining the movement. However, an opportunity arose in 1931, with the death of Mirwaiz Ahmed Ullah of the Jama Masjid. Nearly 100,000 Muslims, led by the Reading Room Party, walked with the coffin toward the graveyard and buried him. His successor, Yusuf Shah, had the full sympathy of the Reading Room Party and promised assistance, including allowing the party to use the Jama Masjid for political activities. Sensing the importance of the Reading Room Party and the gathering storm of activism, the other Mirwaiz also promised to help.

On April 29, 1931, during the Muslim religious festival of 'Id, a Hindu sub-inspector of police tried to stop a prayer leader at a religious congregation from delivering *khutba*, a sermon, at a mosque in Jammu. Protest rallies were held all over the state against this action—an offense that was taken seriously because the officer had interfered with a religious duty. The protests were followed, a few days later, by another incident in which a Hindu constable caused the desecration of some pages of a Quran in Jammu. Though the act was probably not intentional, Muslims again rose in protest, this time all over the state. This was followed by a similar incident at Digore, a village in Jammu: Local police officers prevented a group of Muslims from using a public water tank and the adjoining ground for 'Id prayers.[8] Both Muslims and Hindus had used the water tank and the grounds for religious purposes for several years, and this gave Muslims yet another opportunity to rise against the Dogra rule.

The Maharaja government made several attempts to appease the Muslims. It suspended the Hindu sub-inspector who had tried to stop the prayer in Jammu, and made the police officer in Digore apologize for restricting access to the water tank. The constable who had caused the desecration of the Quran was retired from service. Even this did not pacify the Muslims. The Young Men's Muslim Association of Jammu printed an inflammatory poster that described the events and distributed it all over the state. Reading Room Party members pasted these posters on walls in Srinagar. Police arrested one volunteer of the Reading Room Party hanging the posters, and again thousands of Muslims gathered to protest. On the same day, the Reading Room Party leaders addressed an unprecedented gathering of Muslims at the Jama Masjid, attracting its largest crowd ever, and made a procession through the streets of Srinagar.

The district magistrate reacted by forbidding any political speeches inside the Jama Masjid. The Reading Room Party defied this ban during a religious festival on the following Friday. The festival, held just outside Srinagar, was attended by nearly 30,000 Muslims. The young leaders of the Reading Room Party appeared as heroes, and were cheered as they entered the festival. Party members asked people to go from the festival to the Jama Masjid, where they would hold a political meeting. This was the first time that the Reading Room Party deliberately violated the law. By doing so, they further cemented their position as a rebellious and powerful voice for oppressed Muslims in the valley.

The Reading Room Party met to formally elect representatives on June 21, 1931, in the open compound of the shrine of the Khanqah-i-Mualla, in what would turn out to be the most important meeting in the history of anti-Dogra agitation. For the first time, leaders of all sects gathered at one place. They elected seven leaders: Shaikh Mohammad

Abdullah, Mirwaiz Yusuf Shah, Mirwaiz Hamdani, Khawaja Said-ud-Deen Shawl, Agha Syed Hussain Shah Jalali, Khawaja Ghulam Ahmed Ashai, and Munshi Shahab-ud-Deen. When the meeting adjourned and people started to leave, a previously unknown Pashtun attendee took over the stage and delivered an inflammatory speech in which he denounced the Hindus and the Hindu Maharaja. The man was named Abdul Qadir and had come from the North-West Frontier Province, now in Pakistan, to Srinagar, with a European cook.

The state government arrested Qadir and, prosecuted him in Sessions Court from July 6 to 9, 1931, for his political speech. The early part of the trial attracted huge crowds, which obstructed traffic while the accused was brought into court and returned to the judicial lock-up. There was unrest outside the trial and frequent clashes with the police. Under these circumstances, the state government ordered the continuation of Qadir's trial to be held in secret in the Central Jail. Word, however, leaked out and crowds started gathering outside the Central Jail on July 13, 1931, the first day of the secret trial. The crowd swelled to some 7,000. According to the jailor, the crowd wanted to enter the jail and see the face of the accused. When the crowd forced its way into the outer compound, the district magistrate ordered the arrest of the leaders in the crowd. But the mob became furious and started throwing stones at the police and other officials. They also cut the telephone lines, ransacked police barricades, and attempted to set them on fire. Police finally fired on the crowd, killing twenty-one and wounding many more. This would be remembered as the "Revolt of July 13."

The crowd carried the dead bodies on cots and proceeded en masse through the city. In front of the procession
they carried a banner soaked in the blood of one of the July
13 victims, and they raised anti-Dogra slogans along the
march route. This incident crystalized the impression that
the Dogra rulers and the Hindu minority were in concert:
The Maharaja was a Hindu and all of the police officials
were Hindu, while all the agitators were Muslim. When
the mob reached Maharaj Gunj, a busy trading center, they
broke into and looted Hindu shops. Near-simultaneously,
a wave of anti-Hindu riots broke out at several places in
the city. Mobs looted hundreds of Hindu houses, murdered
three Hindus, and wounded 163.

The Revolt of July 13 paved the way for months of
mass agitation. The government imposed martial law on
September 24, 1931, to control the situation. And Muslim
shopkeepers observed a complete strike over the following several days. Hindu shopkeepers also shuttered their
businesses for fear of reprisals. Hundreds of large protest
meetings were held as Muslims marched throughout the
state. They burned down a bridge over the River Jhelum
at Sangam, twenty-six miles outside Srinagar. To take advantage of the situation, the Majlis-i-Ahrar organized several demonstrations in Punjab. They sent parties of Muslim
activists—known as *jathas*—to create unrest in Jammu and
Kashmir and put pressure on the government. The state
police arrested more than 2,500 members of these jathas
in September and some 2,000 more in the vicinity of Suchetgarh, the frontier post between Sialkot in Punjab and
Jammu between October 29 and November 2, 1931.[9] The
diplomat Joseph Korbel estimates that tens of thousands

of Punjabi Muslims came to help their Kashmiri cousins during the revolt of 1931. The Maharaja did succeed in quelling the revolt, but the Valley of Kashmir remained in a state of wide unrest thereafter.[10]

Besides imposing martial law, the Maharaja also put Shaikh Abdullah behind bars for several weeks, earning him the name *Sher-i-Kashmir*, the Lion of Kashmir. After his release, emboldened by the attention and success, Abdullah went on to found the All Jammu and Kashmir Muslim Conference, which attempted to unite Muslims in the state with those throughout the subcontinent in the struggle for the rights of Muslims in Kashmir. Its first session was held from October 15 to 17, 1932 and was attended by thousands. Mirwaiz Yusuf Shah and his group participated in the first session but refrained from attending subsequent ones.[11] In the growing communalist atmosphere in the subcontinent, Abdullah faced a dilemma in choosing between nationalist and secular politics. The decision was not easy, but Abdullah eventually renamed his party the All Jammu and Kashmir National Conference in 1939, attempting to push his movement away from emerging religious tension in British India and broaden its appeal. A small group resisted and maintained its identity as the All Jammu and Kashmir Muslim Conference.

Mirwaiz Yusuf Shah parted ways with the mainstream Muslim leadership at the end of 1931. From then onward, he focused on representing upper- and middle-class Muslims, while Abdullah attempted to represent the oppressed. The Mirwaiz was successful in winning a few leaders and a large number of workers to his side, thanks to his religious status, but the majority of the poor continued to follow Abdullah. The division became more pronounced at the end of 1931, when the state government vehemently supported the Mirwaiz. When a punitive tax was imposed on the Muslim residents of Maisuma in Srinagar, the followers of Yusuf Shah were exempted. In 1936, the Mirwaiz presented an address of welcome to the Maharaja on his return to Srinagar, widely seen as an attempt at reconciliation. Ultimately, the government granted Yusuf Shah a jagir as a reward for his ongoing collaboration.

Soon the Abdullah faction was also influenced by a more mainstream politics and moved closer to the Indian nationalist parties. In May 1946, Abdullah launched a "Quit Kashmir" campaign, much along the lines of the Indian National Congress's "Quit India" movement. The Indian National Congress ran its campaign against the British; the All Jammu and Kashmir National Conference ran their campaign against the Hindu Maharaja. Though he was quite popular, Shaikh Abdullah found himself remaining, for the most part, a leader only of Kashmiri Muslims; he had difficulties endearing himself to the Hindus and others. Some of his Hindu colleagues, such as Prem Nath Bazaz, even suspected that his "Quit Kashmir" campaign, although it attempted to appeal to all residents, was actually aimed at winning back some of the Muslim followers that Abdullah had lost. In July 1946, the All Jammu and Kashmir Muslim Conference ran a direct-action campaign along the lines of the All India Muslim League's campaign in British India.

The directness of Abdullah's "Quit India" campaign further distanced him from the Hindus and other non-Muslim subjects—and he soon found himself in trouble with the police. He was tried and sentenced to a sixteen month jail term, which lasted until September 1947.

At the time of the partition of the subcontinent in August 1947, there were at least 562 princely states, though the exact number remains in dispute.[12] They were spread over one-third of the British Indian colonial territory.[13] The states could be broadly divided into three categories. There were some 140 major states with full legislative and jurisdictional powers, such as Jammu and Kashmir. There were about another 140 states in which the British colonial government exercised varying control over internal administration; the British Indian government had reached formal agreements with such states. The remaining states were jagirs, small areas deeded temporarily to army officials; these had few governmental powers. The princes of all such states were part of the British Empire because they owed their allegiance to the British Crown, willingly or under duress, and not to the British government in Delhi. With the departure of the British from India in 1947, these states were to become fully sovereign, at least in theory. The British made this clear to the leading princes in a meeting on May 12, 1946, during which the princes were advised to join one of the successor states, either India or Pakistan.

The Government of India Act of 1935 had provided the constitutional mechanism for the integration of states in the successor Indian Dominion. The rulers in the first category of states, if they wished to join either India or Pakistan, were to sign an Instrument of Accession in which they were to transfer whatever limited constitutional powers they had to the Dominion. Another Instrument of Accession was devised for the second category of states, making it clear that, with the departure of the British, they did not acquire any constitutional powers that they had not hitherto exercised. The states in the third category posed little or no problem and would be easily absorbed by the successor states, since these third-category states were deeded to their rulers only on a temporary basis. The 1947 provisions also offered a possibility for a state to sign a "standstill agreement" if substantive issues remained unresolved.[14]

With the exception of three states, each of the princely states falling within the Indian Dominion territory chose to accede before August 15, 1947. The Muslim Raja of Junagarh in western India, with a population of 700,000, nearly 80 percent of them Hindu, chose to accede to Pakistan. The Nizam of Hyderabad, with a Hindu-majority population, wanted to remain independent, as did the Hindu Raja of Jammu and Kashmir. The first two states were surrounded by Indian Union territory, and there was no realistic option for them to remain sovereign. However, the state of Jammu and Kashmir had borders with both India and Pakistan, as well as with Tibet, China, and, arguably, Afghanistan. It also came close to the former Soviet Union.

In Junagarh, India imposed a binding plebiscite; nearly 99 percent of the population voted to join India, and the state was later incorporated into the Indian Union. Indian forces occupied Hyderabad in a military operation under the command of Major General "Jimmy" Chandhuri in September 1948 and deposed the local government, thereby forcing the state to join India. The state of Jammu and Kashmir, with a Hindu prince and a Muslim majority, was the most complicated matter and obviously the source of greatest dispute between India and Pakistan, the two successor states.

Unlike in India, the future leaders of Pakistan had shown little interest in negotiating terms with the princely states before August 14, 1947. Indeed, none of the states within the territorial limits of what was to become Pakistan acceded before independence; they were incorporated much later, some through the use of force. Mohammad Ali Jinnah, who served as Pakistan's first governor-general and was known as "the father of Pakistan," laid his claim to Junagarh, in spite of the plebiscite, in an effort to uphold the Nawab of Junagarh's right to join whichever dominion he chose—but Jinnah's claim and the Nawab's rights could not pull the state to Pakistan after the Indian vote. Though Jinnah rejected the people of Junagarh's right to self-determination, he had a contradictory position on Jammu and Kashmir. There, he argued, the state must join Pakistan, no matter the Maharaja's wishes.

That the Maharaja of Kashmir opted for an independent and sovereign state of Jammu and Kashmir after the departure of the British was a vote, more than anything, for inaction. In the words of M.J. Akbar, "Frightened by Jinnah's Islam in Pakistan and Nehru's democracy in India, he [the Maharaja] opted for procrastination."[15] Two days before partition, he offered a standstill agreement to both India and Pakistan. India refused, but Pakistan accepted. The Maharaja's government and Pakistan signed their agreement on August 14, 1947. Under the agreement, the responsibilities of the British Indian government, such as running communications, postal, and telegraph services, were to be transferred to Pakistan. However, the position of Shaikh Abdullah, the most popular political leader, was ambiguous.

Abdullah wanted to establish a democratic government in Kashmir, but there were subtleties to his public position. Although he had appeased the Maharaja in order to be released from jail after his direct-action campaign, his public statements also took direct aim at the Maharaja. Just before the partition of the subcontinent, Abdullah argued that the rulers of the Indian states "who possess one-fourth of India have always played traitors to the cause of Indian freedom." "No sale deed, however sacrosanct," he said, referring to the British sale of the valley in 1846, "can condemn four million men and women to the servitude of an autocrat when the will to live under his rule is no longer there. We, the people of Kashmir, are determined to mould our own destiny."[16] Abdullah had also become close to Jawaharlal Nehru, who would become the first Indian prime minister. Nehru had traveled to Kashmir to support Abdullah during his 1946 trial, and an emissary in contact with Abdullah had reported that Abdullah had agreed to support Kashmir's accession to India.

The Muslims in Jammu and Kashmir, particularly in the valley, had become more rebellious since 1931. The Maharaja was completely aware of this situation; he strengthened Hindu and Sikh garrisons in the Muslim-majority areas and ordered citizens to deposit their arms with the police. There was also a brutal pattern of aggression against the Muslim population. Where the government suspected Muslim rebels were hiding, the Maharaja's army set entire villages on fire. The Muslims in many parts of the state, many of whom had served in the British Indian army, organized against this brutality. They sensed the opportunity for partition and took aim at the Maharaja. Fearing reprisals, these activists took their families to West Punjab and returned to organize a resistance. The people in Pooncch completely defied the Maharaja's orders and started organizing themselves into guerrilla units. Some of them went to the tribal areas, looking for arms.

Meanwhile, the British colonial government, bankrupted by World War II, was hastening the process of dismantling its portion of the Indian Empire, which, in addition to the princely states, included 17 provinces. The British planned to divide these colonial possessions into India and Pakistan. To formally make the division, the British set up two boundary commissions under Vice Chairman of English Bar Council Sir Cyril Radcliffe, who arrived in New Delhi on July 8, 1947, and prepared the final award on August 12. The award shocked Pakistani leaders, because it awarded three key subdivisions of the Gurdaspur district to India, although two of the three had clear Muslim majorities. The award also gave India the crucial land-route access to Jammu and Kashmir, without which it seemed impossible to physically control Jammu and Kashmir.[17]

There was no legal means to protest Radcliffe's commission, but Pakistan would devise a radical course of action on Kashmir.

On October 24, 1947, barely seventy days after Pakistan's founding, a group of *mujahideen*, or freedom fighters, supported by Pakistan was sent into Jammu and Kashmir. It is unclear when the planning for the operation began, but it was clearly the work of elements of the Pakistani military. During the planning for the attack, the leaders of the nascent state of Pakistan were also engaged in hectic diplomatic missions in an attempt to secure the accession of Jammu and Kashmir to Pakistan. *Jihad*, holy war, and diplomacy were thus the first elements of Pakistan's foreign and defense policy—and they remain so more than sixty years later.

The story of Pakistan's first jihad starts with a meeting between Pakistan's Colonel Akbar Khan, who would manage the jihad under his nom de guerre of "General Tariq," and Sardar Mohammad Ibrahim Khan, a young rebel. [18] Sardar Ibrahim was an elder of the Sudhan tribe and an elected representative of Pooncch, a jagir of Jammu and Kashmir. Earlier, he had served as a legal officer in the government of the Maharaja, and he would later become the first president of Azad Kashmir.

Throughout 1947, Sardar Ibrahim was involved in the search for weapons to wage a war against the Maharaja. He had been touring Jammu and Kashmir extensively, attempting to arouse rebellion. Sardar Ibrahim's Pooncch was an extremely agitated region during this period and united against the Maharaja; there were between 60,000 and 80,000 ex-servicemen there. And the region was very much pro-Pakistan: Its people celebrated secession from the British Empire by waving Pakistani flags and holding demonstrations. Again the Maharaja imposed martial law with the outbreak of political rallies, and there were clashes between the people and the state army at the end of August 1947. The seriousness of the situation in Pooncch had encouraged Sardar Ibrahim to come to Pakistan seeking assistance.

During a meeting with Colonel Khan, Sardar Ibrahim declared that 500 rifles would be sufficient to liberate the state of Jammu and Kashmir. Khan thought this too modest an estimate. The situation at the time was complicated for Colonel Khan because, although he wanted very much to assist Sardar Ibrahim, the commanders of the nascent Pakistani army were not willing to assist outsiders, since the commander-in-chief and other senior members of the army were British and remained under the British army and the supreme command of General Sir Claude Auchinleck. (They would remain so until November 1947.) Colonel Khan, who was junior to at least twenty army officers, mostly British, decided to support Sardar Ibrahim without arousing the notice of senior Pakistani officers. He was ideally positioned to assist, however: As director of weapons and equipment at the General Headquarters of the Pakistani army, he was able to send 4,000 rifles to the Punjab police and pressure them into distributing the weapons to a large group of tribesmen that Sardar Ibrahim had recruited. Colonel Azam Khanzada, of the Ordnance Corps of the Pakistani army, also secretly gave old ammunition, which was not technically fit for army use, to the tribesmen—documenting the ammunition as "discarded" in his logs.

Colonel Akbar Khan had written a secret plan for "Armed Revolt Inside Kashmir" to justify his actions and assistance to the government. The plan proposed strengthening the Kashmiri civilians against the 9,000-strong army of the Maharaja of Jammu and Kashmir. Khan's plan foresaw that 2,000 Muslim soldiers in the Maharaja's army would remain passive, or even desert. It also foresaw that the armed people of Kashmir could slowly overpower the remaining 7,000 soldiers, who were widely scattered across the state. However, the success of the plan depended on blocking reinforcements from India, which could come easily from Kathua to Jammu in good weather. Khan's plan envisaged deploying a band of guerrillas to prevent this, while also assuming that any Indian army units taking this route would be blocked by bad weather. Khan predicted that coming rains, followed by snowfall in winter, would block the route until the spring of 1948. (As it turned out, his certainty was unfounded.) The plan also called for deploying about 200 armed men to take the landing field, which was just outside Srinagar, thus discouraging Indian troops from approaching by air. The plan also envisaged giving some 1,000 rifles to civilians who were to block the Kathua-Jammu track, and 200 rifles to those who were to stop the landing of any transport planes from India, with the remaining rifles to be distributed among the civilians fighting throughout the state.

In Murree, a summer resort near Rawalpindi, Colonel Khan met Mian Iftikharud Deen, a Muslim League politician who was returning from a diplomatic mission in Srinagar, where he had gone on the orders of Governor-General Jinnah. Colonel Khan sent twelve copies of his plan to the government through Deen.

Colonel Khan was subsequently called for a series of meetings with government leaders, including Pakistani Prime Minister Liaquat Ali Khan, in Lahore. There, Colonel Khan discovered that Sardar Shaukat Hayat, a provincial minister, already had an alternative plan in mind.[19] His plan envisaged the deployment of former Indian National Army soldiers and officers under the command of Zaman

Kiani across the Punjab border. (The Indian National army [INA] had been formed during World War II with the aim of overthrowing the British Raj in colonial India.) It also called for the forces under the commander of Khurshid Anwar, a commander of the Muslim League National Guard, to move across the borders north of Rawalpindi. As it turned out, Colonel Khan was not alone, and these forces were added to Colonel Khan's plan.

By the time the first shots were fired, several other Muslim officers in the Pakistani army had been taken into confidence and added to the planning. Multiple cells worked on strategy. However, Colonel Khan appears to have remained the chief player in the game. The Pakistani army's director of intelligence, Brigadier Sher Khan, supported the effort by passing intelligence reports to Colonel Khan. Elements within the army also diverted army ammunition to Zaman Kiani and Khurshid Anwar. The divisional commissioner of Rawalpindi, Khawaja Abdur Rahim, collected funds, weapons, and other goods for volunteers in Kashmir. In the North-West Frontier Province, Chief Minister Khan Abdul Qayyum Khan recruited tribesmen to join the fight. Several *pirs*, or religious men, most prominently the Pir of Manki Sharif, helped by promising the jihadis *houris*—virgins in paradise—and worldly riches if they joined the jihad. The government also inducted the Swat army of the North-West Frontier Province to join the fight. Many former INA officers were recruited to lead tribesmen. Colonel Khan had fought against the tribesmen in the late 1930s as an officer of the British Indian army, and he was convinced of their valor.

According to an American mercenary, Russell K. Haight Jr., who served in the militia for two months, Pakistani army personnel also ran the Kashmiri militants' radio operations. They used army receivers to relay messages and organize encampments inside Pakistan. The Army also supplied food, uniforms, arms, and ammunition through a variety of off-the-books methods, including "such subterfuges as the 'loss' of ammunition shipments."[20] The minister of health in Sindh also appealed "to all trained and demobilised soldiers to proceed as volunteers to the Kashmir front."[21]

A militia of tribesmen, mostly Afridis from valley of Tirah in the Khyber Agency and Mehsuds from Waziristan Agency, entered the state of Jammu and Kashmir on October 22, 1947. Just before the tribal raids, Pakistan imposed an unannounced economic blockade of the state of Jammu and Kashmir by cutting off supplies of essential goods such as kerosene oil, gasoline, and food. Pakistan also stopped private trucks and cars from going beyond Rawalpindi and suspended the railway link between Sialkot and Jammu. The main group of fighters drove down the Domel-Baramula road that led to Srinagar. The small town of Domel was the first town to fall. Brigadier Rajinder Singh, chief of the Jammu and Kashmir state army, put up resistance by blowing the bridge Uri in Garhi, and he succeeded in halting the invading militia temporarily, before he was killed at Rampur.

Sensing the danger, the Maharaja sent his Deputy Prime Minister R.L. Batra to New Delhi with the offer to accede to India in exchange for Indian military support. On the same day, the rebels in Pooncch declared their independence from the Maharaja and set up a liberated government of the state Jammu and Kashmir, headed by Sardar Ibrahim. Mirwaiz Mohammad Yusuf Shah joined the liberated government as education minister.

Maharaja Hari Singh had not learned of the approaching raiders until October 24, when they blew up the Mohore power station and blacked out Srinagar. He had sent his message to New Delhi, pleading for military assistance, and fled Srinagar for his palace in Jammu, on October 26, the fourth day of the tribal invasion. Tired and nervous, the Maharaja realized that only the Indians could stall the invasion. He decided to go to sleep, asking his deputy not to wake him. If the Indians refused to come, he would lose everything—and he ordered his deputy to shoot him in his sleep. If the Indian army came, victory was assured. In neither case, he said, would he need to wake early the next day.[22]

India was also watching the situation with great nervousness. The Indian army and air force sent out reconnaissance missions, and Indian Dominion Governor General Mountbatten, on Prime Minister Nehru's advice, summoned a meeting of the defense committee at 11 a.m. on October 25. Mountbatten thought that Indian troops should be dispatched only if the Maharaja signed an Instrument of Accession. However, Mountbatten wouldn't consider any agreement to be final: If Jammu and Kashmir signed an accession agreement, India would hold a plebiscite to ascertain the wishes of the people, as the Indians had done in other contested states.

On learning that the raiders were almost knocking at the doors of Srinagar, the Army reconnaissance mission, headed by V.P. Menon, returned to New Delhi with a request from the Maharaja for military help, and offering accession. The Indian government was already preparing to dispatch troops, and the government rushed Menon back to Jammu to get Maharaja Hari Singh's signature on the Instrument of Accession. Menon reached Jammu the next day and woke the Maharaja. The nervous Maharaja apparently took little time to sign the Instrument of Accession, and India sent troops the same day.

The invading tribesmen reached Baramula on October 26. The demoralized state troops were retreating. They were only thirty-five miles away from Srinagar and could reach there in less than two hours, and had an easy path ahead because of good roads and little resistance from state troops. The militias moved on October 28 and first met resistance from the Indian troops. They overcame the Indian army ten miles outside Baramula and managed to advance to Srinagar on October 29.

Baramula turned out to be the Waterloo for the raiders. The fighters took up residence there, targeting many local residents, many of whom were in sympathy with their cause. Non-Muslims suffered particularly. At Saint Joseph's Franciscan convent, tribesmen shot a twenty-year old Indian nurse, Philomena, who tried to protect a Muslim mother who had just given birth. The mother was their next target. They shot whoever got in their way: Mother Superior Aldetrude; Assistant Mother Teresalina; a convent official named Colonel Dykes; his wife, Gee Boretto; and nine other nuns.[23]

Margaret Bourke-White, an American journalist, narrated the story of a brave young Muslim shopkeeper named

Sherwani. On hearing of the invasion by the raiders, Sherwani tried to rally frightened villagers to resist them until the Indian army could come to their assistance. When the army finally arrived, Sherwani helped the force capture bands of tribesmen. However, he was then captured himself by the tribesmen, who took him to the town square and asked him to declare that Pakistan was the best choice for the Kashmiris. When he refused, the tribesmen tied him to porch posts in the convent and drove nails through his palms. They put a plaque on his forehead that read "The punishment of a traitor is death" and shot him.[24]

The Indian army had entered Baramula on November 8, proceeding quickly with the invasion, but it soon lost momentum. There was a serious shortage of gasoline, and Indian army vehicles could not pursue the retreating tribesmen. The under-clothed soldiers found it difficult to keep fighting, as they were confronted with hundreds of dead and unprecedented evidence of brutality. When the Indian army regained Rajauri, then a small town of 5,000 people, in April 1948, soldiers were shocked by the devastation. According to an eyewitness, upon entering the town, the Indian army thought it had been abandoned, but soon found the situation to be much worse: "We found [the] grotesque sight of dead and dying huddled in dark corners; men in heaps, women with their hair on their heads trembling in the breeze in mute appeal, and undernourished children. Some of the women had committed suicide by throwing themselves into wells rather than continue to suffer the ordeal they were undergoing. Cases were reported of young girls who were lucky enough to escape, more dead than alive, who had been assaulted by ten, twenty, thirty or more men. Others, we were told, had been dragged away screaming or unconscious."[25]

When Colonel Khan learned about the arrival of Indian troops in Srinagar, he and Divisional Commissioner of Rawalpindi Khawaja Abdul Rahim gathered about one hundred ex-soldiers to go to Srinagar under the command of Muslim League National Guard officer Latif Afghani. There they would attempt to stop Indian transport planes from landing. Thirty of Khan's force died on the way, and when they did reach Srinagar, they found that Indian troops had already taken control of the landing ground.

Pakistan entered the war over Kashmir when the tribesmen failed to take over the valley. The Maharaja of Jammu and Kashmir acceded to India on October 27, 1947; that evening, Pakistani Prime Minister Liaquat Ali Khan convened an unofficial meeting of ministers, along with intelligence director Brigadier Sher Khan and Colonel Akbar Khan. Colonel Khan proposed that they should formally enter the war by founding a committee that would be tasked with the liberation of Jammu and Kashmir. His proposal was accepted, and he was named the military member of the committee; he would also become the military advisor to the prime minister on the Kashmir question.[26]

As a final military move, Colonel Khan proposed a drastic escalation of the fighting. He recommended that the retreating tribesmen be tasked with liquidating Jammu, in the hopes that a focused attack on the Hindu population there would cause an instantaneous stream of refugees, which would choke the only road link between India and Jammu and Kashmir. Colonel Khan thought that 3,000 tribesmen, divided into three groups, were needed for the job. He offered to lead the troops on the battlefield.

From the very beginning, planning for a final operation in Kashmir was based on the premise that India could not afford a total war with Pakistan. On this point, Colonel Khan argued that even the liquidation of Jammu would not provoke India into full-scale war. The tribesmen had already penetrated eighty miles into the state after traversing Pakistani territory, and India appeared to make the mistake of believing that the tribesmen had also besieged the towns of Mirpur, Pooncch, Kotli, Jhangar, Naushehra, and Bhimber. And still the conflict appeared to be limited. The Indian army was also, in the eyes of the Pakistani army and Colonel Khan, too far extended to launch a full-scale war. India's forces were stretched, positioned to defend against the potentially hostile army of the state of Hyderabad in Southern India; and they also had troops massed near East Pakistan, now Bangladesh, and East Punjab. It appeared unlikely that India could make a full commitment to defending Kashmir.

On October 29, tribesmen again started pouring into Jammu and Kashmir. They came in packed, broken-down trucks, carrying an eclectic mix of weapons ranging from European guns to locally made rifles. Pakistani irregulars and tribesmen were estimated to need some three million rounds of ammunition, if the force was to be maintained. And they once again attacked the civilian population.

The practicality of unofficially supporting such a force was immediately called into question. Colonel Akbar Khan set off to Srinagar and sensed, upon learning of the scale of

the Indian force, that the tribesmen were not likely to defeat
the Indian troops. On his return to Rawalpindi, he again
attempted to further Pakistani military involvement by re-
questing a squadron of armored cars from his military unit.
The soldiers, he proposed, should be given civilian clothes,
and be sent without official permission from the army headquarters, and fight at their own risk. Brigadier Sher Khan
and politician Raja Ghazanfar Ali Khan, whose approvals
were needed, rejected the proposal, realizing the risk of having Pakistani regulars fighting in Kashmir. Both Brigadier
Khan and Raja Ghazanfar Ali Khan believed they could
bring about a full-scale war between the two countries.

By November 5, most of the tribesmen had withdrawn
to Uri, sixty-five miles from Srinagar and the fighting. From
there, they were returning to the Pakistani tribal areas, realizing that the fight was lost. Colonel Akbar Khan and a
dozen other irregulars remained to resist the Indian army.
However, on November 7, India pushed through the enemy
line and struck the remaining tribesmen, just four miles
outside Srinagar, with three battalions and a squadron of
armored cars. The battle lasted twelve hours. The tribesmen left nearly 500 dead behind, and the Indian army finally captured Baramula the next day.

Another meeting of Pakistani high officials was held
on December 4, 1947, at the Circuit House in Rawalpindi,
with Prime Minister Liaquat Ali Khan leading the meeting.
Colonel Akbar Khan was also there. The government had
finally taken the commander-in-chief of the Pakistani army,
General Messervy, into full confidence, telling him of their
support for the militias that had invaded Kashmir. Although
General Messervy did not attend the meeting, greater Pa-

kistani military involvement was sanctioned. Colonel Khan was promised one million rounds of ammunition, and he was given twelve volunteer officers to coordinate the ongoing offensive, or what was left of it.

In the spring of 1948, India launched an offensive to evict the remaining resistance. Pakistan followed by finally committing its own military forces to Kashmir at the end of April 1948 to, in the words of Colonel Khan, "stay behind the Azad forces, to be there only to prevent any sudden break through to the Pakistan borders by the Indians." With this, the overall command of the troops passed to the Pakistani army.[27] Pakistan started inducing the militias, including the Kurram Militia, the Swat Army, the Frontier Scouts, and the Azad forces, to come under its command. As the fight progressed and a military victory began to seem more unlikely, more and more of the Pakistanis forces abandoned the fight. Retreating Frontier Scouts refused to return to the front. And soon the Pakistani military settled into holding the established military lines, depending less and less on the original jihadi forces.

Pakistan and India stayed locked in battle over Jammu and Kashmir for the next eight months. In August 1948, the United Nations handed over proposals for a cease-fire to the two counties. The timing was very much in Pakistan's favor: Their forces were retreating while the Indians were advancing. But India accepted the proposal in December, and a cease-fire went into effect at midnight on December 31, 1948. India had occupied the Valley of Kashmir, Jammu, and Ladakh. Pakistan succeeded in occupying only the outlying areas of the erstwhile state of Jammu and Kashmir. But here the conflict would sit.

CHAPTER TWO

THE POLITICS OF PLEBISCITE
"RAISE A PEOPLE'S MILITIA"

When the news of Maharaja Hari Singh's acceptance of the Instrument of Accession to the Indian dominion reached Karachi, Pakistan's Mohammad Ali Jinnah reacted by ordering acting commander-in-chief General Sir Douglas D. Gracey to send Pakistani troops to Jammu and Kashmir. Jinnah was ready to launch a full-scale war. But General Gracey refused to follow the orders; he wanted the approval of Marshal Sir Claude Auchinleck, the supreme commander overseeing the partition of the British Indian armed forces, who would have control over the army until November 1947.

General Auchinleck flew to Lahore immediately. He sat down with Jinnah and pressured him to rescind the order. Jinnah obliged, but he wanted quick movement on the Kashmir issue. Former British viceroy Lord Mountbatten had accepted the Maharaja's accession by proposing that a plebiscite be held to ascertain the wishes of the people in Jammu and Kashmir, in view of its Muslim majority, and Jinnah wanted to hold him to this. He invited Lord Mountbatten and the Indian prime minister, Jawaharlal Nehru, to Lahore for talks.[1]

Lord Mountbatten arrived alone in Pakistan on November 1, 1947. When the two met, Jinnah made a three-point proposal: First, the governments should issue a proclamation to implement a cease-fire within forty-eight hours. Second, the Indian Dominion forces and the tribesmen should withdraw from Jammu and Kashmir. And finally, the two governments should empower their governors general to restore peace, take over the administration, and hold a plebiscite in the state of Jammu and Kashmir. On the final point, Mountbatten dissented from Jinnah's proposal. In one of the key turns of the conflict, Mountbatten instead proposed that a plebiscite be held under the auspices of the newly founded United Nations. The next day, Prime Minister Nehru concurred, formally proposing that the plebiscite be executed by the UN.

For the next ten days, the two governments exchanged ideas via telegram. Then, suddenly, in a press statement on

November 16, 1947, Pakistan's prime minister, Liaquat Ali Khan, accepted Nehru's proposal of referring the issue to the UN. In the statement, Khan proposed that

> [T]he United Nations Organisation immediately to appoint its representative in the Jammu and Kashmir State in order to put a stop to fighting and to the repression of Muslims in the State, to arrange the programme of withdrawal of outside forces, set up an impartial administration of the State until a plebiscite is held, and undertake the plebiscite under its direction and control for the purpose of ascertaining the free and unfettered will of the people of the State on the question of accession.[2]

Nehru, however, disagreed with the specifics; he didn't think "the United Nations had enough forces at its disposal" to put an end to the fighting:

> This can only be done by an organised military force and is being done by our troops. The fighting would also stop as soon as raiders were made to withdraw....the people of Kashmir should decide the question of accession by plebiscite or referendum under...the United Nations only after the raiders were withdrawn.[3]

Nehru made another about-face on December 12, 1947. In a telegram sent to Karachi, he wrote, "We are prepared to invite the United Nations observers to come here and advise us as to the proposed plebiscite, it is not clear in what other capacity United Nations help can be sought." [4] India wanted to handle the specifics of the plebiscite.

On January 1, 1948, India formally called upon the United Nations Security Council to intervene in the Kashmir conflict under articles 34 and 35 of the United Nations Charter. In its complaint, India requested that the Security Council prevent Pakistani civil and military officials from participating in or assisting the occupation of Jammu and Kashmir in any manner. In the complaint, India also once again pledged to give the people of Kashmir the right "to decide their future by the democratic method of a plebiscite or referendum which...might be held under international auspices."[5] President of the UN Security Council F. Van Langenhove immediately appealed to both governments "to refrain from any step incompatible with the Charter and liable to result in an aggravation of the situation."[6] But the fighting in Jammu and Kashmir continued.

The UN Security Council, with the agreement of both governments, succeeded in forming a three-member commission, which was "to proceed to the spot as quickly as possible," investigate the complaints of the two governments, and exercise "mediatory influence likely to smooth away difficulties." After inaction for several weeks, India again asked the UN Security Council to send a group to the subcontinent to supervise the cease-fire and mediate between the two countries, this time stipulating that the fighting must stop and that the invaders and all Pakistani nationals withdraw before India would go forward with the UN plan; India further demanded it maintain its external security forces, since it was responsible for the defense of the state, and that refugees be able to return. Finally, India demanded that Shaikh Mohammad Abdullah be appointed prime minister of Jammu and Kashmir. With regard to the plebiscite, the Indian delegation proposed to elect a national assembly, which would then constitute a national government. The national government would hold the plebiscite under the supervision of the UN Security Council.

On the floor of the Indian parliament, Prime Minister Nehru said:

> In order to establish our bona fides, we have suggested that when the people are given the chance to decide their future, this should be done under the supervision of an impartial tribunal such as the United Nations organisation. The issue in Kashmir is whether violence and naked force should decide the future or the will of the people.

Pakistan, however, objected to these new stipulations, demanding that the UN Security Council be empowered to create an impartial interim administration in the state and to supervise the withdrawal of all the troops and the return of refugees, and then hold a plebiscite.[7]

The United Nations passed its first resolution on the matter on January 17, 1948, and a more important resolution was passed on April 21, 1948. The resolution outlined the position of the UN Security Council on the Kashmir issue and recommended a method of resolution. According to Josef Korbel, the resolution became "the principal term of reference for various United Nations representatives who ever since have been trying to bring about a peaceful and final settlement of the problem."[8] The council asked Pakistan "to secure the withdrawal from the State of Jammu and Kashmir of tribesmen and Pakistani nationals not normally resident therein who have entered the State for the purpose of fighting and to prevent any intrusion into the State of such elements and any furnishing of material aid to those fighting in the State." It also pushed India to "put into operation in consultation with the [UN] Commission a plan for withdrawing their own forces from Jammu and Kashmir and reducing them progressively to the minimum strength required for the support of the civil power in the maintenance of law and order." After achieving these goals, the UN resolution stipulated that India hold a free and fair plebiscite under a plebiscite administrator, who was to be a nominee of the secretary general of the United Nations.

When the UN Commission finally reached Pakistan in July 1948, Foreign Minister Sir Zafarullah Khan told its members that Pakistan had sent three brigades to Jammu and Kashmir in May 1948, reacting to a large-scale Indian army offensive in the spring 1948 that had pushed the tribesmen toward the Pakistani borders. Khan, defending the troop movement, told the Commission that Pakistan could not sit still, wait for the UN, and watch an emerging situation. General Gracey, who in October had refused to accept orders from Governor General Jinnah to send troops to Kashmir, confirmed this, telling the Commission that the Indian army had been preparing to launch a general offensive to reach strategic positions in the areas bordering Pakistan to the northwest and southwest, a move that

General Gracey thought would put Pakistan at the mercy of Indian military forces.[9]

From Pakistan, the Commission traveled to India. Nehru told the Commission that India could not negotiate until Pakistan withdrew its forces. He said,

> We do not insist upon the right of our army to advance and occupy the territory which would be evacuated. On the other hand there must not be a vacuum there and we shall be satisfied with the recognition of the authority of the State over all its territories and with the occupation of advanced position important to us strategically and economically.[10]

The strong positions of both states stalled the Commission for a time, but the UN committee intervened with another resolution, adopted on August 13, 1948, asking both India and Pakistan to agree upon a cease-fire within four days of their acceptance of the resolution. It asked Pakistan to withdraw all troops from Kashmir "as the presence of troops of Pakistan in the territory of Jammu and Kashmir constitutes a material change in the situation since it was represented by the Government of Pakistan." Tribesmen and other Pakistani citizens were to be withdrawn. The evacuated territory, according to the Committee's resolution, would be administered by local authorities, under the supervision of the Commission. India was also to start evacuating its forces, after the tribesmen and other Pakistani nationals had withdrawn. Both India and Pakistan were to agree that the people of Kashmir would determine the future of the state.

In spite of all the difficulties, the Commission did succeed in making the two countries agree to the proposal and a cease-fire, which came into effect one minute before midnight on January 1, 1949. The Commission met in Lake Success, New York—the temporary home of the UN—to translate its proposal into a UN resolution on January 5, 1949.

The work of the Commission had been supported unanimously by the UN Security Council up to this point, but the political climate had shifted since January 1948, with the Cold War quickly solidifying and slowing the work of the UN. India had also become close to the Soviet camp and, sensing a superior position on the Kashmir issue, it moved to stall the progress of the Commission. Working on behalf of India, the Czechoslovakian delegation put every possible hurdle in the way of the resolution, and it eventually stalled the process completely. The specifics of a plebiscite wouldn't, after all, be decided by the UN. The UN Security Council remained engaged with the Kashmir issue until 1951 and passed two more resolutions in favor of demilitarization and plebiscite, on March 14, 1950, and March 30, 1951, but failed to implement the resolutions' objectives. Indeed, the Cold War completely overtook the UN Security Council agenda and the Kashmir conflict was put on a back-burner.

Even in an hour of panic, Maharaja Singh tried to keep a measure of independence and sovereignty for his state. When he signed the Instrument of Accession with India, the seventh clause read, "Nothing in this Instrument shall be deemed to commit me in any way to acceptance of any future Constitution of India or to fetter my discretion to enter into arrangements with the government of India under any such future constitution." Clause Eight stipulated that "nothing in this Instrument affects the continuance of my sovereignty in and over this state, or, save as provided by or under this Instrument, the exercise of any powers, authority and rights now enjoyed by me as Ruler of this State or the validity of any law at present in this State." Jammu and Kashmir, to use the words of M.J. Akbar, "had joined the Union of India, but not the law of India."[11] The Jammu and Kashmir Constitution Act of 1939, which governed the state's internal administration including the legislature, remained intact, but the Indian Union took over responsibility for foreign affairs, defense, and communications. (In October 1949, the Indian Parliament adopted article 306A in its draft constitution, which later became Article 370, guaranteeing full autonomy to the state of Jammu and Kashmir.) It was declared a victory for the Indian union. Maharaja Hari Singh also defended his jagirdars' property rights in Clause Six of the Instrument of Accession, stipulating that "Nothing in this Instrument shall empower the dominion Legislature to make any law for this State authorizing the compulsory acquisition of land for any purpose."

Immediately after Shaikh Abdullah's September 1947 release, he again started organizing public meetings, this time delivering decidedly anti-Pakistan speeches. He had refined his message, declaring that only representatives of the people had the right to accede to Pakistan or India, though he threatened both the Maharaja and the Indian government. He took aim at the despotic rule of the Maharaja and the lack of direct rule.

Throughout the fall of 1947, Indian Prime Minister Nehru pressured Maharaja Singh to appoint Shaikh Abdullah to a senior position. Abdullah had been the Maharaja's political opponent for some twenty years—and Nehru's pressure did little to bring the Maharaja closer to India; Nuhru and the Maharaja had little rapport. On November 13, Nehru wrote, saying that "The only person who can deliver the goods in Kashmir is Shaikh Abdullah. He is obviously the leading political personality in Kashmir... Full confidence must be placed in him....I would suggest to you to keep in close personal touch with him and deal with him directly and not through intermediaries."[12] On October 30, the Maharaja finally obliged, and Abdullah was appointed head of the Emergency Administration, which was established to run the government with the Maharaja's prime minister.

But Shaikh Abdullah was not a trained bureaucrat, and he clashed with Singh and the prime minister of Kashmir, Mehr Chand Mahajan. As the political crisis in Kashmir deepened, Maharaja Singh even considered retracting his accession to India. Eventually, amidst great turmoil, Prime Minister Mahajan sought permission to resign, and did so on March 2, 1948.[13] Just weeks later, Shaikh Abdullah replaced him as prime minister.

In October 1949, a special session of Abdullah's National Conference confirmed the provisional accession of the State to India, and pledged full support of a full accession to India. The aim of the National Conference was to create a new Kashmir. And the most important pillar of his reform program was fair land reform. The Dogra princes and their jagirdars, as well as a class of minor landlords, had usurped most of the 2.2 million acres of cultivable land in Kashmir, while the Muslims had been mostly reduced to tillers.

Shaikh Abdullah started a new program of land reform to reverse this situation. He also put an immediate moratorium on the execution of peasants and workers and set up debt conciliation courts to alleviate the burden on usury-ridden Muslims. Maharaja Hari Singh had not foreseen such radical reforms and could do little to stop them. (In reaction, the Hindus set up a communal party, Praja Parishad, with the aim of removing Shaikh Abdullah.) The total amount of outstanding debt in the country was brought down from 11.1 million rupees to 2.4 million rupees as a result. Peasants also regained their rights in mortgaged property, and new rules preventing peasants from being evicted by Hindu landlords were instituted; their share of crop profits increased from half to two-thirds, and production costs were also now to be split. Abdullah also created a Land Reform Committee that slashed the maximum land holding to 22.75 acres, transferring the rest to tenants.

The campaign was enormously popular in Kashmir, and it was also strongly supported by India. The interests of Shaikh Abdullah and the Indian Union had converged on the issue, because Abdullah's land reforms further marginalized Maharaja Hari Singh, who had become a major obstacle in Jammu and Kashmir's final union with India. The land reforms consolidated Shaikh Abdullah's political power, but they also turned Kashmiri peasants strongly toward India because, as Abdullah correctly told them, such reforms would not have been possible in Pakistan. Maharaja Singh, who became the sadr-i-riyasat, or regent, after accession to India, could not endure Abdullah's political popularity; he abdicated his position, leaving Kashmir for Mumbai, and left his post to a son, Yuvraj Karan Singh, on June 9, 1949.

But Abdullah had still not achieved independence for the state, and he remained constrained by the newly appointed sadr-i-riyasat. In 1950, he broached the idea of an independent state of Jammu and Kashmir with Sir Owen Dixon, who had been appointed the UN representative to mediate between India and Pakistan over Jammu and Kashmir. And he increasingly clashed with India, even publicly criticizing Nehru in 1950 for advising him on matters outside defense, external affairs, and communications. Nehru reacted by advising Abdullah not to "attach any value to any friendly advice we might give." But Abdullah responded curtly: "I cannot barter away [Kashmiris'] cherished rights and privileges."

In 1952, Abdullah stepped up the war of words when the Indian government tried to extend the jurisdiction of the comptroller and auditor general to Kashmir. Abdullah threatened Delhi, saying that the Kashmiris "have to provide for all eventualities." And in a speech on Martyrs' Day, July 13, 1953, to pay tribute to the martyrs of July 13, 1931, he said, "It is not necessary that our state should become an appendage of either India or Pakistan."

Open talk of independence was too much for Sadr-i-Riyasat Karan Singh, who finally dismissed Abdullah on August 8, 1953. Singh appointed a dissident cabinet minister, Bakhshi Ghulam Mohammad, prime minister. Bakhshi, who had been collaborating with Delhi and the sadr-i-riyasat until then, refused to form a government before Abdullah was jailed and taken off the political scene. Abdullah was arrested on charges of conspiracy against the state just past the midnight on August 9, and Bakhshi became the second prime minister of Jammu and Kashmir just before dawn. Abdullah was to remain behind bars for the next eleven years, with only a brief release, from January to April of 1958. (Delhi unsuccessfully tried to prove his complicity with Pakistan.)

The arrest of Shaikh Abdullah had a far-reaching impact on the region's subsequent history, and arguably, on the rest of the world. And with Abdullah behind bars, Delhi finally forgot its promise of holding a plebiscite in Jammu and Kashmir for good.

Colonel Akbar Khan's dream of engineering an armed revolt in Kashmir did not come to an end with the 1948 cease-fire. A few months after it took effect, he wrote another plan under the title "What Next in Kashmir?," followed by a paper titled "Keep the Pot Boiling in Abdullah's Kashmir."[14] In the first paper, he argued that there was no compelling reason for India to hold a plebiscite and predicted it wouldn't. He also opposed the argument that Pakistan should strengthen itself militarily to snatch Jammu and Kashmir from India. Instead, he thought the best option available to Pakistan was to support proxy forces: Pakistan could give military training to residents of Pakistani-controlled Kashmir, and from Pakistan, and "raise a people's militia." The plan was influential, and

Khan succeeded in persuading the prime minister to allocate 1,000,000 rupees (less than US $200,000 at that time) to manufacture small arms. Factories started producing sten guns and .303 cartridges during the early 1950s.

In 1956, Colonel Akbar Khan wrote yet another pamphlet, in which he argued that mere appeals to the United Nations and the UN Security Council would not bring about a plebiscite. Pakistan, Khan wrote, must help the people of Jammu and Kashmir revolt against India in order to have any chance of pushing a vote. Khan's logic was that such an intervention would be viewed as a threat to international peace and would force the UN to again take notice of the situation: "If the worst happened and India committed aggression against Pakistan, the world would be forced to intervene against her." Responding to Khan's writing, Pakistan's President Iskandar Mirza summoned him and asked how such a plan could be carried out. Colonel Khan told him that only 500 young men at a time would be needed to wage a guerrilla war and carry out sabotage inside Jammu and Kashmir. They should be local people or dressed in local clothes, but he imagined that the forces could eventually be spread across the state and carry out sabotage activities that would encourage and eventually lead to a popular revolt. The forces should be given dynamite, to blow up bridges and other strategic locations, and equipment to cut wires and disable communication systems. They should also have knives and arms to protect themselves, though they should avoid direct encounters with Indian troops or police. Their targets should be "unguarded bridges, isolated wires, and unprotected transport." And Pakistan should have another cadre of 500 young men ready to replace them if they were eliminated in encounters with the Indian security agencies, and a third group of fighters under training. Akbar Khan told the president that there were industrialists ready to fund these operations.

Little is known about the implementation of these plans. However, circumstantial evidence shows that Khan's plans were indeed implemented. There were explosions in the Valley of Kashmir throughout the 1950s, including a devastating bomb explosion in the Palladium Cinema building in Srinagar on June 28, 1957.[15]

The *moe muqaddas,* a strand of hair from the beard of the Prophet Mohammad, is by far the most important Muslim relic held in Kashmir. Indeed, it has been an important religious and political symbol for centuries, held in the shrine of Hazratbal in Srinagar. The moe muqaddas is held in a specially designed quartz container and can be seen only from one side. It is displayed rarely, during religious festivals, and on occasion for private viewings.

On December 26, 1963, the custodian of Hazratbal, Nishandez Rahim Bandey, held a private viewing of the moe muqaddas in the evening. After the viewing, he carefully locked it and left the shrine. Early the next morning, he discovered that someone had broken into the shrine and stolen the relic.

For the first time since 1931, the entire valley went into an uproar. Immediately, protests broke out across the country, with people demanding that an investigation be launched immediately—and that the thief be caught and hanged. There was a general strike. And in no time, a religious event had become a political cause célèbre. It was rumored that somebody close to Prime Minister Bakhshi, who had just been ousted from power, had stolen the moe muqaddas.

Sensing an opportunity, Prime Minister Nehru sent his best intelligence officer, B.N. Mullick, to Kashmir to investigate and find the holy relic. On December 31, 1963, Mullick left for Srinagar. There, he was joined by the inspector general of police, Lakshaman Das Thakur. The protests over the disappearance of the holy relic had turned into communal protests during the early days of 1964; Muslims stated attacking Hindus, with protests spreading to nearly every village in the Valley of Kashmir. The scale of the violence was unprecedented, creating a huge refugee population that sent Hindus fleeing the valley to Jammu. Seeing the unprecedented unrest, Pakistan also made a move, using the theft to stoke communal tensions in East Pakistan. There, Hindus started fleeing to West Bengal in India.

Protestors everywhere demanded Bakhshi's head and the release of Abdullah, and the protests became more organized with each passing day. Urban demonstrations drew enormous crowds from remote villages, with local Muslims feeding and housing the out-of-town protestors. How the holy relic reappeared in its shrine remains a mystery even today, but, according to press reports from the time, Mullick, the Indian intelligence official, and Thakur, the police inspector, evacuated the Hazratbal shrine on the evening of January 4, 1964, having been promised that the holy relic would be returned during the night. In the morning, the holy relic was indeed returned in its original quartz tube.

How Mullick and Thakur eventually recovered the holy relic is still unknown.

The most lasting impact of the theft, however, is that the situation did much to weaken Kashmiri links with the Indian Union. Aging Prime Minister Nehru was deeply shaken by the anti-Hindu violence, and he decided to reverse his policy on Kashmir and try to bring Shaikh Abdullah back into the political process. With pressure from Nehru, G.M. Sadiq was sworn in as the new prime minister of Jammu and Kashmir, and he announced a complete withdrawal of the conspiracy charges against Shaikh Abdullah on April 5, 1964. Abdullah was set free three days later, after eleven years in prison.

Abdullah traveled first to Srinagar, then to Delhi on April 29. In Delhi, Nehru and Abdullah seriously discussed a peace plan with Pakistan, and it was agreed that Abdullah would go to Pakistan as Nehru's emissary. Nehru wanted him to go to Pakistan as soon as possible, because he himself was ill and knew he was running short of time. Abdullah arrived in Rawalpindi on May 23, 1964.

There, Abdullah convinced Field Marshal Ayub Khan, who had become military ruler of Pakistan in October 1958, to agree to a summit with Nehru. Nehru also agreed, sending his official consent to Karachi on May 27. It would be his last act in office. He died on the morning of May 27. With his death, another chance for peace was lost.

The death of Nehru and the election of Indian Prime Minister Lal Bahadur Shastri in June 1964 further worsened

India-Pakistan relations, especially after plans to fully in-
tegrate Jammu and Kashmir into India gained momentum under Shastri's government. In early January 1965,
the prime minister further undid Article 370 of the Indian
Constitution by applying Articles 356 and 357, which made
the Indian governor's rule possible without the consent of
the local legislature. India's Congress Party also launched a
Jammu and Kashmir chapter on January 26, 1965—further
evidence of the state's intensifying alignment with India.
The convergence of these events alarmed Field Marshal
Ayub Khan.

To address ongoing questions in the state, Ayub Khan
set up a "Kashmir cell" consisting of the foreign secretary, the defense secretary, the director of the intelligence
bureau, the chief of general staff of the Pakistani army,
and the director of military operations. The group would
keep the Kashmir situation under constant review. Foreign
Secretary Aziz Ahmed was made chairman, and the meetings of the cell were to be held at the residence of the
secretary of education, in order to keep them an absolute
secret. According to General Gul Hasan, a former chief
of Army staff, Aziz Ahmed informed the cell sometime in
1964 that the "President had ordered the GHQ [the General
Headquarters of the army]" to prepare two plans, one to
encourage sabotage activities across the cease-fire line and
the other to provide "all-out support for guerrillas to be
inducted into Kashmir." The GHQ assigned Army Division
12, stationed in the hill town of Murree, to prepare the
plans and train personnel.[16]

The Kashmir cell's assumption was that Muslims in
the Valley of Kashmir would spontaneously revolt once

trained Pakistani soldiers reached them. This would give the Pakistani army the opportunity to drive Indian forces out of Indian-controlled Jammu and Kashmir, while fear of China would prevent India from opening battle-fronts on the international borders. (In 1962, India had lost a war with China, over a border conflict, and relations between China and India had since deteriorated.) The Inter-Services Intelligence agency (ISI), the main branch of Pakistan's intelligence infrastructure, in collaboration with the Pakistani foreign office, secretly prepared a military plan that reflected the thinking of the Kashmir cell, which the ISI then presented to Ayub Khan at the end of December 1964.

Khan postponed action on the report after Information Secretary Altaf Gauhar advised him that it was a quixotic plan, differing little from one he had already rejected. But Khan put the plan before the intelligence committee of the cabinet anyway sometime during the second week of February 1965. Commander-in-Chief of the Pakistani army General Musa Khan and his senior aides, as well as Foreign Minister Zulfikar Ali Bhutto and Foreign Secretary Aziz Ahmed, were present, though the commanders-in-chief of the air force and the navy were excluded. T.S. Jan, deputy director of the ISI, briefed the cabinet.

Ahmed said that India was in a highly vulnerable position. A feeling of popular revolt, he claimed, was sweeping the valley, making India's position indefensible. If the Indian forces were diverted by sabotage and subjected to armed harassment by trained soldiers, Kashmir could soon be liberated. Pakistan's rapidly growing friendship with China was the most powerful factor in favor of Pakistan's plan and would stop India from retaliating across the international borders. At the end of the briefing, Field Marshal Ayub Khan, surprised at complexity of the plan, sensed new forces at work; he thought he hadn't authorized the preparation of any such plan: "All I asked them was to keep the situation in Indian-controlled Jammu and Kashmir under review. They cannot force a campaign of military action on the Government."[17]

The plan for what was called Operation Gibraltar was kept top secret: Even corps commanders and the chiefs of the air force and navy were kept in the dark. Only two civil officers, the foreign secretary and the defense secretary, had knowledge of the plan. It had been difficult to fully convince Ayub Khan of the potential success of such an operation. He had rejected a similar plan once before, and he had been skeptical of the specifics: He had asked Army Lieutenant Colonel A.O. Mitha to examine the possibility and implications of an uprising. Mitha had concluded that the Pakistani army could indeed create an uprising if given sufficient time. However, he reported, the Indians were likely to attack across the international borders if they lost control in Kashmir. Defending the plan, Foreign Minister Bhutto wrote a letter to Ayub Khan, arguing the opposite, that India was in no position to go into a general war. He summarized the situation by saying that Pakistan had only two alternatives: "to react now boldly and courageously in self defense," or to "allow the initiative to move irrevocably to India, who would then proceed to launch her final attack for the liquidation of Pakistan subsequently at a place and time of her own choosing." The message echoed that of a handful of military officers with whom Bhutto had become close, and with whom he met regularly at his residence. While these generals had little political access to Ayub Khan, they found an invaluable ally in Foreign Minister Bhutto.

According to sources, however, Ayub Khan eventually became convinced of an operation like that described to the intelligence committee. On May 13, 1965, Major General Akhtar Malik briefed Ayub Khan on the specifics of Operation Gibraltar. Toward the end of the briefing, when Ayub Khan signed off on the plan, he asked General Malik to target Akhnur, a town of great strategic value in Indian-controlled Kashmir. General Malik asked for additional money and forces, and he got both.

In late 1964, Malik started training a force to launch Operation Gibraltar. He organized ten forces of about 500 men each. The groups were called Khalid, Tariq, Qasim, Salahuddin, Ghaznavvi, Khilji, Murtaza, Babar, Nusrat, and Sikandar.[18] The first five made up the Gibraltar forces, and the last five made up the "Nusrat" forces. General Malik recruited personnel and former army officers from the villages of Pakistani-controlled Jammu and Kashmir. Personnel were also recruited from the Pakistani army and from associations of former soldiers. The operation called for Pakistani army officers to command the companies; force commanders would be drawn from the army of Pakistani-controlled Jammu and Kashmir. Forces started training in March 1964 at Kotli, Mongbajri (near Rawalakot), Shinki-ari, and Ratu in Gilgit. The training was to end by June 1965 but was extended to July 1965.[19]

The situation on the India-Pakistan border, in an area called the Rann of Kutch, started becoming hostile in early 1964. The Rann of Kutch was a deserted inland lake situated between the Pakistani province of Sindh and the erstwhile princely state of Kutch, which had been incorporated in the Indian state of Gujrat in 1947. Pakistan claimed the northern 3,500 square miles, while India claimed the entirety of the 8,400-square-mile area. Villagers there, however, moved with their cattle freely across the undemarcated border. In 1956, the Indian forces expelled Pakistani villagers from long-used grazing areas and impounded their cattle. Pakistan reacted by forcefully evicting the Indians from the area. In 1965, the Indian forces started obstructing the movement of the Pakistani border patrols south of Kanjarkot, a half-ruined fort in the jungle. In March 1965, the Indians set up new posts opposite the Pakistani posts and brought in an infantry brigade to hold their positions in an exercise code-named "Arrow Head." On April 8, Indian troops fired on the Pakistani posts. Recurrent skirmishes followed between the Pakistani and Indian armies until April 26. The Indians suffered heavy losses during the operation, with Indian attacks declining dramatically by late April. A de facto cease-fire was in place by June 6 and a formal one in operation on July 1. According to Altaf Gauhar, "The euphoria over the Pakistan army's performance in the Rann of Kutch must have persuaded Ayub to allow the army to prepare a war plan."[20]

With the death of Prime Minister Nehru, Shaikh Abdullah had lost hope. Hawks under the leadership of Prime Minister Shastri had taken the reins of government in Delhi. And without a clear option in sight, Abdullah sought help from Pakistan. In early 1965, Abdullah announced a pilgrimage to Mecca. He used the trip as a goodwill tour, seeking Arab sympathies and openly discussing achieving self-determination for the people of Jammu and Kashmir. Throughout his trip, he openly used Pakistani embassy facilities during his meetings. Pakistan's Foreign Minister Bhutto also arranged for Shaikh Abdullah to meet other world leaders, including China's Zhou en-Lai, on March 31 in Algiers. In the meeting, China openly announced its support for the Kashmiris' right of self-determination.[21]

In April 1965, Ayub Khan had asked the director of the Pakistani Intelligence Bureau, Ayub Awan, to contact Shaikh Abdullah and offer him cash, with the goal of adding Abdullah as a paid agent. Ayub Awan made his approach during Abdullah's visit to Saudi Arabia. In their meeting in Mecca, Abdullah told Awan that he had learned about Operation Gibraltar and cautioned him that the Kashmiri people might not welcome Pakistani soldiers. To Awan's surprise, however, Abdullah offered to give his support to the operation. "If I call upon them to rise in support of the plan, their response could be overwhelming," Abdullah told Awan. But Abdullah had a request: "Please do not let me go back to India. Keep me anywhere you like in your Northern Areas, or locate me in Sinkiang [China] and let me call upon the Kashmiris from there to give you their full support." Awan came back to Pakistan and conveyed Abdullah's message to Field Marshal Ayub Khan, who showed no interest in Abdullah's offer.[22] Apparently disheartened, Abdullah returned to India.

The Indians, who had considered blocking Abdullah's trip to Saudi Arabia in the first place, were outraged by intelligence reports of his meetings there; they cancelled his passport and arrested him at the Delhi airport when he returned on May 8. Open planning for independence was too much: He was again thrown into jail, this time with a two-and-a-half-year sentence. Pakistan protested unsuccessfully by calling the arrest "reckless" and lodging a protest with the UN Security Council on May 20, 1965. Delhi also used Abdullah's actions as an excuse to replace the title of sadr-i-riyasat, another symbol of Jammu and Kashmir's special status, with the title of governor.

Field Marshal Ayub Khan gave the final go-ahead to Operation Gibraltar in a meeting on July 24, 1965, and the operation was launched on August 8. All the forces started moving to forward positions on July 24, and they reached their destinations on July 28. From these forward positions, they infiltrated across the cease-fire line. Success was sporadic: The force commander of the "Tariq" unit and twenty-one other men died due to failure to acclimate while they were moving into the Himalayan range at 17,000 feet, and the force had to be withdrawn. "Qasim," which operated north of Bandipora, found it difficult to live off the land and withdrew on September 4, with the Indians closing in. "Khalid" attacked an Indian battalion at Trehgam, but the commander lost control of his companies, who retreated in small groups. "Salahuddin" was attacked by the Indians at Tanmarg, after a shepherd boy refused to be bribed and reported the presence of strangers to the Indian security forces. The force was to withdraw in total disarray. "Ghaznavi," however, inflicted heavy casualties on the enemy. It continued to dominate the wide region in western and southwestern Jammu throughout the operation and was not withdrawn until after the cease-fire. The "Nusrat" forces were directed to attack enemy communication centers and supply lines immediately behind the enemy positions along the cease-fire line. None succeeded, and they eventually merged with the Gibraltar forces.

The propaganda war was an important part of the operation. After the meeting that set the operation in motion, Ayub Khan told Information Secretary Altaf Gauhar, "a great deal will depend on how we handle the propaganda." The army acquired a mobile transmitter to broadcast the "Voice of Kashmir" radio program, although the information secretary himself was not briefed about the details of the military operation. Brigadier Irshad told him, "In less than twenty-four hours some important targets will be captured by the freedom fighters and I will give you all the news you want to keep the world humming." ISI Brigadier Riaz Husain was even more upbeat and claimed that he had a whole range of equipment with which to learn about every development inside Jammu and Kashmir. He told the information secretary, "I shall flood you with information. We have our contacts."[23]

The Indians had overcome all the forces except "Ghaznavi" by August 16. The Indian army launched its biggest attack against Bedori Bulge, and it occupied the Haji Pir Pass on August 28. Pakistani Commander-in-Chief General Musa Khan rushed to Foreign Minister Bhutto's house, and told him, "My boys have nothing but stones to fight with," and asked him to obtain Field Marshal Khan's permission to launch a second operation, Operation Grand

Slam, which appeared to be the only way to reverse the situation. Operation Grand Slam required Pakistani troops to cross a small section of the international border between Jammu in Indian-controlled Jammu and Kashmir and the Pakistani city of Sialkot. Earlier, General Malik had also advised that Operation Grand Slam be launched immediately. The operation, which aimed at capturing Akhnur, was not a clearly defined military plan. Though there was some speculation that the operation was intended to isolate the five Indian divisions in Kashmir by cutting off the only rail link between India and Kashmir, this is unlikely, as such an operation would have been more advisably launched before Operation Gibraltar. The more likely goal was for the operation to build pressure on the Indian army while the Gibraltar forces carried on their work. There was still optimism that the Gibraltar forces could create an uprising the Valley of Kashmir, if given time.

Field Marshal Ayub Khan had gone to Swat in the North-West Frontier Province, in hopes that such a trip would help conceal the Gibraltar plans from the Indians. Foreign Minister Bhutto flew to Swat and came back with a directive approving Operation Grand Slam, which was signed on August 29. The directive was addressed to the foreign minister and the commander-in-chief and was titled the "Political Aim for Struggle in Kashmir." The plan aimed at taking

> such action that will de-freeze the Kashmir problem, weaken Indian resolve and bring her to the conference table without provoking a general war. However, the element of escalation is always present in

such struggles. So whilst confining our action to the Kashmir area we must not be unmindful that India may in desperation involve us in a general war or violate Pakistani territory where we are weak. We must, therefore, be prepared for such a contingency. To expect quick results in this struggle, [India] has much larger forces than us, would be unrealistic. Therefore, our action should be such that can be sustained over a long period. As a general rule Hindu morale would not stand more than a couple of hard blows at the right time and place. Such opportunities should, therefore, be sought and exploited.

The Pakistan army launched Operation Grand Slam on August 31. The Indians put up fierce resistance, forcing the Pakistanis to halt the operation in one sector and delay it in another. The situation was fairly chaotic by the morning of September 2, when Pakistani GHQ asked Major General Malik to hand over command of the operation to Major General Yahya Khan, who later became the commander-in-chief of Pakistani Army and imposed the second Martial Law regime in 1969.

Major General Khan's job was to wind up Operation Grand Slam. According to a study done by Staff College in Quetta, there was a breakdown of communications between Major General Malik and his commanders that sparked a final blow to the operation.[24] The Pakistani army had assumed that the Indians were vulnerable at Akhnur, while the reality was just the opposite. The Indians were prepared for the Pakistani army at Munawwar Gap, through which the Pakistani army had planned to advance to Akhnur.

Operation Gibraltar had failed. Pakistan had miscalculated the reaction of Kashmiris to its military adventure: they did not rise to revolt against Indian rule. Pakistan had also failed to calculate the reaction of the Indian government. At 3:30 a.m. on September 6, 1965, the Indian army crossed the international border in Punjab and caught Pakistan unaware. The two armies fought for another seventeen days. This time, India's victory was nearly total: India accepted cease-fire only after it had occupied 740 square miles, though Pakistan had made marginal gains of 210 square miles of territory. Despite the obvious strength of the Indian wins, both countries claim to have been victorious.

The failure of the Operation Gibraltar showed that outsiders could not easily stir the people of Indian-controlled Jammu and Kashmir on a small scale, though there were many discontented Kashmiris.

As part of an ill-conceived and stubborn strategy to make the people of Indian-controlled Kashmir rise against Indian rule, the Pakistani army continued sending operatives across the cease-fire line to recruit Kashmiri Muslims after the 1965 war came to an end. There were about eighty underground cells active in the Valley of Kashmir between 1965 and 1971, and the ISI did succeed in winning over some of these cells during the late 1960s.[25]

One of these groups was al-Fatah, founded by Ghulam Rasool Zahgir in the mid-1960s.[26] Later several smaller groups joined it and turned it into the most important group active during the late 1960s. Al-Fatah was the first organization from Indian-controlled Kashmir to establish formal links with the ISI, a relationship that al-Fatah had initiated. The ISI provided weapons, training, and sanctuaries to al-Fatah's fleeing fighters, though the ISI did not take a direct role in its militant actions. The ISI also provided little or no money; al-Fatah funded its subversive operations by looting Indian government departments and robbing banks. The al-Fatah militants looted over 70,000 rupees from the subdivisional education office in Pulwama in April 1970 and some 100,000 rupees from a local Hazratbal bank, using agents disguised in police uniforms, in January 1971. The police later arrested a handful of the al-Fatah fighters, which led to a raid of the group on January 13, 1971 and caused the arrest of nearly its entire membership. [27] The Indian government also expelled the first secretary in the Pakistani High Commission in New Delhi on January 24, 1971 for alleged "involvement in this subversive outfit."[28]

Another important group was the Plebiscite Front (for Azad Kashmir and Pakistan), formed just before Operation Gibraltar. The group was founded by Kashmiris in Pakistani-controlled Kashmir at a convention convened by Mir Abdul Mannan in Sialkot on April 4, 1965.[29] The first meeting nominated Abdul Khaliq Ansari its president, G.M. Lone its senior vice president, Ghulam Nabi Gulkaar its vice president, Amanullah Khan its secretary general, Majeed Amjad Bhat its joint secretary, G. M. Khan its assistant secretary, Mir Abdul Qayyum its treasurer, and Maqbool Bhat as publicity secretary. As soon as the convention was over, the participants boarded buses and traveled to an unguarded India-Pakistan boundary at Socheet Garh, twenty kilometres from the city of Jammu. One of them crossed the no man's land and brought back soil from across the working boundary. With the earth from "occupied" Jammu and Kashmir in their hands, the newly elected office-bearers of the Plebiscite Front (for Azad Kashmir and Pakistan) took an oath to work exclusively for the liberation of Jammu and Kashmir.[30]

The Plebiscite Front was not a homogenous group. Indeed, there were two currents of thought dividing it. The office-bearers for the most part rejected militancy, while members led by Amanullah Khan and Maqbool Bhat, who would become the best-known members of the group, wanted the group to pass a resolution for the establishment of a legislative assembly in Pakistani-controlled Azad Kashmir and to finalize a program for armed struggle for *azaadi* (liberation).

Discouraged by their colleagues, Amanullah Khan and Maqbool Bhat decided to found an underground group within the Plebiscite Front to plan for an armed struggle in Indian-controlled Kashmir. They won some of the members of the Plebiscite Front to their side. In a meeting in Peshawar from August 12 to 13, 1965, they named their underground group the National Liberation Front (NLF). The one-point program of the NLF was "to create such conditions through every means including the armed struggle for the people of the state of Jammu and Kashmir in which they can determine the future of their motherland."[31] Inspired by and organized on the model of the Algerian National Liberation Front, also called the NLF, the new group was divided into four wings. The military wing was headed by a Major Amanullah; a political wing was led by Amanullah Khan; a financial wing was headed by Mir Abdul Qayyum; and a *rabita,* or coordination wing, was put under Maqbool Bhat. All the members of the NLF were required to sign an oath in blood that they would not hesitate to sacrifice their lives to achieve the NLF objectives.

In a meeting in Karachi in November 1965, the NLF decided to send two groups to Indian-controlled Kashmir. One of the groups, headed by Maqbool Bhat, was to recruit young Kashmiris, and the other group, headed by Major Amanullah, was to give them military training. The two groups crossed the cease-fire line on June 10, 1966, at Dudhial.[32] Maqbool Bhat, Kala Khan, Ghulam Muhammad Dar, and Mir Ahmed set up underground cells in cities of Srinagar, Sopur, Baramula, Bandipura, and Anantnag. But as they left Srinagar to return to Pakistani-controlled Kashmir in September 1966, Indian intelligence agencies learned of their presence.

Sensing their vulnerability, they preemptively kidnapped a police inspector, Amarchand, from his house on their return to Pakistani-controlled Kashmir. When the inspector tried to escape, they pursued and killed him. The Indian army cordoned off the entire area and, with the help of a double agent, Ghulam Mohammad Dar, zeroed in the house where the group had taken sanctuary. In a subsequent clash with the Indian army, Kala Khan was killed and Maqbool Bhat, along with his comrades, surrendered, after they realized that it was not possible to escape.[33] The Indian security agencies later arrested hundreds of Kashmiris on suspicion of being NLF members, and some of them would remain behind bars for up to four years. They also registered cases against Maqbool Bhat and others for inciting the people against the state of India and the murder of Inspector Amarchand. Following an earlier plan, the other NLF faction, led by Major Amanullah, stayed near the cease-fire line to receive new recruits and give them military training. However, after learning about the clash between the NLF group and the Indian army, they withdrew to Pakistani-controlled Kashmir, where they were arrested by the Pakistani army.

The arrest of Maqbool Bhat in Indian-controlled Kashmir and the revelation about the existence of the NLF divided the Plebiscite Front into two clear groups, headed by Amanullah Khan and Mir Abdul Aziz respectively. The division came into the open at a meeting of the central working committee of the Plebiscite Front in September 1966. The position of the Amanullah-led group was that the establishment of the NLF aimed at putting the freedom struggle on the revolutionary track and that armed struggle must be part of the Plebiscite Front's program. The majority of the Plebiscite Front sided with Mir Abdul Aziz's group and "banned" the NLF as an unconstitutional body.

The Amanullah-led group, however, was slowly becoming stronger and their opposition quickly declined. The strengthening of the pro-militancy group disheartened Mir Abdul Aziz, and he left the Plebiscite Front in March 1968.

In August 1968, an Indian Kashmir court sentenced Maqbool Bhat and Mir Ahmed to death for killing Inspector Amarchand and Kala Khan to life in prison. But in December 1968, Maqbool Bhat, Mir Ahmed, and Chaudhary Yasin, another fighter who had been imprisoned in the Srinagar Central Jail since 1966, broke out of prison and reached Pakistani-controlled Kashmir after a harrowing sixteen-day trek through snow-covered mountains. They were arrested on reaching Pakistani-controlled Kashmir, though the Pakistani government released them under the pressure of agitation from the Plebiscite Front in March 1969.

The jailbreak by Maqbool Bhat and his comrades made the group famous, and it increased their power within the Plebiscite Front. In a convention held in November 1969, the Plebiscite Front finally abandoned its opposition to the NLF, declaring that Kashmir could only be liberated through an armed struggle. The convention also elected Maqbool Bhat president of the Plebiscite Front. Bhat then moved to publicly declare the NLF to be an armed wing of the organization, despite opposition from Amanullah Khan and other leaders. The Plebiscite Front, which had been inactive for the last two years, once again started working.

It sponsored a series of bomb explosions in Jammu, in the cities of Jammu and Pooncch, during the following summer. The group had particular success through contracting local mercenary Sikhs and Christians to carry out their actions. Targets included public places, such as a railway station and a bus station, as well as military installations, including the transit military camp at Satwari Cantonment, near Jammu; the divisional headquarters of the Indian army in Jammu, and an ammunition depot in the Kamial village in Pooncch. The NLF thought these bombing campaigns would draw the attention of the international community, but when the frequency of these operations increased, India imposed a curfew in and around Pooncch.[34] And although the Pakistani government was tolerant of the activities of the Plebiscite Front, it very often advised the local press to suppress news about their operations inside Indian-controlled Kashmir, fearing Indian reprisals.

To the disillusionment of the Plebiscite Front, the Kashmir issue did not attract international attention, and the organization soon began looking for ways to escalate their work, hoping to eventually carry out a dramatic act that would draw the world's attention to the Kashmir issue. In September 1970, the Popular Front for the Liberation of Palestine hijacked four jets bound for New York and successfully landed two of them at Dawson's Field in Jordan. They used the hostages to negotiate the release of Palestinian prisoners, and they were soon joined by a third hijacked jet. The operation was stunningly successful, attracting international media attention that climaxed with the detonation of three jets at Dawson's Field. The Plebiscite Front decided to try a hijacking of its own.

In the fall of 1969, Hashim Qureshi came from Srinagar to attend the wedding ceremony of his sister in Peshawar. There, he also met Maqbool Bhat. The two held several meetings and discussed the situation in Indian-controlled Kashmir, and during the meetings, Qureshi expressed his desire to join the NLF. Maqbool Bhat appointed Qureshi as the head of the NLF in the Valley of Kashmir. Qureshi went to Rawalpindi in April 1970, illegally crossing the cease-fire line. In Rawalpindi, he underwent physical training under the supervision of Subedar Yar Mohammad, a retired army soldier. By mid-1970, NLF leaders had developed confidence in Hashim Qureshi and asked him to lead the hijacking of an Indian airplane. Qureshi agreed.

Jamshed Manto, who was a former Pakistani air force pilot, trained Qureshi for his mission, which was planned for August 1970. Qureshi crossed the working boundary in Sialkot with the help of a professional smuggler after completing his preparations for the hijacking. However, the Indian Border Security Force, the BSF, arrested him in transit to Jammu, and confiscated the arms and equipment he was traveling with. Maqbool Bhat had instructed Hashim Qureshi to lie to Indian interrogators if he was arrested, to claim in particular that two other hijackers had crossed into Indian Kashmir on the same mission. Under torture, Hashim Qureshi fed his interrogators the misinformation. It turned out to be a key negotiating chip; Indian security officers eventually offered Qureshi a safe release if he would assist in the search for other conspirators. Qureshi agreed and asked for an appointment as an inspector in the BSF. The BSF complied and issued Qureshi a letter of appointment.[35]

Hashim Qureshi soon learned that the Indian security forces had also intercepted arms that Maqbool Bhat had separately sent to him. However, he continued preparations for the hijacking. With no access to weapons, Qureshi and three collaborators, Ashraf Qureshi, Jamil, and Gilani, decided to use toy weapons during the operation. They bought an authentic-looking toy pistol but could not find a toy grenade, which they eventually had fabricated for the operation. Ashraf Qureshi bought two air tickets to travel on an Indian Airlines flight from Srinagar to Jammu city on January 31, 1971 for what would be known as the Ganga hijacking. Hashim Qureshi traveled under a fake name, Mohammad Hussain. All this time, he was still working as an agent for the Indian BSF.

As soon as the pilot announced that the airplane was to land at the Jammu airport, Hashim Qureshi entered the cockpit with the toy pistol; Ashraf Qureshi stood outside the cockpit threatening the passengers and cabin crew with the toy grenade. The pilot, however, succeeded in informing the control tower in Jammu city that the airplane had been hijacked. Within a few minutes, Indian air force fighter planes surrounded the hijacked airplane. They demanded that the hijackers turn back. By this time, however, the airplane had entered Pakistani airspace near the city of Wazirabad in West Punjab, and Pakistani air force fighter planes took over and surrounded the airplane. The pilot told the hijackers that there was not enough fuel to go to Rawalpindi but that they could make it to Lahore. The hijackers agreed that the pilot would land at the Lahore airport.

The hijacking apparently took the Pakistani government by surprise. General Yahya Khan, who had been handed the presidency after the resignation of Ayub Khan in 1969, was alarmed. The Pakistani security agencies took over the hijacked airplane as soon as it landed in Lahore; hundreds of security personnel surrounded the plane.

Hashim Qureshi got out of the airplane at the airport and called Dr. Farooq Haider, a key NLF leader in Rawalpindi, to tell him that the "bird" had landed. Dr. Haider promised to call back in ten minutes, after consulting Maqbool Bhat, who had gone to Peshawar. Later a caller, who pretended to be Dr. Haider, told Hashim Qureshi to let the passengers get off the airplane. The hijackers wanted to use the passengers as hostages to get Kashmiri fighters released from the Indian jails, but they complied with what they thought to be Dr. Haider's orders. As it turned out, the caller had been an impostor—a Pakistani agent. The hostages had also been transported back to India, on February 2, despite the hijackers' understanding that they would be held in Lahore.

For three days after the plane, a Fokker F27, landed at the Lahore airport, the security agencies thoroughly searched it. They combed through documents and opened mail being transported on the airplane. According to witnesses, both the hijackers and the security personnel came in and out of the airplane without any hindrance. After the security agencies finished searching the airplane, they maneuvered the hijackers to set it on fire. The airplane turned into ashes in a few minutes, eighty hours after it had landed. The fire destroyed any evidence that Pakistani officials had broken international law by removing papers and opening postal bags.

The hijacking of the Ganga airplane instantly turned Hashim Qureshi, Ashraf Qureshi, Maqbool Bhat, and other NLF leaders into national heroes in Pakistan, particularly in Punjab and Pakistani-controlled Kashmir. Thousands of people turned up at the airport to celebrate. Political leaders, including Pakistan Peoples Party Chairman Z.A. Bhutto, whose party had emerged as the biggest political party in the general elections, supported the hijacking. Bhutto even came personally to congratulate and meet the hijackers. Before the fire, he asked them not to let the airplane go back to India because "that would be our defeat."[36] For weeks, the hijackers were free and welcomed as heroes wherever they went. They led mammoth public processions in Lahore and elsewhere, and they were showered with rose petals, with PPP members forming a majority of those in the processions.

The celebrations became political. Shaikh Mujibur Rehman, whose Awami League had won a landslide victory in what was then East Pakistan, believed that President

Yahya Khan, in collusion with Z.A. Bhutto, was behind the hijacking, and he demanded an inquiry. The military regime also backed away from the hijackers, even starting a smear campaign against them in the press by March 1971. The statements in the Pakistani press also started to cast doubts on the intentions of the hijackers. The press began to describe them as Indian agents who wanted to give India an excuse to cut the air links between East and West Pakistan, the most immediate result of the hijacking. A one-member investigation commission, headed by Justice Noorul Arifeen, declared the hijacking an Indian conspiracy and accused the NLF of working for Indian interests, a fact supported only by Hashim Qureshi's BSF appointment.

Instead of trying the hijackers in an ordinary court, the military regime constituted a special tribunal consisting of Justice Yaqub Ali Khan of the Supreme Court and Justice Abdul Qadir Shaikh of the Sindh High Court to try the NLF leaders. Initially, the government rounded up some 150 NLF fighters, including Hashim Qureshi, Ashraf Qureshi, and Maqbool Bhat. However, only six men were brought to trial in December 1971. The others remained in custody without trial—and were forced to undergo brutal treatment by the security agencies, including torture in the Lahore Fort, until December 1971. (Reports indicate that the prisoners were physically brutalized and forced to drink urine and eat excrement.)

The prosecution contended that Indian officials had helped Maqbool Bhat break out of the Srinagar jail in December 1968 and flee to Pakistan so that he could work as an undercover agent. In a 407-page verdict, announced on May 17, 1973, the tribunal acquitted Maqbool Bhat and collaborator G.M. Lone. Mir Abdul Qayyum and Mir Abdul Mannan were convicted of assisting the operation by sending unlicensed arms to Indian-controlled Jammu and Kashmir. Ashraf Qureshi was released a hero, but Hashim Qureshi was sentenced to fourteen years in prison—though there was little difference between their actions. Interestingly, Z.A. Bhutto, who had become president by the time the sentence was handed down, had declared that the government would free one of the accused and convict the other—in a careful balancing act, which seemed to neither favor nor condone the hijacking. Amanullah Khan and Maqbool Bhat appealed to the Supreme Court against the verdict within a few days on behalf of Hashim Qureshi, but the Supreme Court would not release Hashim Qureshi until 1980, some nine years after he was arrested.

In 1970 residents of the former East Pakistan, now Bangladesh, rose against the military rulers, and a prolonged civil war in East Pakistan followed. In December 1971, the Indian army intervened in support of the Bengali secessionists and pushed the breakup of Pakistan. The Pakistani army eventually surrendered.

India had finally taken revenge for Pakistani interventions in Jammu and Kashmir. The eventual defeat and partition of Pakistan in 1971 shocked Muslims in Jammu and Kashmir. Shaikh Abdullah had been wandering in political wilderness since he had been released by Prime Minister Indira Gandhi in 1968, and he was looking for a new political role in the changed political and geo-strategic situation. The events of 1971 shook him profoundly. He saw that the political landscape had changed once again—and Pakistan, with whom he was in occasional talks, was now badly crippled and would not be able to intervene again.

He was also in talks, sometimes direct and sometimes indirect, with the Indian leaders. The beginning of a solution to the Kashmir question had been slowly coming into focus. Under such circumstances, Shaikh Abdullah made one last effort to reach out to Pakistan. For the mission, he called his son and political heir, Farooq Abdullah, to Pakistan. Farooq Abdullah arrived from England, where he had been living, in late 1974. In Pakistan and Pakistani-controlled Jammu and Kashmir, Farooq Abdullah's hosts were the Plebiscite Front leaders, who tried to convince him of continuing to struggle for a sovereign state of Jammu and Kashmir. The young Abdullah also met high officials, including Prime Minister Z.A. Bhutto, who told him that a final solution had been more or less arrived at: The recognition of the LoC as an international border, he conceded, would need to be a final solution.[37] Prime Minister Bhutto also told Farooq Abdullah that Pakistan would not be able to give any help to the Kashmiris for another ten years, and that the Kashmiris should take whatever they could from India.[38] Farooq Abdullah then flew to Delhi, where he briefed Prime Minister Gandhi in the presence of his principal secretary, P.N. Dhar, and left for Srinagar.

After debriefing his son, Shaikh Abdullah's romance with the concept of plebiscite was finally over, and he accepted the ratification of the accession to India. Mirza Afzal Beg and Indian Union leaders had been discussing the possible accord for the last few years. Prime Minister Gandhi announced the five-point Accord in the Indian Parliament on February 24, 1975. First, they had agreed to keep Article 370. Second, the Indian Union was to retain control of legislation dealing with the sovereignty of India while residuary powers were to remain with the Jammu and Kashmir Assembly. Third, the Jammu and Kashmir Assembly could alter any future provision with the consent of the president of India. Fourth, the State could review the legislation after 1953 on the concurrent list; the president's assent was to be considered sympathetically. Fifth, Article 356 and the powers of the Indian Election Commission were to remain as they were.

In other words, the Accord changed little for Kashmir and its people, but it did pave the way for Abdullah to become chief minister. After signing the Accord, Shaikh Abdullah went from Jammu to Srinagar. The people of Kashmir seemed to understand the limitations of their leader, but there was jubilation. People thronged to the street to see Abdullah pass.

The gulf between the pro-militancy and anti-militancy groups within the Plebiscite Front increased in the wake of the Ganga hijacking, and the conflict between the two factions nearly paralyzed the organization. The anti-militancy group held most of the offices of the party, but both groups appear to have concluded by the mid-1970s that they could not continue to work together. The anti-militancy group demanded the formation of a committee to finalize a clear policy on armed struggle.

Before the committee could be constituted, however, Maqbool Bhat, along with Hameed Butt from Jammu and

Riaz Dar from the valley, once again went to Indian-controlled Jammu and Kashmir in May 1976 to recruit new members and set up cells. Bhat sent at least one group of young Kashmiris into Pakistani-controlled Kashmir to undergo military training. (Most of the Kashmiris interested in military training at this time came to Pakistan with Indian passports; from there they could go to Pakistani-controlled Jammu and Kashmir for training.)

During the recruitment mission Maqbool Bhat ran short of money; indeed the Plebiscite Front was always short of money. This time Bhat planned to rob a bank in a village. Unfortunately for Bhat, the bank employees resisted, and, in a shootout that followed, the bank manger was killed. Bhat tried to flee the scene, but the Indian security agencies soon arrested him.[39] The Plebiscite Front immediately dissociated itself from Bhat and the armed struggle. Bhat, having narrowly escaped severe sentences on several occasions, was sentenced to death, and the Indian government eventually transferred him to the Tihar jail in New Delhi in 1981 to await execution.

From the time of Bhat's arrest in 1976, a group of young Kashmiri expatriates in the United Kingdom worked in particular to defend Bhat. The group had been set up in 1971 as the United Kashmir Liberation Front; they had organized in the aftermath of the government crackdown on the NLF and the Plebiscite Front after the Ganga hijacking.[40] Originally they organized demonstrations against the physical and mental torture that members of the Plebiscite Front were undergoing in Indian and Pakistani jails. They were joined in England in 1973 by a new British wing of the Plebiscite Front. And in June of 1976, Amanullah Khan himself went to the United Kingdom to help organize the Plebiscite Front UK, where he continued to advocate for Bhat's release and the Kashmir issue at large. Amanullah Khan's arrival on the British scene could not have been better timed. Kashmiri expatriates were angry over a 1974 accord between Shaikh Abdullah and Indira Gandhi, and the Plebiscite Front in Indian-controlled Kashmir, now headed by Shaikh Abdullah, also stood discredited in the eyes of the Kashmiris. Khan intended to use his time in England to launch an international campaign for Kashmir and restore his standing.

In England, the leaders of the Plebiscite Front found it difficult to explain the difference between its organization and the United Kashmir Liberation Front. Amanullah Khan and some other members of the working committee of the Plebiscite Front added to the confusion by founding yet another new organization, the Jammu and Kashmir Liberation Front (JKLF) with the active support of Abdul Khaliq Ansari, president of the Plebiscite Front, on May 29, 1977, in a meeting in Birmingham, England. The Plebiscite Front UK was merged immediately merged into the new organization.

While the total number of original JKLF members did not exceed more than a few dozen, most of whom were drawn from the Plebiscite Front UK, the organization would quickly become the largest and most important, as well as the most iconic, group working on behalf of Kashmiri independence. JKLF leaders spent the next few years in setting up branches in New York, Holland, West

Germany, Denmark, France, Saudi Arabia, and the United
Arab Emirates.

Amanullah Khan and Abdul Khaliq Ansari agreed
that the Plebiscite Front for Azad Kashmir and Pakistan
would continue to work in Kashmir, while the JKLF would
work at the international level. They also agreed that the
Plebiscite Front should become active in both Kashmir and
Pakistan. Amanullah Khan returned to Pakistan in May
1980 and, at a meeting of the Working Committee of the
Plebiscite Front, proposed that the local Plebiscite Front
also merge with the JKLF. Though the leaders refused,
the Plebiscite Front would soon be eclipsed by the JKLF.
At a meeting in Birmingham on April 18, 1982, the JKLF
decided to add branches in Pakistani-controlled Jammu and
Kashmir and Pakistan.

From its inception, the JKLF has not considered the
Kashmir issue a territorial dispute between Pakistan and India. They maintain that neither Pakistan nor India has any
legal claim on any part of the state of Jammu and Kashmir.
Hence, it opposes the Simla agreement of 1972 between
Pakistan and India. The organization instead holds that the
only acceptable solution of the Kashmir issue is to merge
all the parts of the erstwhile state into a single sovereign
nation; they claim to be struggling to liberate the state
from foreign dominance and make it a sovereign nation.
The JKLF believes in waging the liberation struggle on all
fronts, including armed struggle. It has also dedicated itself
to assisting every group struggling for the sovereignty of
the state.

The JKLF, however, did not move quickly to restart
militancy. For several years, it worked more like a political group, bringing out protest demonstrations in European

capitals and in the United States, where there are a large number of Kashmiri expatriates. It held dozens of protest demonstrations between 1977 and 1984. In 1981, it held simultaneous demonstrations in a dozen European capitals. It also continued to hold protest demonstrations against the death sentence of Maqbool Bhat, in front of the Indian embassies in The Hague, London, Paris, Berlin, and Copenhagen. It again demonstrated in front of the diplomatic missions of India and Pakistan in the same countries on the eve of India-Pakistan bilateral talks in December 1982.

Amanullah Khan also gave considerable importance to writing letters to world leaders. He wrote hundreds of letters during the early period of the JKLF. He also wrote for newspapers and magazines throughout the world to create awareness about the Kashmir issue. He also wrote dozens of pamphlets on the subject and half a dozen books on Kashmir. In the early years, the JKLF particularly focused its activities on the United Nations headquarters in New York. Amanullah Khan traveled to New York four times between 1979 and 1984 to campaign among UN delegates for the liberation of Jammu and Kashmir.

On October 3, 1980, it launched a rogue protest at UN headquarters in New York: When the Indian foreign minister rose to speak, four JKLF members raised anti-India slogans, one after the other, from different corners of the Visitors Gallery. The Indian foreign minister had to wait for almost twenty minutes while the security guards overcame the JKLF activists.[41] JKLF activists also threw bundles of leaflets down onto the members seated below and into the halls of the UN.

Though many of the delegates didn't yet know it, an important new organization was announcing itself.

CHAPTER THREE

"I WANT TO FLEX MY MUSCLES"
PRELUDE TO JIHAD

At the end of 1976, confident of his popularity, Pakistani Prime Minister Zulfikar Ali Bhutto decided to schedule general elections for March 1977. Pakistan was experiencing a period of relative political calm. Although there was unrest in many urban areas, Bhutto's Pakistan Peoples Party looked certain to win the elections. Unexpectedly, however, the election announcement caused political turbulence. Dormant political and religious parties suddenly came to life, as well as a new group, the Pakistan National Alliance, or PNA, a collection of right-wing political and religious parties, among them the National Awami Party, a Pashtun nationalist party from the Frontier Province. It was political common sense that the PNA enjoyed the support of the Pakistani army and the ISI, which were not happy with the secularization of the country and wanted to reverse it. Bhutto, however, was sure that the army would not move against him; it was headed by Mohammad Zia-ul-Haq, an unusually obedient general who had been chosen personally by Bhutto to be chief of the army staff.

The elections themselves brought even more turbulence, with the PNA refusing to accept the results and holding demonstrations in cities throughout Pakistan. The protests turned violent in April 1977, and, under popular pressure, Bhutto started negotiations with the opposition. An agreement between Bhutto's government and the PNA was almost agreed upon and ready to be signed when General Zia declared martial law.

Zia had been a junior general when Bhutto tapped him to lead the army, and in taking the post he superseded a half-dozen more senior officers. Bhutto was attracted to Zia because he showed unusual respect to his political seniors, and because he was unlike other senior members of the army: Zia rejected the British pretensions of his colleagues, many of whom were trained at England's Sandhurst Royal Military Academy. But there was another side to General Zia: he was known to be exceedingly religious and close to the Jamat-i-Islami of Pakistan, a conservative religious party.

Bhutto saw General Zia for the last time before the coup at a diplomatic reception in Islamabad hosted by

U.S. Ambassador Arthur W. Hummel, Jr. on July 4, 1977. There, Bhutto watched Zia and the other members of the army leadership closely, hoping to catch any sign that a plot was in the works. Bhutto didn't see anything out of the ordinary and was confident of his army chief when he left the reception after dinner; he had gone to sleep without any worries. Bhutto was proved wrong. Late that night, he and members of his cabinet, as well as the members of the provincial cabinets, were awakened and arrested by junior army officers, who took them to safe houses in and around the capital. Zia took the reins of government on July 5 and he later chose cabinet ministers from the opposition alliance of PNA, and particularly from the Jamat-i-Islami of Pakistan.

Jamat-i-Islami had been founded in 1941 by Maulana Syed Abul A'ala Maududi, an Islamist writer who advocated revolutionary tactics for the Islamic movement. His first book, *Jihad in Islam*, published in the late 1920s, borrowed from vanguard revolutionary tactics and the Islamists' moral call. His writings advocated an Islamic state in India and, later, Pakistan and echoed the calls of the Saudi clergy in their demand for a return to Islamic law and politics. In 1947, Jamat-i-Islami opposed the creation of Pakistan under the rule of the secular Mohammad Ali Jinnah, though it favored making the Muslim population a separate state. Over time, the organization expanded, though its electoral successes were limited. Six independent parties were established: in Pakistan, India, Bangladesh, the United Kingdom, and both the Indian- and Pakistani-controlled zones of Kashmir. Each organization was a separate entity, with its own decision-making structure and process, though the group was united by ideology. The Pakistani Jamat-i-Islami remained the most important.

During the late 1960s, Jamat-i-Islami started coming closer to the Pakistani Army. The Pakistani Jamat-i-Islami and its student wing, Islami Jamiat Tulaba (IJT), under the names "al-Badr" and "al-Shams," fought alongside the army against the secular Bengali freedom fighters in Bangladesh. It was here that the Pakistani military realized it had an ally in Jamat-i-Islami. When Zia took the reins, he further elevated the organization, bringing its representatives into the government. Indeed, the Jamat-i-Islami of Pakistan became integral to the Martial Law regime, and the alliance between the Pakistani military and the Islamist parties has survived to this day.

In advance of the Iranian revolution, the *Tarjamanul Quran*, the official publication of the Jamat-i-Islami of Pakistan, had also been a powerful voice in support of the Ayatollah Khomeini. In 1978, to recognize the support from Maulana Maududi, Khomeini sent two of his representatives from Paris, Kamal Kharazi and Mohammad Jalali, to meet Maududi. They were brought to the offices of the Jamat-i-Islami of Pakistan at Icchra in Lahore in a large, public procession.

Jamat-i-Islami of Azad Jammu and Kashmir was founded in 1974, in hopes of slowing the rise of secular ideas in the region. Along with partners in Pakistan's Jamat-i-Islami, they also hoped to eventually liberate Indian-controlled Jammu and Kashmir and merge them with Pakistan. A veteran jihadi, Maulana Abdul Bari, who had participated in the 1947 jihad as well as in Operation Gibraltar in 1965, was named founding amir. Bari had close links to the Saudi establishment, having joined the Muslim World League in Saudi Arabia in 1974, just a month after the foundation of the new chapter of Jamat-i-Islami.

The key meeting is still shrouded in secrecy. But according to several sources, General Zia-ul Haq called a meeting with Jamat-i-Islami's Maulana Abdul Bari in Rawalpindi in early 1980.

According to Bari, the general stated his intentions plainly: he had decided to contribute to the American-sponsored war in Afghanistan in order to prepare the ground for a larger conflict in Kashmir, and he wanted to involve the Jamat-i-Islami of Azad Jammu and Kashmir. To the general, the war in Afghanistan would be a smokescreen behind which Pakistan could carefully prepare a more significant battle in Kashmir. The general said he had carefully calculated his support for the American operation, predicting that the Americans would be distracted by the fighting in Afghanistan and, as a result, turn a blind eye to Pakistani moves in the region. Bari was skeptical. The Afghan operation was enterprising, but it didn't necessarily give Pakistan the room to make a move.

"But how can the Americans stop us from waging jihad in Kashmir when they themselves are waging jihad in Afghanistan?" the general asked.

There was also, according to Zia, a financial dimension. The cost of Pakistani military aid and support for the war in Afghanistan—to be reimbursed by the CIA and the

Saudis—could be greatly inflated, and General Zia promised to give a large portion of the profit to Bari's Jamat-i-Islami. Guns and ammunition could also be diverted to Kashmir.

The beginnings of the plan had already been set in motion, and Zia dictated Abdul Bari's role: he was to gather international support for the Kashmiri cause, from international Islamic movements in particular.[1] And he was to bring the Jamat-i-Islami of Azad Jammu and Kashmir into cooperation with the Pakistani army.

Bari agreed.

As Zia and Bari got up to leave the room, Bari asked, "Who in the Afghan jihad will receive the biggest share of the international arms and American financial assistance?" Zia smiled, and said, "Maulana! Please leave that to us!" He paused and, seeing Bari's blank face, added, "Whoever trains the boys from Kashmir." A triumphant smile appeared on Bari's face. Kashmir had determined the direction of the Afghan jihad.

General Zia arranged a series of meetings for Bari with ISI officials at the office of the military secretary in Rawalpindi. During one meeting Bari realized that ISI officials did not have a clear plan for Kashmir. Their goals, as stated during meetings with Bari, chiefly involved intelligence: they wanted Bari and his group to survey the political mood of the Kashmiri leaders in Indian-controlled Kashmir and report back. They advised Bari on how to go about making approaches.

The ISI wanted to be able to predict how local Kashmiris would react to a Pakistani-supported war. In this role, Bari had some experience. In 1980, after meeting Zia, he had traveled to Mecca to attend a meeting of the Rabita Alam Islami (Muslim World League).[2] There he sought help from the leaders of international Islamic movements in liberating Indian-controlled Kashmir. Though no firm commitments were made in 1980, Bari was encouraged—and encouraged to return.

When Bari traveled to Indian-controlled Kashmir, he held meetings with a wide array of politicians and activists. He also met many in the underground movement for Kashmiri independence. Typical was a meeting with Maulana Sa'adud Din, the founding amir of the Jamat-i-Islami of Indian-controlled Kashmir.

Their meeting was held in secret, in the house of a Jamat-i-Islami official, in a small village called Ajis, fifteen miles outside Srinagar. Din had many reservations about involving Pakistan in Jamat-i-Islami's struggle for Kashmir. He argued that Pakistan had never been transparent with the Jamat-i-Islami during their previous military campaigns. And during Operation Gibraltar, some fifteen years earlier, Pakistan had not even informed the Kashmiri leadership of their plans. Kashmiri leaders had been ignored again during the 1971 war. It was India that had inflicted all kinds of atrocities on the Kashmiris who cooperated with the Pakistanis during the Gibraltar operation and later—but such atrocities, Din argued, had only been possible because the Pakistanis had abandoned their Kashmiri comrades.

To Din, the Pakistani army simply wasn't a wise course for Kashmiri independence. And certainly not for an organization like the the Jamat-i-Islami—which struggled independently.

Nonetheless, Din and Bari agreed that a decision should be made by the larger group—and Din proposed that Bari present his case before the officials of the Jamat-i-Islami of Indian-controlled Kashmir. In Bari's address to a closed-door meeting at the offices of Jamat-i-Islami, he demanded realism: "If you think the Pakistan army will come and fight in Srinagar to liberate you, it is not possible." After Pakistan's two overt attempts at military intervention in Kashmir, Bari insisted that a new strategy was necessary. This time he proposed that the Pakistani army could support their cause but without troops. They would of course have the support of the two Jamat-i-Islamis, one in Azad Jammu and Kashmir and one in Pakistan. But, relaying General Zia's message, Bari said they would also have the support of the Pakistani military and the ISI. "You yourselves will have to rise to get freedom," he declared. But the ISI would pay the bill, and stand behind them with other kinds of support.

As he recalled later, the strategy was simple: "You will have to do the fighting, and they provide all assistance."

As soon as Bari returned to Pakistan, he was summoned by the ISI. Officials there asked if he had formulated a plan— and they wanted to know the results of his meetings.

Bari said that he felt he had the support of the Jamat-i-Islami of Indian-controlled Jammu and Kashmir, though no overt endorsement had ever been given. The ISI still had work to do to move the Kashmiri movement toward Pakistan, but his contacts had, in the end, reacted positively to the offer of support from General Zia. They would, he thought, provide the manpower for a new military operation in Kashmir.

The trip had been dangerous for Bari, as well as for the leaders on both sides of the Line of Control. Bari told ISI officials that as he had moved around, he had encountered intense media and intelligence attention. He had entered Indian-controlled Jammu and Kashmir legally, with a visa to visit family in the territory. But he couldn't afford to keep operating out in the open.[3]

Further negotiations in Indian-controlled Jammu and Kashmir would require more precaution. It was decided that the best way to avoid the Indian intelligence services was for the ISI to arrange for large meetings in Saudi Arabia, where participants could travel under the cover of hajj, religious pilgrimage.

Within a week of his second round of meetings with ISI officials, Bari was in Saudi Arabia meeting with Kashmiri leaders. During his stay, he was the chief go-between for the ISI and the Kashmiris.

These indirect negotiations continued through September 1982, when the ISI invited Kashmiri leaders to Pakistan for direct negotiations and final planning. Again, there was great effort taken to avoid the notice of the Indian intelligence services. Leaders traveling from Indian-controlled Kashmir went through Saudi Arabia, with the full cooperation of the Saudi intelligence. Neither Saudi nor Pakistani officials stamped their passports.

Kashmiri leaders soon held detailed meetings with the ISI. At these first direct meetings, some consensus was reached. Their plan was the product of many conversations, but it lacked detail. The strategy was jihad—a holy war waged against Indian oppression, a campaign for "freedom." Members of Jamat-i-Islami were to return to Indian-controlled Kashmir and begin the recruitment of young Kashmiris— who would, the plan went, be sent at first opportunity for military training.

This series of meetings was kept in absolute confidence. Senior members of Jamat-i-Islami were not informed. Even Din, the founding amir of the organization, was in the dark.

Din, the earliest critic of the plan to collaborate with the Pakistani army, turned out to be one of its most influential opponents. Because of his continued opposition to new military action with the Pakistanis, he was summoned by the ISI to Saudi Arabia in late 1982. Again, the pretext was a pilgrimage—though the real purpose of his visit was quickly revealed after his arrival.

In a meeting on January 17, 1983, Din voiced many of the same concerns to the ISI that he had in his earlier meetings with Bari. Din believed that no action should begin until victory was assured. Little agreement could be reached, but Din did agree to one point: he would meet personally with General Zia-ul-Haq.

A preliminary meeting between General Zia and Bari was held on February 27, 1983. Bari coached the general on what arguments needed to be made to Din and stressed the importance of having the support of the Jamat-i-Islami of Indian-controlled Jammu and Kashmir. He requested that Din be made a guest of state during his visit. General Zia agreed.

In a series of meetings between May 4 and May 10, 1983, Din moved quickly to define the respective roles of his Jamat-i-Islami and the Pakistani army in the preparation for an armed struggle. Din had come around to accepting some Pakistani involvement in future efforts, but he would be slow in committing to General Zia.

Din's position was somewhat modified. He conceded that the Pakistanis now held a stake in what was obviously an emerging and influential plan. But, in exchange for his support, he wanted to drastically limit the role of the Pakistani army in the conflict. In his mind, the army should provide only military training and financial support. Everything else must be left to Jamat-i-Islami.

General Zia pressed Din to come to an agreement. Zia and ISI were willing to agree to a limited role, but they wanted a firm commitment that Jamat-i-Islami would send its units for training. Din resisted such a commitment on this point and the talks stalled for a time; Din said he had to return to Kashmir and speak with the leaders there.[4] General Zia was bitter about Din's lack of enthusiasm, and his inability to sway Din in the meetings engendered a long-term resentment. He thought of Din as an oddball, telling aides that Din "comes from a cold region. He starts coughing when he comes here."[5]

Despite the tension, Din did indeed return, three days later—and he finally made a deal with General Zia. Din would direct his Jamat-i-Islami members to begin receiving military training immediately. After nearly three years of planning, the Jamat-i-Islami of Indian-controlled Jammu and Kashmir had a pact with General Zia.

Din sent his son with the first group of volunteers set to receive military training.[6]

On October 13, 1983, the Indian XI cricket team led by Kapil Dev faced the West Indian XI team at the Amar

Singh Club Stadium in Srinagar. Throughout the stands, fans hoisted huge portraits of Imran Khan, the Pakistani cricket hero, and shouted anti-Indian slogans. Supporters of Jamat-i-Islami, sprinkled throughout the crowd, waved party flags—green and nearly identical to the Pakistani flag. Spectators threw eggs and rotten fruit at the Indian team, and they rushed the field at one point, beating and bloodying Indian players.[7]

Throughout Srinagar and Indian Kashmir, the mood was shifting. There was a rise in anti-Indian sentiment, and a turn toward Pakistan. It could be seen in the streets as well as at cricket matches. It also manifested itself in a stunning series of terrorist bombings in 1983 and 1984.[8] Three bombs exploded in the stands of the Bakhshhi stadium in Srinagar on August 15, 1983, Indian Independence Day. Five days later, four JKLF activists were arrested on charges of involvement in the violence.[9] Communal riots broke out in Bhiwandi in May 1984; there, too, the crowd raised Pakistani flags, praised Pakistan, and destroyed Indian army vehicles. The marchers also set fire to a number of buildings on their route.[10] The violence repeated itself in Anantnag in February of 1986, where Hindu temples were destroyed and Hindus were forced to flee the city.[11]

Rhetoric heated up everywhere. A notable activist, Azam Inquilabi, one of the first Kashmiris to work directly with the Pakistanis, made a public show of writing "Long Live Pakistan!" in his own blood. He also claimed that Kashmir was more important to Muslims than Mecca or Medina.[12] Throughout Kashmir the mood was shifting, the message turning against Indian rule. In the run-up to elections in 1977, Shaikh Abdullah had run a campaign against the Indians with the slogans "Hold the plebiscite!" and "Indian dogs go home!" But now the movement was turning more religious, and it shifted increasingly toward Pakistan.

It was also a period of political unrest. Shaikh Abdullah died on September 8, 1982, and the position of chief minister of Jammu and Kashmir was transferred to his son, Farooq Abdullah, a relatively inexperienced politician who had spent most of his life in England. The young Abdullah was known as the "disco chief minister" and was often seen riding through the streets of Srinagar on a motorcycle. Farooq Abdullah was caught in the middle of evolving political turmoil, depicted as a stooge of the Indian government by some and a defender of Kashmiri sovereignty by others. He negotiated a degree of self-government for Jammu and Kashmir, but he faltered in his negotiations with both Pakistan and India. His father had negotiated a resettlement agreement before his death, a piece of legislation that would have allowed any Kashmiri to return to his or her home. But the Indian government objected to the legislation, which acquired the approval of the New Delhi government, on the grounds that citizenship was a question for the national government. Abdullah also locked himself in battle with Indian Prime Minister Indira Gandhi, who vowed to run Congress Party candidates in Jammu and Kashmir. Abdullah's National Conference Party rejected a major compromise with Gandhi's Congress Party, antagonizing Gandhi personally. The young Abdullah was eventually forced from power, accused of supporting Sikh nationalists and allowing them to train in Jammu and Kashmir, an accusation that he denied. Thirteen members of the Kashmiri legislative council withdrew their support for Abdullah, and he was replaced by his brother-in-law, G.M. Shah, in July 1984.

Abdullah's dismissal set off another wave of protest and strengthened a coalition of new players. Among them was the Islami Jamiat-i-Tulaba, the Islamic Organization of Students or IJT, which became a vehicle for an emerging coalition that opposed the Indian Union government. The IJT was founded in the 1960s, but it remained mostly inactive and lacking support until 1980, when it became active under the leadership of Shaikh Tajamul Islam. Tajamul Islam was immensely inspired by the political writing of Jamat-i-Islami's Maulana Maududi, as well as with the success of the Islamic revolution in Iran. Shaikh Tajamul Islam questioned Jammu and Kashmir's accession to India and called the Indian troops "an occupation army." At a press conference in March 1980, he vowed to establish an Islamic state in Jammu and Kashmir, and in August 1980, he announced he would work toward an Iranian-style Islamic revolution. The group's aim was to keep the freedom struggle rooted in Islam. In the words of Innayat Ullah Andrabi, an Islamist ideologue active in the anti-India movement, "It combined the causes of liberation and Islam." [13] Shaikh Tajamul Islam also ran campaigns against video stores and the sale of liquor; he was arrested and held by Indian authorities on several occasions during the 1970s and 1980s.

The IJT remained at the center stage of Islamist politics until 1989. By 1991, the group had grown to be more than a student association and its target audience had expanded to include the entire the Muslim population. In 1991, the Islami Jamiat-i-Tulaba converted itself into Mahaz-i-Azadi.

And in 1991, more than twelve organizations including the Mahaz-i-Azadi set up the "Forum Against Sellout" to keep pressuring for the implementation of the UN resolutions. IJT believed in Jammu and Kashmir's integration with Pakistan in the short term, but its main goal was to establish a pan-Islamic state.

Another group that played on nationalist sentiments among the Muslims of Kashmir was the Islamic Students League, or ISL. It had a humble beginning but became a major group during the late 1980s. Its origins were in the Tula Party, an informal clandestine group formed by a number of young students in Srinagar in 1985.[14] Much as the Islamic revolution of Iran had impressed the IJT, the Palestinian struggle and Afghan war inspired the boys who formed Tula.[15] The party included both Islamist and secular students, many of whom later played key roles in the militancy. Some of them went to meet Palestinian fighters in New Delhi, took portraits of the fighters back to Srinagar and exhibited them on the polo grounds for the Muslim festival of 'Id, and used the exhibition to raise funds for the Afghan mujahideen, some 9,000 rupees in total.[16]

In its early days, the group adopted the slogan "Say with pride we are Muslims" and jihad as its goal. They also used the slogan *Kashmir baney ga Pakistan*, "Kashmir will become part of Pakistan." [17] The ISL never boasted a large membership; it numbered around eighty, mostly based in Srinagar, Baramula, and Anantnag. The group, however, played a seminal role in introducing the culture of violence to Jammu and Kashmir. Its flag explained its ideology: it featured a world globe, on top of which sat a Kalashnikov rifle with a flag affixed to its bayonet. The flag carried the words "There is no god but Allah and Mohammad is the prophet of Allah." Below the globe is written "Muslims of the world, unite."

Ansarul Islam ("the helpers of Islam") also played a decisive role in converting the nationalist movement into a jihadi movement. It came into being under the name of Shubbabul Islam ("the youth of Islam") sometime in 1984 but later took on the more Islamist name. The founder of the group was Hilal Ahmed Mir, who used the aliases Nasirul Islam and Abu Jihad, "father of jihad." He came into politics in 1977, the year in which Shaikh Abdullah came into office for the last time and banned the teaching of Islamic studies in public schools. Mir was studying at the Hanafia Arabia College in Srinagar at that time and led his religiously motivated friends to the main gate of the government secretariat in Srinagar to protest against the decision. The police arrested him along with other protestors. After his release, he founded Shubbabul Islam on December 15, 1977.[18] A three-day meeting of the majlis-i-shoura, or consultative council, of the Shubbabul Islam in September 1983, which took place in Baramula, renamed Shubbabul Islam as Ansarul Islam and elected Mir as its amir. In a communiqué issued at the end of this secret meeting, the group pledged to work for the unity of the "ummah [Muslim nation] and the establishment of a caliphate in addition to push the usurping India out of the state of Jammu and Kashmir." Most importantly, the majlis-i-shoura also decided to provide rudimentary military training to its members. They selected the forests of Khansahib in Budgam and Pehelgam in Islamabad to set up training camps. The initial training consisted of handling of local guns. However, the members soon started demanding training in automatic arms, which was possible only in Afghanistan. In a meeting in Srinagar on August 5, 1985, the majlis-i-shoura decided to look for unguarded routes from Kashmir to Afghanistan. The organization spent many months searching for such routes, with the first batch of the mujahideen crossing the line of control and reaching Pakistani-controlled Jammu and Kashmir in the middle of 1986. From there, they went to Afghanistan to get further military training.

In September 1986, a dozen Islamist parties that had shown little promise in the past elections organized themselves under the umbrella of the Muslim United Front (MUF) on the eve of the state assembly elections.[19] The ISL decided to join the MUF, and the group played a key role in organizing and disciplining the public rallies.[20] Since Prime Minister Gandhi's assassination by Sikh nationalists in October 1984, Farooq Abdullah had slowly reemerged on the political scene, under the banner of a combined National Conference-Congress party. When the elections finally came on March 23, 1987, some 75 percent of the voters participated. Farooq Abdullah's combined party won sixty-six seats (the Congress Party won five out of six seats its candidates had contested), while the MUF won just four seats. It had hoped to win about ten seats, having run forty-four candidates. However, the MUF did succeed in unleashing the pro-Pakistani sentiments of young people. They openly sang and played Pakistani national songs at the MUF rallies—another sign of growing dissatisfaction with Indian rule.[21]

There was also widespread rejection of the election results. The MUF thought that the election had been rigged, and there was anger about Farooq Abdullah's coalition with the Congress party, which he later admitted had been a serious political error. It tainted his reputation, putting him too close to India. Though calm settled for a moment, dissent throughout the valley soon erupted. In May 1987, Farooq Abdullah's motorcade was attacked while in transit to a mosque. The parties associated with MUF were angry.

By the mid-1980s, the JKLF was ineffectual. It was badly beaten, and its leadership didn't have the manpower or the resources to make a move, to influence policy. It had been at the center of a movement for Kashmiri independence for so long that it had become a center of attention, vulnerable and under heavy surveillance. Both Pakistan and India had tried to crush it. For a while, a calm fell over the organization.

But during the JKLF's dormancy, something surprising happened. Elements within the group struck out on their own, frustrated by JKLF inaction. On February 3, 1984, a group of militants, who called themselves the Kashmir Liberation Army, kidnapped the assistant high commissioner of India in Birmingham, England, Ravindra Mhatre, without the permission or knowledge of the JKLF leadership.[22] In exchange for the commissioner, they demanded the release of Maqbool Bhat and other JKLF fighters held in jails in New Delhi and Kashmir within twenty-four hours, along with one million dollars. When the deadline expired, the kidnappers killed Mhatre. India, which had recently reinstated the death penalty, retaliated by hanging Maqbool Bhat on February 11.

The kidnapping and murder of Mhatre once again brought the JKLF into the headlines and revealed the potential of its fighters. The ISI in particular was watching the group closely, frustrated with Din and Jamat-i-Islami—which had yet to make a move. ISI officials were looking for other actors who would involve themselves in armed resistance. In May 1984, Director General of the ISI Lieutenant General Akhtar Abdur Rehman went so far as to make contact with the JKLF leadership. He and other ISI officials held several meetings with the group during the later part of 1984. Most of these meetings took place at the Margalla Motel in Islamabad. General Rehman attempted to conceal his identity from the JKLF leaders, but he was recognized almost instantly. He offered financial and other assistance to the JKLF so they could continue their struggle and offered to help start an armed revolt. He proposed a scenario very much like what had been proposed years earlier to the Jamat-i-Islami. The two sides used these meetings to weigh their options, but neither side committed to any action. The ISI broke away from the meetings suddenly at the end of 1984 because Jamat-i-Islami again made significant moves toward planning a jihad. But it again went back on its promise and stalled.[23]

On September 5, 1985, British police arrested Amanullah Khan and a handful of JKLF militants. Within a few days, they were released—with the exception of Khan, who was charged with possession of chemicals that could be used to manufacture explosives. The charges couldn't be proven in court, though the Thatcher government subsequently ordered Khan's deportation on national security grounds in December 1986. By the time he landed at the

Karachi airport, Khan himself had come full circle: he had gone to England in 1976 to organize the Plebiscite Front, a political solution. But the organization had run out of options, and now here he was—deported. He had come to believe that armed struggle was really the only option left to the JKLF. Khan realized the importance of the JKLF's position and its potential role in a military conflict. It was the only organization in Kashmir with an organizational structure and a high profile. But it was lacking resources and its future was uncertain.

Khan had not yet heard of the ISI's salvo and its potential support, a topic that was back on the table; the ISI had restarted talks with the JKLF in 1986. It reached out to JKLF leaders, including Dr. Farooq Haider, in Rawalpindi. Haider had taken two key associates, Raja Muzzaffar and Sardar Rashid Hasrat, into confidence by this time, and the three were now very much inclined toward accepting whatever help the ISI could give. Haider thought it necessary to talk to Amanullah Khan and get his approval for the collaboration, so he asked Khan to come to Rawalpindi, where some "new developments" were taking place. Frustrated and embittered, Khan assumed that Haider was talking about an alliance of political parties in Pakistani-controlled Kashmir. Since he was unable to go to Rawalpindi at that time, he asked Haider to make decisions at his discretion after consultation with other JKLF leaders in Rawalpindi.[24] In the fall of 1986, the ISI and the JKLF finally agreed to cooperate. They decided to accelerate their activities in Indian-controlled Jammu and Kashmir, to give guerrilla military training to Kashmiri youth, and to form secret, underground cells of the trained Kashmiris, which would be activated later. The JKLF leaders believed that they would be able to create enough subversion in Kashmir to attract international attention if they succeeded in recruiting even fifty fighters.[25]

The two groups sent Rauf Kashmiri to assess the situation in Indian-controlled Kashmir and to survey opportunities for alliances and recruitment. There, he met many Kashmiri leaders, but he later reported that he was not taken seriously, nor impressed. On his return to Rawalpindi, Kashmiri advised JKLF leaders to ignore the more prominent Kashmiri leaders and concentrate instead on young students who had expressed interest in the JKLF's plans.

Amanullah Khan went to Rawalpindi in March 1987 and was shocked to learn about the "new developments" with the ISI. "How could we trust and cooperate with the ISI, which had stabbed us twice in the past?" he angrily asked Haider. However, he soon realized the ISI's potential for helping the JKLF to create an independent state in Kashmir. He recognized that Haider's move was a smart bet. Khan decided to gamble as well, asking Haider to arrange a private meeting with ISI officials so Khan could go over the details of the collaboration.[26] A meeting was arranged between Khan and a brigadier of the ISI, and subsequent meetings followed.[27] At a second meeting, the brigadier informed Khan that General Zia himself had made the decision to cooperate with the JKLF. He also assured Khan that the ISI would give the organization a free hand, with the ISI promising to not interfere with JKLF organizational matters.

Khan also confirmed the terms and conditions for cooperation with the ISI, which the ISI had already agreed to during meetings with Haider. In his meeting with the

brigadier, Khan bluntly insisted that the relationship between the JKLF and the ISI would not be that of a master
and a slave, nor that of employer and employee. The role
of the JKLF was to be limited to bringing young Kashmiri
boys to Pakistan for military training, while the role of the
ISI would be restricted to training and arming them. The
JKLF was to decide upon the strategy for armed struggle
inside Indian-controlled Jammu and Kashmir. And Khan
warned the brigadier against giving any direct orders to
the JKLF, since they were under separate authority. There
was considerable tension between the two organizations,
with each having its own goals. There was also an ideological difference: ISI officials saw the conflict over Kashmir in religious terms, whereas the JKLF had a secular
agenda. Khan told the brigadier, "As a Muslim, I believe in
the *kalima*" (the belief that there is no god but Allah and
Mohammad is his Prophet) "as a Kashmiri, I believe in a
sovereign Kashmir." [28] Khan also got the brigadier to agree
that the ISI would not try to pass money to any member of
the political or diplomatic wing of the JKLF.[29] The JKLF
and the ISI conferred on other points, such as the slogan of
the movement: "*azadi*," freedom. For JKLF leaders, *azadi*
meant an independent state of Jammu and Kashmir, while
for the ISI the slogan could mean secession from India and
accession to Pakistan.[30]

This was what Amanullah Khan called a "gentleman's
agreement." And soon the collaboration got under way.
The ISI published and smuggled into Indian Jammu and
Kashmir two booklets by Khan in Urdu, and in large quantities. These booklets, *The Ideology of Sovereign Kashmir*
and *Why Sovereign Kashmir?* inaugurated the new move-

ment and explicated the JKLF's fundamental ideology.[31] The JKLF started recruiting young Kashmiris in the spring of 1987. And the ISI went one step further than its agreement, pushing militants it was already handling to join the JKLF. This included many small groups of Kashmiri mujahideen, operating at district, subdivision, and neighborhood levels. All of these forces were directed to take militant training in Pakistan, Afghanistan, and Pakistan-controlled Jammu and Kashmir under the JKLF flag.

Khan also set up the Jammu and Kashmir Students Liberation Front (JKSLF) in Karachi on April 17, 1987. The prime objective of the JKSLF was to recruit young men from Pakistan and Pakistani-controlled Kashmir. In 1989, the JKLF opened a separate chapter of the JKSLF in Indian-controlled Jammu and Kashmir, headed by Hilal Ahmed Beg. The openings were part of the larger recruitment drive on both sides of the Line of Control, which was put into motion during 1987 and the first half of 1988.[32] Recruits were brought to Pakistani-controlled Jammu and Kashmir and Rawalpindi, where they received guerrilla training. They then returned home to set up underground sleeper cells. The JKLF had set up some 300 such cells in the Valley of Kashmir by mid-1988, and it later shifted its attention to Jammu and Ladakh. It had set up about 10 cells in Kishtwar and Doda, four in Jammu city, four in Pooncch, and three in Ladakh. However, the JKLF still wanted more time to extend its network to other parts of the Jammu and Ladakh divisions. They also wanted to set up hideouts for retreating fighters in the Pir Panjal region.[33]

During the planning stages, the militants were strictly forbidden to carry out any military action. Instead, they were asked to give ideological and militant training to others and wait for directions from the JKLF leadership in Pakistan. The first batch of fighters from Indian-controlled Jammu and Kashmir under the JKLF flag traveled to Pakistani-controlled Jammu and Kashmir for specialized training in February 1988.[34]

On the morning of April 10, 1988, an explosion shook the streets near Pakistan's Ojjhri ammunition depot in Rawalpindi. Within seconds, a chain reaction of detonations began, with thousands of small arms, bombs, and missiles exploding in the sky. Projectiles landed scattershot on the twin cities of Rawalpindi and Islamabad. Witnesses assumed that it was a catastrophic attack; the sky was full of missiles. About one hundred buildings were damaged and dozens were killed as explosions filled the sky with debris for nearly twenty-four hours. The Ojjhri depot was used to store weapons for the Afghan mujahideen, collected from the CIA and other sources. The Afghan and Kashmir cells of the ISI were housed in the same camp. It was a sensitive facility, but it had somehow been compromised.

In Srinagar, a huge, violent crowd took to the streets. Kashmiris had heard that India was behind the attack—and they didn't hesitate to protest. Members of the Islamic Students League joined the protests and actively participated in the violence.[35] JKLF leaders watching events unfold were encouraged—the population seemed ready to take to the streets to protest what seemed to be insignificant events and suspicions. Violence again broke out in Srinagar on June 9, 1988, to protest a hike in the electricity rates, a not unusual occurrence. The protest lasted for nearly a week; five people were killed and nearly one hundred injured during the chaos. JKLF took this ongoing unrest to be a sign that an independence movement had the potential for mass appeal; the population was becoming more and more disenchanted with the state and union governments. A rebellion might have a chance to succeed.

By the spring of 1988, General Zia's regime had also started pressing the JKLF leaders to begin the armed campaign. In a meeting in Rawalpindi with JKLF leaders early in the summer of 1988, an emissary of General Zia quoted the general as saying, "I want to flex my muscles because we have already sent a lot of arms and ammunition."[36] But, despite the encouraging response the JKLF had received from the Kashmiri youth—and the protests they saw unfolding—the organization's leadership still didn't think the timing was right. They hoped to train more fighters and create more cells. And there was still more planning to be done.

Encouraged by the events in Srinagar, the ISI pushed the JKLF leadership to call Ghulam Nabi Butt, S.M. Afzal, and Ghulam Hasan Lone, important JKLF operatives who had been tasked with launching the armed struggle, to Pakistani-controlled Jammu and Kashmir for consultations. At the end of these discussions, they reluctantly agreed to set the Martyrs of 1931 Day, July 13, as the formal start of the campaign. Fazal Ahmed Wani and Manzoor Ahmed of Pakistani-controlled Jammu and Kashmir were sent to Srinagar to prepare for the launch of the fighting.[37] Wani reported that there were approximately 10,000 trained militants, working in some fifty units.

Within the JKLF, there was still apprehension about the premature launch of the conflict. In Srinagar, Azam Inquilabi even stopped Bilal Siddiqui, another key militant, from carrying out orders for the planned July 13 action, because he thought it premature.[38] But plans were soon back on track. ISI pressure to coordinate attacks by the end of July was significant. According to JKLF's Hanif Haidery, senior JKLF members sent Nazimud Din to push the militants forward, saying that if they didn't move by the end of July, the JKLF would hand over a dossier containing photographs and information on all militant operatives to the Indian security forces.[39] With this, final plans for action were set for July 31, 1988.[40] Four bombings were carried out, though only two were successful.

In Srinagar, there were two explosions: one outside the Central Post and Telegraph office and the other near the Amar Singh Club. Two more bombs, one affixed to a wall of the Congress Party headquarters and the other to the walls of the Radio Kashmir building, failed to explode. The attacks were eventually linked the al-Hamza group, working alongside JKLF. Amanullah Khan took credit for the attacks, though other factions tried to disassociate themselves from the actions. The explosions triggered large-scale Indian arrests of Muslim youth—and the JKLF was marked, linked to the ongoing violence. Now the fight was in the open. It was a mostly symbolic beginning, but a new war had started.

CHAPTER FOUR

"A NEW GAME HAS STARTED"
THE RISE OF HIZBUL MUJAHIDEEN

At 3:36 pm on August 17, 1988, the Pak One, an American-made C-130 and the official plane of General Muhammad Zia-ul-Haq, took off from a military base just outside the small desert city of Bahawalpur in Pakistani Punjab, on a return flight to Islamabad. General Zia had been invited to witness the desert test of the Abrams tank, which the Americans were trying to sell to the Pakistani Army. The test had been an unmitigated disaster—the tank hadn't hit a single target. Less than five minutes outside Bahawalpur, the plane exploded, nose-dived, and crashed. All thirty-one passengers were killed. On board were eight other Pakistani generals, as well as former ISI chief Lieutenant General Akhtar Abdur Rehman, who had run the Afghan jihad for more than eight years. Also on board were Arnold Raphel, who was the American ambassador to Pakistan, and General Herbert M. Wassom, the head of the American military aid mission. The bodies of everyone on board were burned to char.

General Mirza Aslam Beg, who had been at the Abrams demonstration but had chosen not to fly with General Zia, took over the command of the army. Fearing a coup, he ordered troop movements, including sending units to guard government buildings. Because of the unexplained explosion at the Ojhri depot in Rawalpindi in April 1988, many suspected a conspiracy. The surviving army generals assumed that the Americans were behind the crash, though no evidence of this was ever located, and many argued against the idea since it seemed unlikely that the Americans would sacrifice two senior officials. Some suspected General Beg's involvement. Others suspected the Indians. Or the Soviets.

Zia-ul-Haq had been the country's military dictator for eleven years. He was the father of the Afghan and Kashmir jihads—but he was no more. The Kashmiri groups deeply mourned his loss, and the crash sent jitters throughout the movement. The violence that had erupted on July 31 now intensified. Increased militant activities coincided with Zia's death, with JKLF militants accelerating a campaign of terror, carrying out bombings and other high-profile militant actions through the fall of 1988. By the end of the year, militants had conducted six direct assaults on the Indian security forces and bombed or set fire to nearly 150 buildings.

Maqbool Alai, masterminded the first high-profile attack of the insurgency. Alai was a guerrilla strategist and Islamist. On the night of September 17, 1988, he led militants in the attempted assassination of the deputy inspector general of the police, the number-two official in the force, Ali Muhammad Watali. JKLF members attacked his residence in Srinagar, but the operation failed amid heavy resistance and fighting. One JKLF militant, Aijaz Dar, was killed and soon became celebrated as the first JKLF martyr. The militants struck a week later, on September 22, 1988, firing on the house of N.K. Ganjoo, a retired sessions judge, who had sentenced Maqbool Bhat to death. A day later, the militants fired indiscriminately on the road between the offices of the inspector general of the police, the top police official, and the Criminal Investigation Department, which is tasked with investigating terrorism related crimes. And the frequency of these operations slowly increased.

Beginning on January 26, 1989, Indian Republic Day, the JKLF successfully inaugurated a long series of general strikes, which were declared to vocalize the Kashmiri people's disillusionment over Indian rule. Riots that accompanied the Indian Republic Day strikes led to an attack on a state cabinet minister, P. L. Handoo; the crowd set fire to his office and other state buildings. The strikes consumed some one-third of working days in 1989 and provided a powerful symbol of resistance, and of solidarity with the JKLF fighters. On July 13, 1989, in another high-profile attack, JKLF militants fired on a bus filled with members of the Central Reserve Police Force, a paramilitary police division. Two constables were killed, ten were injured, and four civilians were killed in the crossfire. A number of other political activists were also targeted: On August 21, militants killed activist Mohammad Yusuf Halwai; on September 14, they killed BJP's Tika Lal Taploo; and N. K. Ganjoo was again targeted, this time on a public street, though he narrowly escaped again.

There were also more bold acts of terrorism. On September 18, 1989, the anniversary of the death of Aijaz Dar, the first martyr, there was a swell in the violence in Srinagar. Amidst fears of bombings, markets were closed. JKLF militants carried out two grenade attacks on the police at Nawakadal, killing ten. On November 16, 1989, JKLF operatives planted a bomb in a state passenger bus, which JKLF officials claimed was being used to transport troops. Twenty-four passengers were injured. Later that same day, a bomb was detonated in the public works department.[1]

The Indian government was slow to react to the increased violence. Inside India, a political sea change was taking place with the Janata Dal party coming into power during elections in 1989. The party unseated the ruling Congress Party under the leadership of Prime Minister Rajiv Gandhi, amidst charges of corruption in a defense deal that came to be known as the "Bofors scandal." The Janata Dal, under Prime Minister Vishwanath Pratap Singh, formed a center government with the help of small parties. In hopes of appeasing the Kashmiri Muslim population and halting the rising swell of violence, the Janata Dal government appointed Mufti Mohammad Sayeed, a Muslim politician, who had defected to the Janata Dal, sensing that his Congress Party was falling from favor, to serve as the first union home minister on December 2, 1989. The position of home minister was symbolically responsible for most functions of the security apparatus in Indian Kashmir: from issues of law and order; to issuing passports and visas; to guarding international borders. Sayeed was born in Indian Kashmir, and the Janata Dal government thought his appointment would demonstrate its concern for the Muslim population, which had long been disenchanted with the policies of the ruling Congress Party.

The gesture did not, however, appease India's critics or the JKLF. On December 8, four JKLF militants kidnapped Rubaiya Sayeed, Mufti Sayeed's 23-year-old unmarried daughter, who worked as an intern at Lalded Memorial Hospital in Srinagar. She was returning home from the hospital when militants stopped her van and took her at gunpoint.[2] In an anonymous call to the *Kashmir Times,* the JKLF claimed responsibility for the kidnapping and demanded the release of five of its militants in return for her safe release.[3] Sayeed was moved frequently, first held in Sopore at the government residence of Ali Mohammad Mir, an engineer for the government, then transferred to the home of another of the kidnappers. The Indian government finally succumbed to the JKLF demands and released the five militants on December 13, 1989.[4] Thousands of young activists gathered to celebrate the release of the militants, making "V" signs with their hands to celebrate victory.

The JKLF continued its campaign of terror by targeting intellectuals and public figures, in and outside of government. The JKLF targeted an entire class of intellectuals in Indian Kashmir, in hopes of establishing a monopoly on the movement for self-determination and rooting out dissenting groups. The group kidnapped Professor Mushirul Haq, vice president of Kashmir University and a leading Muslim intellectual, along with his special assistant, Abdul Ghani Zargar, on April 6, 1990. The kidnapping took place during a moment of great chaos. Amanullah Khan, who had not been briefed about plans to kidnap the professor, was forced to comment on the action during a trip to New York.[5] Khan later intervened with Farooq Haider—who mistakenly informed Khan that Professor Haq and his assistant had been killed—in hopes of getting them released. A later public announcement of their deaths apparently caused a JKLF official to order their killing. Their bodies were dumped on a roadside outside Srinagar.

The JKLF violence continued apace. According to a study of the period, 390 incidents of terrorist violence were reported in 1988; in 1989, the number rose to 2,154; in 1990 the number peaked at 3,905.[6] The response to the kidnapping of Rubaiya Sayeed, the home minister's daughter, unleashed the anger of a large protest movement that took to the streets and grew throughout December 1989 and January 1990. On January 21, nearly half a million people were reported to have taken to the streets of Srinagar in an anti-India rally. The Central Reserve Police unit reacted violently, firing indiscriminately into the crowd and killing more than one hundred people.

After the formal launch of the armed struggle in July 1988, the slow but growing popularity of the JKLF worried ISI officials. With the death of General Zia, the ISI took even more control over the situation in Kashmir.

The ISI initially backed the JKLF only as a way to push its client, the Jamat-i-Islami, into militancy. Moreover, it had planned to replace the JKLF once Jamat-i-Islami could be pushed into the conflict. The ISI had many concerns about the JKLF: the group was a nationalist, secular party with no particular allegiance to Pakistan. What the ISI envisioned was a new militant organization, sponsored by Jamat-i-Islami, that would replace JKLF and lead the insurgency, as well as represent its interests. What the ISI wanted to prevent, above all else, was the creation of a separate state in Kashmir that would include both the Pakistani and Indian-controlled sections of Kashmir, which was precisely the JKLF's goal. But the rise of the JKLF also created other complications, chief among them that a number of small Islamist militant groups came into the open. There may have been as many as 180 such organizations in operation during the early years of the insurgency.[7] And the ISI supported many of these groups.

The opening salvo of the JKLF's July 1988 campaign took the Jamat-i-Islami by surprise as well. They quickly realized that new players had emerged on the scene and that, in the words of one militant, "a new game has started."[8] Jamat-i-Islami forces quickly surveyed the political landscape and saw that decisive action was needed if it was to take a controlling role in the struggle. Informal relationships with smaller jihadi groups were strengthened, with many of the leaders of Jamat-i-Islami taking direct roles in the activities of underground mujahideen. Key Jamat-i-Islami members including Habib Ullah in Kupwara, Wali Mohammad Shah in Baramula, Riaz Rasool in Budgam, Mir Asad Ullah in Pulwama, and Abdur Rashid Islah in Doda started working with smaller jihadi cells.[9] Involvement with the smaller cells was risky, given the importance of loyalty within Jamat-i-Islami.

The smaller cells on the rise during this period shared the pan-Islamic philosophy of Jamat-i-Islami—even though the outsiders in these groups came to Pakistani-controlled Kashmir under the umbrella of JKLF. One important group, active since 1987, was the Zia Tigers, named after General Zia-ul-Haq. The group was particularly active in Budgam, Baramula, and Kupwara, and was headed by Mohammad Ashraf Dar. Another group, al-Hamza, named after the Prophet Mohammad's uncle, had been active since 1988, led by Maqbool Alai. Muzzaffar Shah led another important group, called Hizbul Ansar.[10] Both the Zia Tigers and al-Hamza looked toward the Jamat-i-Islami of Indian-controlled Jammu and Kashmir for guidance. Though each worked alongside the JKLF, that organization did not recognize the cells as separate entities.

The most important group, the largest and best organized, was Ansarul Islam, which had been active since the mid-1980s. Ansarul Islam was, like the membership of Jamat-i-Islami, opposed to the secular mission of the JKLF.[11] Some of its members worked through the early period of the insurgency to strengthen their ties to Jamat-i-Islami and the ISI. Members of Ansarul Islam also founded a new organization called al-Badr, which the ISI soon pushed them to combine with Maqbool Alai's al-Hamza, another ISI client.[12]

The merging of jihadi organizations was very much an open concern for the movement, since the militants saw the need for a large organization to combat the influence of the JKLF. Two clandestine militants, Muzaffar Shah and Masood Sarfraz, also formed a group called Hizbul Ansar, which they hoped to expand further as a united front for the Kashmiri mujahideen.

This vast network of jihadi groups worked within the JKLF for many months; they were among the most active members of the insurgency. It was cadres from al-Hamza that carried out the two sucessful bomb explosions in Srinagar on July 31, 1988, for which Amanullah Khan would later accept responsibility, and which inaugurated the open rebellion in Kashmir. These explosions—at the time obscured behind JKLF—would also change the jihadi movement. Ansarul Islam, which attempted to disssociate itself from the bombings, was held responsible, and the Indian police began a large-scale roundup of Muslim youth. Nearly the entire leadership of Ansarul Islam were arrested, including Hilal Ahmed Mir and Ghulam Rasool Shah, who were not released until 1989.

As the insurgency broke into the open and proceeded in JKLF's name, an Ansarul Islam majlis-i-shoura was called on June 11, 1989, to decide the fate of the Islamist movement. The meeting was held at Hadiderpura, in the Budgam district of Indian Kashmir. The movement was badly crippled, but those gathered at the Hadiderpura meeting decided that their network should take decisive steps to pull the movement out of the JKLF's hands. To broaden its appeal, Ansarul Islam would be renamed Hizbul Mujahideen, "the party of the holy warriors." And the majlis-i-

shoura elected Hilal Ahmed Mir as the first leader of their
newly formed Hizbul Mujahideen; Mir assumed the nom
de guerre Nasirul Islam (helper of Islam).

But, at nearly the same time as the rise of this first
Hizbul Mujahideen, another organization named Hizbul
Mujahideen also sprang up. In August 1989, the Jamat-
i-Islami of Azad Kashmir sent Masood Sarfraz, an articulate and intelligent guerrilla commander, across the line of
control in an effort to raise a serious organization parallel
to the JKLF. Sarfraz was accompanied by another militant, Muzzaffar Shah. Their plan was to form an umbrella
organization for Islamist militants. Sarfraz had been talking privately for some months about naming the organization Hizbul Mujahideen, a fact that leaked, Shah thought,
through the important Islamist Syed Ali Shah Geelani, allowing the name to be appropriated by Hilal Ahmed Mir's
organization.[13] Others thought it was merely a coincidence.
For Sarfraz, the name had an important resonance: it was
derived from the Hizbe Islami party of Afghanistan, a key
group in the fight against the Soviets with which Sarfraz had
been associated since 1985 through Gulbadin Hekmatyar,
founder and leader of the Hizbe Islami and a well-known
rebel military commander in the war against the Soviets.[14]
Hizbe Islami was one of the most influential jihadi parties
in history. It also conjured the name of the Tehreek-ul-Mu-
jahideen, the first major jihadi party, which fought against
the British and the Sikhs in the nineteenth century. Sarfraz
thought the new Hizbul Mujahideen needed to have clear
goals; the central tenet would be militancy, but ideological
differences needed to be put aside if at all possible. And the
group would need not to associate itself with a particular

political or religious party.[15] Its chief priority was bringing fighters to Afganistan and Pakistani-controlled Kashmir for military training. Fazlul Haq Qureshi was appointed the amir of the organization.[16]

The two Hizbul Mujahideen organizations hovered in concert with other new umbrella organizations, including Tehreek-i-Jihad-i-Islami, the TJI. Its founding members came from a number of different organizations, but the new organization had few requirements for membership: members had to believe in militancy as an instrument of politics, and they had to accommodate every fighter, no matter to which organization he belonged.[17] This constellation of new organizations pushed the larger movement into action, and many of the key groups moved to consolidate into a single organization, to be called Hizbul Mujahideen.[18] After three weeks of discussion, Hilal Ahmed Mir brought his group together with Masood Sarfraz's group, thus merging the two Hizbul Mujahideens. The structure of the new, combined group was set up at a meeting of twenty-nine commanders in October 1989. The meeting placed Ahsan Dar as chief commander of the group. Ahmed Alai and Ashraf Dar were appointed to represent the group in Pakistani-controlled Jammu and Kashmir. A later meeting placed Hilal Ahmed Mir as amir. The group also established a twenty-member council and a five-member decision-making group. Yet another section was established to prepare a constitution for the group.

The ISI and the Jamat-i-Islami of Pakistani-controlled Kashmir both watched with some unease as these militants formed Hizbul Mujahideen. It seemed, to senior ISI officials, that their group's efforts in bringing the Jamat-i-

Islami of Indian Kashmir into the armed struggle had been wasted. Among top leaders of the organization in 1989, only Syed Ali Shah Geelani was willing to publicly support armed jihad.

Born in 1929, Geelani was almost universally respected among the militants. He later became the undisputed secessionist leader in Jammu and Kashmir, where he was elected to the state Assembly in 1972 and 1977. He also authored more than thirty pamphlets on his views of the Kashmir conflict, including an account of a long prison sentence that was widely read. During a delegation of fighters, however, even Geelani made clear that he supported the armed struggle only in his individual capacity, and not as a leader of Jamat-i-Islami.[19] The emerging trend was toward the JKLF and its call for an independent state. To ISI officials, only the intervention of Jamat-i-Islami could curb this tendency.

On January 14, 1990, a secret meeting was held in Katmandu, Nepal, to discuss Jamat-i-Islami's role in the growing jihadi movement.[20] Though little has been reported about this key meeting, leaders from all three of the Jamat-i-Islami branches were gathered.[21] The pro-jihad participants in the meeting made clear their fears about the growing influence of the JKLF. And there were still many reservations about Jamat-i-Islami's supporting an open insurgency. Hakeem Ghulam Nabi, the founding leader and amir of Jamat-i-Islami of Indian-controlled Jammu and Kashmir, protested most vocally, arguing that direct involvement would destroy the organization and open it to Indian assault.[22]

A pro-militancy constituency secretly arranged for Syed Ali Shah Geelani to address the group. When negotiations stalled, Geelani appeared suddenly, made an impassioned speech and, according to accounts of the meeting, succeeded in pushing the group toward openly supporting the jihad.[23] The decision would remain secret for the time being, but the group had decided to take an active hand.

All that was left to be worked out were the details.

The Katmandu meeting came at a key moment for the Jamat-i-Islami of Indian-controlled Kashmir, as a number of its own members had deserted the organization and joined the smaller Islamist groups, especially in the period between November 1989 and June 1990. Indeed, there was a mounting fear within the organization that its position of influence might be swept away by a gathering storm of new players. The Jamat-i-Islami leadership now moved on to decisive action, activating a decade of planning. Intense bargaining took place between the ISI and Jamat-i-Islami, with the ISI wanting to connect Hizbul Mujahideen and the other Islamist groups to Jamat-i-Islami. The two-member constitution committee of Hizbul Mujahideen delayed its work in order to incorporate the Jamat-i-Islami demands in the group's constitution and to facilitate the ISI's demands. A constitution was finalized on June 10, 1990, nearly six months behind schedule; it allowed the Jamat-i-Islami of Indian-controlled Kashmir to nominate one of its own members as the leader of Hizbul Mujahideen, and virtually turned the organization into a subsidiary of Jamat-i-Islami.

The constitution created the offices of a patron, an amir, and a chief commander, who together made up the new group's executive leadership. It also established a central majlis-i-shoura with two representatives from each district of the Valley of Kashmir. The patron was to nominate the amir of the organization, after holding consultations with the majlis-i-shoura, while the amir was to nominate the chief commander under the counsel of the patron. As a result, the power to appoint the patron meant nearly total control over the organization. Under the terms of the new constitution, Jamat-i-Islami appointed Yusaf Shah, alias Pir Syed Salahuddin, the Jamat-i-Islami's district amir in Srinagar, as the first patron of the Hizbul Mujahideen.

Salahuddin was not a high-profile leader—and, in the eyes of many Jamat-i-Islami leaders, a peculiar choice to become the patron of Hizbul Mujahideen. He rode a motor scooter, and was renowned and mocked for his baldness, as well as for his peculiar demeanor. In the streets of the Batmaloo neighborhood, children taunted Salahuddin with the cry "*khairia, khairia,*" a diminutive of *khor*, the balding disease alopecia.[24] But Salahuddin acted ruthlessly in taking the reins of Hizbul Mujahideen. Though he initially kept Ahsan Dar on as chief commander, he soon decided to consolidate Jamat-i-Islami control over the new organization and demote him. Dar reacted strongly against his dismissal from the position, and his removal created the first major schism among the jihadis.

In a power play, Dar protested his removal from his post by holding a press conference in July 1990 and announcing that Hizbul Mujahideen had formed an alliance with Jamat-i-Islami. Hilal Ahmed Mir, who had first named Hizbul Mujahideen, reacted strongly against the speed of the announcement, denying it outright. Mir also announced Dar's complete expulsion from the organization and claimed that Hizbul Mujahideen was only "the armed wing of Islam and not of Jamat-i-Islami." [25]

By this time, however, both Mir and Dar were effectively marginalized within Hizbul Mujahideen. Mir was soon forced out completely as well, embarrassed by Salahuddin, who was pleased that Dar had announced the Hizbul Mujahideen–Jamat-i-Islami alliance.[26] Hilal Ahmed Mir left Hizbul Mujahideen, along with several key associates—including Ghulam Rasool Shah, Ajmal Khan, and Manzoor Ahmed Shah—though his faction continued to fight for control of Hizbul Mujahideen for several years. Mir appointed Ajmal Khan as the chief commander of his breakaway group and then immediately left for Pakistani-controlled Kashmir, where, after conversations with the ISI, he renamed his faction Jamiatul Mujahideen on June 17, 1991.

Jamat-i-Islami again used Masood Sarfraz, along with a colleague, Syed Saleem Gardezi, to strengthen the new organization. The two were sent to Indian Jammu and Kashmir in September 1990 with the objective of uniting the different Islamist guerrilla groups under the umbrella of the new Hizbul Mujahideen. Under persuasion, Ghazi Ilyas of the Allah Tigers, a small jihadi group, and Abdul Hameed Fayyaz and Saifullah Khalid of al-Badr agreed to merge their groups into Hizbul Mujahideen at a meeting in Ganderbal in mid-October 1990. Sarfraz and Gardezi organized another meeting, in Sopur, during the last week of October 1990, in which Muzaffar Shah and another jihadi, Abdul Majeed Dar, who had merged their groups into Tehreek-i-

Jihad-i-Islami, agreed to merge into Hizbul Mujahideen.[27] Salahuddin also agreed to appoint Abdul Majeed Dar as the secretary general of the Hizbul Mujahideen.[28]

After bringing Hizbul Mujahideen under the control of the Jamat-i-Islami, Salahuddin crossed into Pakistani-controlled Jammu and Kashmir at the end of October 1990. He spent the next year organizing Hizbul Mujahideen in Pakistani-controlled Jammu and Kashmir and in Pakistan itself. He also established links with the Jamat-i-Islami of Pakistani-controlled Jammu and Kashmir and the Jamat-i-Islami of Pakistan. During his one-year stay in Azad Kashmir and Pakistan, Salahuddin also focused on Hizbul Mujahideen's relations with the ISI.

After cobbling a coalition of jihadi groups into Hizbul Mujahideen, the ISI set its targets on the JKLF. There had been significant tensions between the ISI and JKLF officials during the latter half of 1989, and, in the fall of 1989, the ISI attempted to force the JKLF to change its public message. According to Amanullah Khan, the ISI requested that the JKLF stop calling for "sovereignty" for Kashmir and instead focus on "self-determination." The ISI also demanded the appointment of an ISI representative to sit in on the JKLF Central Committee as an observer. Khan rejected both ideas outright: though he said he'd consider allowing the ISI to sit in on the Central Committee meetings if they allowed him to sit in on meetings of the Pakistani army.

By early 1990, the ISI had cut off all funds to the JKLF.[29] Amanullah Khan sought help from Benazir Bhutto, who became Prime Minister of Pakistan in 1988 at the age of 35. But the ISI blocked all communications with the prime minister; it appears none of his messages actually reached Bhutto. In attempting to bypass the ISI, Khan asked Shaikh Rashid, an ethnic Jammuite and rightwing member of the Pakistan Muslim League, to set up a controversial training camp for Kashmiri militants on property he owned inside Pakistan. Rashid's Rawalpindi compound on Fateh Jang road became so controversial that a coalition of Pakistani officials attempted to have it closed: Prime Minister Bhutto, President Ghulam Ishaq Khan, Chief Minsiter Nawaz Sharif, and chief of the army General Mirza Aslam Beg all personally intervened before the facility was finally closed.[30]

Amanullah Khan and the JKLF also came under assault from other fronts. In April 1990, Khan learned that the Indian government had sent agents to assassinate him. He went into hiding immediately, knowing that throughout the 1980s and '90s the Indian government had carried out assassination plots at political rallies, including bombing plots. Khan emerged from hiding in mid-June 1990, planning to speak at an important rally ·at Kotli, in Pakistani-controlled Kashmir. But JKLF members pressured Khan to cancel.

By the time Khan emerged from hiding, the scales had tipped decidedly away from the JKLF. On June 15, Khan received a phone call from an associate, Raja Muzzaffar, who demanded that he cancel the rally and meet in person, since Muzzaffar assumed that Khan was under surveillance. When Khan met with Muzzaffar three days later, he was informed that the Jamat-i-Islami was planning to announce a provisional Kashmiri government in Jedda,

Saudi Arabia, on June 19. The effort was led by Dr. Ayub Thakur, who had the support of key sections of the Saudi clergy and the ISI. Amanullah Khan saw that he had few options. But he moved decisively: he called JKLF's Dr. Farooq Haider and Sardar Rashid Hasrat and asked for permission to preempt the Jamat-i-Islami announcement: he would announce his own provisional government for Jammu and Kashmir. Both Haider and Hasrat, seeing that there was no time to convene about the matter, gave Khan approval. Khan announced his provisional government the next day.

Khan quickly shaped a twenty-three-member cabinet of ministers and advisors into a provisional government, which included representatives from all regions of the state except Ladakh, whose representative was added later.[31] The cabinet also represented almost all major religions and political points of view. The announcement of a provisional government was a masterstroke and sabotaged the Jamat-i-Islami–backed plan to take the lead of the armed struggle, at least for a time.

But despite the operational provisional government, the Indian government continued its military focus on the JKLF. By 1990, the organization's militancy had reached its height, and the Indian army responded with incredible strength, and attempted to brutally repress the organization.[32] They rounded up most of the active militants by the end of the year. Among them was Yasin Malik, a key JKLF militant and one of the planners of Rubaiya Saeed's kidnapping. Malik would later prove to be a huge embarrassment to the organization. He announced, outside the chain of command, a cease-fire with the Indian army shortly after being released from prison in May 1994. He also claimed publicly to be renouncing violence and embracing Gandhi's philosophy. During the waning years of the JKLF, there had also been other defections: Farooq Haider and Sardar Rashid Hasrat broke away from JKLF, though they rejoined it in January 1992.

In the end, it was Yasin Malik, the militant-turned-Gandhian, who pushed the JFLF into total disarray. Amanullah Khan eventually lost patience with the commander and replaced him with Shabir Ahmed Siddiqui in September 1995. But the expulsion backfired: Malik founded his own faction of JKLF. Amanullah Khan was called "the enemy of the freedom movement." For a time, Radio Pakistan and Pakistan Television (PTV) recognized Malik as the leader of the legitimate JKLF. A little later, JKLF leaders Raja Muzzaffar and Farooq Haider also joined Malik's JKLF faction.

But the new leadership had little chance to succeed. The Indian security forces killed Basharat Reza in the Hazratbal shrine on March 24, 1996, and Shabbir Siddiqui and twenty-six other JKLF commanders in their office adjacent to the shrine on March 30, 1996.

To combat the influence of the JKLF, the ISI supported and funded a wide variety of militant organizations; indeed, almost every militant organization active in Kashmir at the time could claim some connection to the ISI. By 1990, the ISI had over 100 militant organizations on its payroll. But with the JKLF removed from the scene, the ISI moved to cease its support of smaller factions, becoming more selective in its support of Kashmiri militants. Reducing payments became a complicated dance: The ISI wanted to move away from the smaller groups, but it also wanted to maintain operational assets in the region. ISI officials still didn't feel confident that Hizbul Mujahideen and the Jamat-i-Islami of Indian-controlled Kashmir would act as pure proxies.

The first challenge to the ISI's work in Kashmir came in 1993, when the United States began pressing Pakistan to rein in militant organizations in Jammu and Kashmir or risk being designated a terrorist state; President Clinton called the region "the most dangerous place on earth." In reaction to U.S. pressure, the ISI decided to continue funding jihadi organizations only if they could gain sponsorship by a client political party. This change in policy could conceal the jihadi fighters from view—and blur the militant organizations' connections to the ISI. If a jihadi organization was unable to find a suitable cover, the ISI would help it find one. The mujahideen commanders were young and immature, the ISI told jihadi commanders, and the world would never accept independent jihadi organizations. In reality, the move was another method of control.

The Awami Action Committee became the sponsor of al-Umar Mujahideen, the Muslim Conference was directed to sponsor the Jamiatul Mujahideen, the Peoples Conference was to sponsor al-Barq, the People's League was to sponsor the Muslim Janbaaz Force (MJF), the Ittehadul Muslimeen was to sponsor the Pasban-i-Islam, and the Islamic Students League was to sponsor the Karwan-i-Mujahideeen. Hizbul Mujahideen was already behind the Jamat-i-Islami. The ISI allowed some factions of the JKLF to remain in the field, since they also functioned as a political party.

Hizbul Mujahideen opposed the ISI's move to fracture the militant movements and put them under the control of regional political organizations. Hizbul Mujahideen envisioned a united front of pro-Pakistani groups under unified command; the organization wanted to eliminate other extremist groups and take the reins of the entire movement. In a September 1990 meeting of Hizbul Mujahideen leaders and MJF commanders in Ganderbal, just outside Srinagar, commanders proposed the merger of all Islamic organizations under one command, meaning the merger of the Hizbul Mujahideen, MJF, TJI, Hizbullah and al-Umar Mujahideen, the five big groups at the time. They came together, in October 1990, into the Muttahidda Jihad Council.

The ISI's effort to further consolidate was considered redundant. The militants argued that the political leadership, with the exception of Syed Ali Shah Geelani, couldn't be trusted by the fighters. Syed Manzoor Ahmed Shah, head of the Islamic Revolutionary Movement, which had been founded in 1991, pushed the ISI to allow mujahideen organizations to form their own political parties, arguing that mujahideen fighters had historically performed political tasks under the Prophet Mohammad. But the ISI would not allow the Islamic Revolutionary Movement to incorporate as a political organization and cut off funds from the organization in 1993; the organization was formally disbanded in 1996. Other organizations protested as well: the Muslim Conference refused to sponsor the Jamiatul Mujahideen. Infighting about the ISI's policy continued through the mid-'90s.

As the jihadi groups consolidated during the early 1990s, the movement also tried to streamline its operational functions. Foremost among the concerns of the militant organizations

was a reliable way to communicate. Communication between fighters on the two sides of the Line of Control was
typically sent by courier and took several days, with Indian
security agencies frequently arresting fighters along with
their messages.

In 1990, the ISI moved to assist, selecting a small group
of young Kashmiris to train in the use of communications
systems.[33] The trainees were selected from militant organizations, though the ISI did not intend for the trainees to
return to their home group once trained; rather, they would
assist the movement as a whole. The ISI intended for their
trainees to handle a wide-ranging flow of information not
only for different jihadi organizations but for the ISI itself.
The ISI trained multiple groups of Kashmiris—but later accounts from Hizbul Mujahideen commanders indicate that
few of the communications operators trained by the ISI
ever actually worked in the field. The ISI apparently leaned
too heavily on the trainees to become ISI assets, and they
defected as a result.

Disillusioned with the ISI's efforts, Ali Mohammad
Dar, vice amir of Hizbul Mujahideen, decided to have his
operatives trained directly. He chose six fighters and sent
them to the Al-Jihad University of Technology outside
Peshawar to learn telegraphic and radio communication
methods. The university was training a large number Afghan jihadis and agreed to keep the training of the Kashmiris a secret from the ISI. Abu Sayyaf, an Arab Chechen,
trained the Kashmiri fighters for several months and passed
them wireless radio sets after they completed the training.[34]
The trainees, however, refused to travel with the radio sets,
fearing they would be intercepted by the ISI. In light of

this, the students contacted ISI representatives and asked them to transport their equipment to Pakistani-controlled Kashmir—but the ISI never did. Frustrated, Hizbul Mujahideen approached Messrs. Micro Electrical International in Lahore, which agreed to supply radio equipment. Again, however, the ISI got in the way by preventing the construction of radio towers, fearing a Kashmiri communications system that couldn't be monitored. Hizbul Mujahideen got around this problem by using the Afghan radio station at the Jallozai camp, an operation that lasted until 1993, when the Pakistanis closed Jallozai.

The group of six that trained at Al-Jihad University developed a close association with the Tanzeem-i-Itlehad-i-Islami, an Afghan mujahideen group operating under the warlord Ustaz Abdur Rabb Rasool Saayaf (who would be elected to the Afghan parliament in 2003). The six were impressed with Sayaaf, and on their return from Peshawar, they asked Ali Mohammad Dar to meet Saayaf and seek assistance from him. A potential relationship was complicated because Jamat-i-Islami was closely associated with Saayaf's rival, the warlord Gulbadin Hekmatyar.

At the continued urging of the six students, Dar finally agreed to meet Saayaf, during a convention of mujahideen in Peshawar. The meeting was also attended by Hizbul Mujahideen leader Ghulam Mohammad Safi—who had to approve the contact between the two organizations. The meeting turned out to be very significant, strengthening ties between the two organizations. Over the next few years, Tanzeem-i-Ittlehad-i-Islami would transfer hundreds of thousands of dollars' worth of arms and ammunition that they received from the CIA and other international donors for the Afghan jihad to Hizbul Mujahideen—as well as to Arab fighters who had been fighting in Afghanistan.

Hundreds of Kashmiri youth had started crossing the line of control every month during 1989 and 1990, entering Azad Kashmir to receive military training. But the ISI had underestimated the number of fighters who could be recruited for military training; they had planned for only two to three dozen militants, but the number would eventually swell to many thousands of fighters by 1990.[35] According to one report, 2,200 fighters once entered Pakistani-controlled Kashmir to receive military training on a single day.[36] Hizbul Mujahideen sent most of these fighters to Afghanistan, to the Hizbe Islami training camp.

In early 1991, a delegation of Hizbul Mujahideen leaders, which included Pir Syed Salahuddin, went to Afghanistan to make further arrangements to train Kashmiri fighters and to facilitate increasing the number of fighters being trained in Afghanistan. According to several Hizbul Mujahideen commanders present at the meeting, Salahuddin spent much of the meeting locked in conversation with Hizbe Islami chief Gulbadin Hekmatyar. According to the commanders, Hekmatyar advised Salahuddin to eliminate all of Hizbul Mujahideen's rivals. Hekmatyar was locked in a civil war with the mujahideen with whom he had fought against the Russians; in retrospect he wished he had eliminated his rivals during that conflict.[37]

Upon returning from Afghanistan, Hizbul Mujahideen intensified its campaign to disarm other militant groups.

Soon after its foundation in late 1989, Hizbul Muhahideen had initiated a smear campaign against the JKLF. Tens of thousands of pamphlets were printed in Pakistan and smuggled into Indian-controlled Jammu and Kashmir. The pamphlets called the JKLF a secular, atheist party, and one with limited aims. One pamphlet noted that the JKLF wanted only to liberate a small territory while the greater Hizbul Mujahideen wanted to impose Islamic law on the entire world. For Hizbul Mujahideen, Kashmir was only the first front in a long battle.

With this smear campaign, the streets of Srinagar filled with new slogans. Gone was JKLF's "What do we want? Freedom!"; the momentum now turned to Hizbul Mujahideen's stark *Azadi ka matlab kia?—La Ilaha illallah*, "What does freedom mean? There is no god but Allah."[38]

Another Hizbul Mujahideen flyer read: "Which system will be allowed to function here? Only the system of Prophet Mohammad." Yet another: "What is our relationship with Pakistan? There is no god but Allah."

But the new campaign was more brutal. Hizbul Mujahideen operatives harassed, beat, and murdered potential rivals, and the scale of the violence was enormous. According to a Hizbul Mujahideen commander, the organization eliminated some 7,000 political rivals.[39] According to Masood Sarfraz, who was once close to Syed Salahuddin but later fell out of favor with him, the actual number is many times higher.[40]

From the beginning of their campaign, Hizbul Mujahideen focused on disarming and kidnapping JKLF members, and many were brutalized in custody and beaten to death. According to Amanullah Khan, Hizbul Mujahideen eliminated more JKLF officials than Indian military agents had. Their purge continued throughout 1991 and 1992. JKLF leader Hameed Shaikh, who was released from captivity in the fall of 1992, ordered a unilateral cease-fire and promised to open negotiations with Hizbul Mujahideen. But even this did not stop the killing spree.

Finally, in the winter of 1993, the JKLF kidnapped Syed Ali Shah Geelani, who was being treated at the Sura Medical Hospital. Geelani remained in the custody of JKLF militants for three days and, during this time, the Hizbul Mujahideen purge finally came to an end, though only temporally. In exchange for the release of Geelani, Hizbul Mujahideen agreed to return a large cache of weapons and declare a truce with the JKLF.[41] The agreement lasted for little more than a month, after which JKLF members were again targeted.[42]

Disillusioned by the ongoing sectarian violence, Ahsan Dar, the founding commander of Hizbul Mujahideen, left the organization. His resignation caused widespread panic in Pattan, his stronghold, and angered leaders in Hizbul Mujahideen, which had him arrested in the summer of 1992, though he was later released.[43] He quickly founded a new organization, Muslim Mujahideen, which would become an influential group for former members of Hizbul Mujahideen. The ruthlessness with which Hizbul Mujahideen had operated prompted defections to Muslim Mujahideen. When Hizbul Mujahideen targeted the family of Ghulam Nabi Azad, beating his brother and sister, he quickly signed up with Muslim Mujahideen. Other top commanders from the organization—including long heralded names Ghulam Nabi Azad and Javed Jahangir—joined the organization. Though Muslim Mujahideen was founded only as a political organization to give its members a platform, many joined the counter-insurgency. The organization also quickly became a target of Hizbul Mujahideen, which killed some fifty Muslim Mujahideen members.[44]

Hizbul Mujahideen also targeted other organizations. Jamiatual Mujahideen was one of its fiercest enemies, considered an archrival. Though the two groups had a common history—and essentially held to the ideology of Jamat-i-Islami—Hizbul Mujahideen stalked Jamiatual Mujahideen, shadowing its fighters and assassinating seven senior members during the early 1990s. Another targeted organization was the Muslim Janbaaz Force (MJF). Some 120 MJF members were killed by Hizbul Mujahideen. Extremists dominated MJF, and the organization eventually merged with a group called Jihad Force and formed a new group called al-Jihad.[45] A bloody battle broke out in Pulwama in 1993 when Hizbul Mujahideen tried to disarm al-Jihad fighters.

Yet another group targeted was the Jammu and Kashmir Students Liberation Front, the JKSLF. The organization's head, Hilal Ahmed Beg, was well known for having kidnapped and murdered the vice chancellor of the University of Kashmir.[46] In the aftermath of the killing, Beg founded a new organization called Ikhwanul Muslimeen. Hizbul Mujahideen targeted the new organization as well, and ruthlessly.

A young JKSLF member, Mohammad Yusaf Parray, who would later go by the name Kukka Parray, was locally known as a dancer and folk singer. A published poet, he was considered by his colleagues to be emotional and sensitive. His harassment by the Hizbul Mujahideen was typical:

though his life was spared, he and his family were tortured for their association with the JKSLF, which Parray joined in Pakistan in 1989, and Ikhwanul Muslimeen, which Parray helped found. Hizbul Mujahideen targeted his sister, cutting her hair off and scalding her back with an iron; and his brother-in-law, by setting fire to his orchid collection. (Targeting siblings was a frequent tactic: according to several accounts, Hizbul Mujahideen lynched family members of Ikhwanul Muslimeen members.) Fierce battles between the two groups took place in the subdivision of Sonarwari in the Baramula district and had far-reaching effects. The Ikhwanul Muslimeen was later renamed the Jammu and Kashmir Islamic Front in 1995. Sajjad Ahmed Keno became its president and Hilal Ahmed Beg its vice president. Parray later estimated that Hizbul Mujahideen had murdered 70 percent of the Ikhwanul Muslimeen membership. After abandoning militancy, Parray launched the Kashmir bachao, Bharat bachao movement ("Save Kashmir, Save India") with the objective of eliminating some of the violence in the region. He distributed cash and clothes to the victims of militancy. (Hizbul Mujahideen finally succeeded in assassinating him on September 13, 2003.)

Hizbul Mujahideen militants also murdered some of the leading political leaders in Kashmir. They killed Dr. Ahad Guru and Professor Abdul Ahad Wailoo (chief commander of al-Barq). They also killed scores of fighters from Muslim Mujahideen, al-Barq, al-Jihad, and JKLF.[47] Mirwaiz Farooq, a leading political personality in Srinagar, was also killed; Syed Ali Shah Geelani ordered his elimination.[48] Hizbul Mujahideen kidnapped Qazi Nissar, one of five secessionist leaders who were imprisoned and later released, on June 19, 1994, and left his bullet-riddled body near Anantnag. The Hizbul Mujahideen also killed Ghulam Qadir Wani; he had publicly opposed Pakistani involvement in the jihad.

The killing was so widespread that even Muslim Kashmiri women sometimes took refuge in Indian army camps to avoid the brutality of Hizbul Mujahideen. [49]

The infighting among the jihadi organizations finally led to the creation of what were known as "renegades," militants with no source of income and who tended to be ill-supplied or ill-armed. It was not only the jihadi infighting that sent militants away from the large organizations; many of them were also disillusioned with the way the ISI handled the liberation struggle. Some could not take the pressure that the Indian security forces put on their families. Eventually the Indian army used these renegades to crush the militants, especially Hizbul Mujahideen.[50] They carried out joint operations since Hizbul Mujahideen's targets were frequently mutual enemies. The fratricidal infighting cost all the Kashmiri jihadi organizations heavily, with the Indian security forces taking full advantage and killing as many political separatists as they could. Hizbul Mujahideen changed course and stopped killing fellow militants only when it became clear that the costs were too high, with both the Indian security forces and rivals targeting their members.

Syed Ali Shah Geelani eventually counted "one thousand Jamat-i-Islami members who had been mercilessly killed by the Indian occupying forces or their cohorts." [51] Only when the organization understood this two-front assault would they finally shift away from targeting their rivals.

CHAPTER FIVE

"OUR AIM IS TO CLEANSE THE SOCIETY"
HOW THE JIHAD WAS WAGED

In June of 1990, the party known as Jamat-i-Islami of Indian-controlled Kashmir had nominated Syed Salahuddin to be the founding patron of Hizbul Mujahideen. But even with this appointment, the party could not fully embrace Hizbul Mujahideen, which was an openly militant group. A connection to Jamat-i-Islami of Indian-controlled Kashmir would likely have proved terminal to the party, exposing them to harassment and further scrutiny by the Indian security forces. As a result, the party only informally participated in the activities of Hizbul Mujahideen, while publicly opposing their jihadi tactics. They ended up playing both sides, disavowing a connection to Hizbul Mujahideen while secretly working to support it.

Hizbul Mujahideen was, however, strongly embraced by the Jamat-i-Islami parties in Pakistan and Pakistani-controlled Kashmir. In 1990, these parties had set constitutional structure in place that allowed them to run Hizbul Mujahideen, including a secret committee, the Jihad-i-Kashmir Committee, which was later established to manage the war in Kashmir. For a time, the Jihad-i-Kashmir Committee, made up of Pakistani and international jihadis, was the most powerful group determining the direction of the jihad.[1]

The tactics of the jihad were obviously brutal: While there was no central front in the war, Hizbul Mujahideen fighters successfully infiltrated Indian-controlled Jammu and Kashmir and carried out their attacks. The organization was responsible for a string of deadly terrorist bombings, acts of arson, kidnappings, assassinations, and threats of further violence. While Indian law applied in Indian-controlled Kashmir, the jihadi forces came to constitute their own order, intimidating residents and targeting their enemies with seeming impunity. The state apparatus could do little to stop them. Muslim police officers refused orders to rein in the violence, and Indian forces struggled to track down shadowy jihadi groups. Though the Indian forces suffered high casualties, little immediate political success seemed to result from the jihadi violence. Indeed, the situation appeared locked in a stalemate, while the jihadi forces continued to make life unbearable in Jammu and Kashmir.

On November 3, 1991, in the throes of militancy, Hizbul Mujahideen met to reorganize itself. The organization knew that it needed to act more like a guerrilla organization, with a unified command structure and precise goals. Its first priority was to cleanse its leadership of members who didn't embrace the Jamat-i-Islami ideology. To accomplish this, it made changes to its constitution, and in so doing did away with the offices of secretary general and patron. But under a new structure, a supreme commander—Syed Salahuddin—was appointed.[2] A permanent majlis-i-shoura was also established in the form of a twelve-member command council.[3] The command council was to be elected by the majlis-i-numaindagan (Council of Representatives), which consisted of two senior commanders from each district in Jammu and Kashmir.

At about the same time, Hizbul Mujahideen also started to grow, benefiting from an influx of young Pakistani fighters from Afghanistan. After achieving victory against the Soviet forces, some of the fighters from the two student wings of Jamat-i-Islami, Islami Jamiat-i-Tulba and Jamiat Tulaba Arabia, joined the fight in Kashmir.[4] The chief organizer of Jamiat Tulaba Arabia, Javed Qasuri, even rose to become a deputy supreme commander of Hizbul Mujahideen.

After having consolidated and restructured for a long period, Hizbul Mujahideen emerged as the dominant player on the jihadi scene—and was able to expand the insurgency that had begun in 1988, particularly through its powerful allegiance with the ISI. It would work to train more fighters, and to push its agenda further. But the newly organized Hizbul Mujahideen would turn out to be an unwieldy force, with competing factions and strong personalities.

Hizbul Mujahideen chief Syed Salahuddin was paranoid. He was also insecure. He had gone from being patron, an honorary office, to supreme commander. And, according to those who knew him well, he suffered from an overinflated ego. He was strongly built and inspired fear in many around him. But he was also bald, peculiar looking, and erratic. He felt uncomfortable around non-Kashmiris. And he worked, from the moment he took the reins of Hizbul Mujahideen, to keep the organization under his tight control. He prevented outsiders from rising in its ranks. (Those outsiders who succeeded—like Masood Sarfraz and Almas Khan, two Hizbul Mujahideen commanders—had hard falls.) And he spied on his fellow fighters whenever he could.

When a group of Hizbul Mujahideen commanders traveled with Salahuddin to the organization's Islamabad headquarters, jokingly called the White House, they were alarmed to find that Salahuddin had had the telephones removed from their rooms to prevent any possibility of their meetings being bugged. According to one Hizbul Mujahideen commander, Salahuddin also asked a "cook in the office, who was also a militant, to keep an eye on all of us. The cook Jehangir himself told us this. He had respect for his comrades but our own amir lacked it."

Many also looked askance at his nom de guerre: The original Salahuddin was the twelfth-century Muslim leader who won stunning victories during the Crusades. On several occasions, Syed Salahuddin told his interlocutors that he would go down in history as Salahuddin the Second. The name, however, seemed to perfectly reflect his inflated self-image.[5]

While Hizbul Mujahideen had suffered a leadership crisis from the very beginning, conflict within the group heated up after its merger with Tehreek-i-Jihad-i-Islami (TJI). Hizbul Mujahideen leaders had promised to give the group a prominent position within their organization and to allow it to help set an agenda and bring in new members.[6] Its leader, Abdul Majeed Dar, was promised a senior position. The conflict simmered for years: in late 1997, it intensified and caused a major schism. That October, Abdul Majeed Dar voiced his opposition to Salahuddin and declared that he wanted to lead Hizbul Mujahideen.

Abdul Majeed Dar was born in Sopore, in the north of the Valley of Kashmir. Before joining the militant movement, he had run a dry-cleaning business. He was revered for his intelligence and enjoyed the wide support of Muslims in the north of Kashmir. His views were radically different from Salahuddin's. Dar was militant, but his affiliation with Jamat-i-Islami was looser; he didn't hold to its ideology.

In 1997, when Dar made public moves away from Salahuddin, Dar's followers moved quickly to support him. At a Hizbul Mujahideen training camp just outside Mansehra, Dar's supporters pelted Salahuddin with stones. And two important groups, the al-Badr Mujahideen and the Pir Punjal Regiment, vocally supported Dar. Dar and Salahuddin eventually reconciled their difference, but only for a time.

Salahuddin, though, expelled al-Badr from Hizbul Mujahideen, and the Jamat-i-Islami of Pakistan stood firmly behind this decision. Al-Badr had been instrumental in recruiting Pakistani fighters to the Afghan training camps—several of which were on the al-Badr complex—and, eventually, to Kashmir. It had been al-Badr, working within Hizbul Mujahideen, that had worked closely in Afghanistan with Hizbe Islami, and an al-Badr operative, Bakht Zamin, had been responsible for making arrangements to train Pakistani and Kashmiri fighters there.[7]

Though Hizbe Islami's Afghan camps and Zamin's jihadi group shared the name al-Badr, they were separate operations, though the group al-Badr had been run in connection with both Hizbe Islami and Hizbul Mujahideen, allowing it to draw on the resources of both organizations. Bakht Zamin, whose father had fought in the 1947 Kashmir war, also used his organization to spread jihadi activities throughout the world: He sent troops to Tajikistan in 1992 and to Azerbaijan and Burma in 1994.[8] And after his expulsion from Hizbul Mujahideen, he quickly reorganized a separate organization.

After Salahuddin purged his organization of al-Badr and the followers of Bakht Zamin, he moved to expel another dissident commander, Masood Sarfraz, and his Pir Punjal Regiment. (Sarfraz is the nephew of Sardar Sikandar Hayat Khan, former president and prime minister of Pakistani-controlled Kashmir.) He was an intelligent and articulate guerrilla commander. In 1985, he had left his university studies to join the Afghan jihad under the command of Hizbe Islami and Hekmatyar and fought at different fronts throughout Afghanistan. He was one of the few Kashmiri mujahideen from Pakistani-controlled Jammu and Kashmir who fought in Afghanistan. He had also recruited a large force of fighters from Indian-controlled Kashmir, and he was one of the earliest jihadis active in the conflict, responsible for recruitment and training of fighters. From the early 1990s on, he had played a central role in the jihadi movement, and he had run some of the most important missions of the fight, though he avoided press coverage of his activities for more than fifteen years, fearing such coverage would fuel jealousies within the movement.

In the early morning hours of October 1, 2000, the Jamat-i-Islami of Pakistani-controlled Kashmir, led by the group's amir Abdur Rashid Turabi, gathered a group of 500 heavily armed militants in Kotli, near the headquarters of the Pir Punjal Regiment. Before the regiment had awakened, Hizbul Mujahideeen took the group hostage, disarmed them, and announced that Masood Sarfraz had been dismissed and replaced with a new commander, Shamsher Khan.

Masood Sarfraz's forces, however, attacked the Jamat-i-Islami forces within hours of the initial attack. This led to a pitched battle between the two groups that lasted for more than twenty hours. The fighting spread to towns and villages throughout Pakistani-controlled Kashmir, including Khui Ratta, Sehnsa, Samahini, Nakial, Saida, and Andarla Katehra. The two rival militias remained locked in battle for several weeks.[9] The battle came to an end when the army moved in to disengage the two militias, and after the fighting had taken the lives of about a dozen civilians. A final resolution to the conflict was negotiated by the Kashmir Cell of the ISI, which divided the assets of the two groups. The training camp at Sehnsa was given to the Hizbul Mujahideen, and Masood Sarfraz was asked to open a new camp at Gul Pur, outside Kotli. The ISI would prevent Sarfraz from calling his forces the Pir Punjal Regiment, but he would reorganize under the name Hizbe Islami, in homage to his colleagues in Afghanistan.

Another important factional struggle in Kashmir has to do with Sunni-Shia divide. The majority of the Muslim population in Kashmir is Sunni, but a small minority—estimated at between 8 and 20 percent of the Muslim population—is Shia Muslim. Shias in they valley are poorly regarded, widely considered backward, tribal, and overly loyal to a small cadre of important Shia families. In an effort to keep the Shia leadership fixed, education is mostly discouraged. One important Shia political organization was Ittehadul Muslimeem, founded in the aftermath of the Hazratbal crisis. The organization was founded by Mohammad Abbas Ansari, whose followers numbered around 200,000. The organization eventually developed links with the Pakistani army, but the collaboration was not to be long-lived.[10] After the execution of Z.A. Bhutto, Ittehadul Muslimeem launched a protest campaign that took aim at the Jamat-i-Islami, among others. A Jamat-i-Islami school in Indian-controlled Kashmir was burned to the ground by Ittehadul Muslimeem forces. Perhaps because of the support of Bhutto and the assaults on Jamat-i-Islami, talks between the army and Ittehadul Muslimeem eventually broke down.

With the rise of the militancy, the ISI supported Ansari's rivals, who eventually formed an organization called Hizbul Momineen. The goal was to use the organization to limit Shia influence, especially Ansari. Other small Shia organizations also sprang up, but none would prove to be long-lasting. Hizbul Momineen, however, was widely credited with preventing the Kashmiri jihad from falling into Sunni-Shia sectarian violence. Though the organization never had much influence, partly because the ISI refused to fully support its activities, it remained an important player until 2001, when it started to decline.

In the early days of the fighting, Hizbul Mujahideen had all of its fighters trained at camps in Afghanistan run by the Hizbe Islami party. In particular, they made use of al-Badr in the Khost province of southern Afghanistan, a training center that remained in use by Kashmiri militants until the Taliban closed it in 1996. [11] (The Taliban raided the camp, saying that Hizbe Islami was working against its government.) Hizbe Islami's operational director at the camp was Khalid Farooqi, one of their top commanders. Kashmiri fighters also made use of other camps in Afghanistan, including, Khalid bin Walid, Al-Farooq, and Abu Jindal. Abu Jindal, known as a site for the training Arab fighters, was made famous in May 1998, when Osama bin Laden held a press conference there and promised to launch attacks against the U.S.

But the training camps in Afghanistan proved too small to house the growing number of fighters recruited to the movement after 1988. In 1988 and 1989, Hizbul Mujahideen started sending its fighters to newly established camps in Pakistani-controlled Kashmir that were operated by the ISI. Beginning in 1990, the Jamat-i-Islami of Pakistan also established independent camps in Pakistani-controlled Kashmir. Jamat-i-Islami had been unable to persuade the ISI to train Pakistani nationals who wanted to fight in Kashmir, and some of these recruits could not be persuaded to travel to

Afghanistan. The Jamat-i-Islami-operated camp established in 1992 at Sehnsa in Pakistani-controlled Kashmir alleviated this problem, and it eventually started training Pakistanis directly. Organizers say that 10,000 militants were trained at the camp before it was shut down in 2000. In 1999, another Jamat-i-Islami camp was established near Muzaffarabad.[12]

The largest camps, however, were established directly by Hizbul Mujahideen, which set up a large jihadi network throughout Pakistan and Pakistani-controlled Kashmir. In addition to these training camps, they established a whole infrastructure to support the jihadi fight. There were living quarters for jihadis, publishing houses to disseminate their literature, and private communication systems to support their network.[13] In Pakistan and Pakistani-controlled Kashmir, most of the Jamat-i-Islami offices party offices housed Hizbul Mujahideen offices as well, greatly expanding its reach and recruitment capabilities. Hizbul Mujahideen also established some fifty detachment camps along the LoC, where, after fighters were trained, they were given arms, ammunition, and money before crossing into Indian-controlled Jammu and Kashmir. Units also waited at these detachment camps until suitable openings in the LoC were discovered.

In addition to camps, the Jamat-i-Islami of Pakistan also established the Pakistan Islamic Medical Association (PIMA) to treat its wounded fighters. Its main project was the construction of the Kashmir Surgical Hospital. The hospital, a modern medical complex, survives on the generosity of Jamat-i-Islami supporters—including donations of 54,718,485 rupees through the end of 2002.

PIMA's activities are not restricted to Jammu and Kashmir. It functions as a kind of medical jihadi unit, always ready to send a delegation wherever Muslims are suffering for Islamic causes. (On April 1, 2003, PIMA announced that it had sent 300 doctors to Iraq via Iran.[14] PIMA also sent relief goods to Indonesia in January 2005, to help the victims of the Tsunami.) In more recent years, some PIMA doctors have been discovered to have substantial links with terrorist groups inside Pakistan. On June 17, 2004, Pakistani agents kidnapped Dr. Akmal Waheed and Arshad Waheed, with a formal arrest following on July 2, 2004. The two were charged with having links with the terrorist group Jindullah, which attacked a convoy of Pakistani army troops in Karachi. They were also accused of providing medical help to fighters wounded in the attack. They were further believed to have provided medical help to al-Qaeda members, as well as facilitating escape routes for fleeing al-Qaeda fighters, in the aftermath of the September 11 attacks.[15]

In addition to PIMA and the Kashmir Surgical Hospital, the Jamat-i-Islami of Indian-controlled Jammu and Kashmir set up a charity, the Relief Organization for Kashmiri Muslims, to benefit casualties of the Kashmir jihad. Later, the Jamat-i-Islami of Pakistan set up another foundation, Shuhdai Islam Foundation, or the Martyrs of Islam Foundation, to raise funds.

Though there had been little friction between Muslims and Hindus in the Valley of Kashmir until the 1980s, this changed dramatically with the launch of the jihadi violence.

In particular, the Jamat-i-Islami of Indian-controlled Kashmir inflamed tensions between Muslims and Hindus.

By the early 1980s, relations between the two communities had become so precarious that even a rumor could unleash widespread violence. In February 1986, a rumor was circulated that Hindus had massacred pilgrims and other Muslims in Jammu. Though the rumor could not be corroborated, Muslim rioters started attacking Hindus and their property. They looted nearly 500 houses and set 50 of them on fire. They also looted Hindu shops and other properties. Hindu activists, in particular, were targeted and severely beaten. The Muslim rioters also targeted Hindu temples. Temple property was looted and idols desecrated. Three villages with Hindu majorities were completely destroyed, and another twenty-four were attacked. In all, nearly 800 villages and hamlets in the valley were affected. The Jamat-i-Islami of Indian-controlled Kashmir directed many of the rioters.[16]

Another significant early act was the murder of Keshav Nath Pandit, who was the first Hindu killed in the violence inaugurated after July 1988. A follower of the Jamat-i-Islami of Indian-controlled Jammu and Kashmir, Constable Mohammad Yousuf, was on duty guarding a temple in Vicharnag. After a dispute, he dragged Mahant Keshav Nath Pandit out of the temple on the morning of December 9, 1988 and asked him to convert to Islam. When he refusal, Yousuf killed him by beating him with the butt of his gun. In the fall of 1989, militants also finally succeeded in murdering N.K. Ganjoo, the judge who had sentenced Maqbool Bhat to death; Ganjoo had been the object of numerous attacks.

Later, on December 27, 1989, militants murdered Hindu political activist Premnath Bhat, and on September 13, 1989, they murdered another activist, Tika Lal Taploo. On October 31, yet another politically active Hindu, Sheela Koul, was murdered.

In many cases, killers left JKLF tags on the bodies, claiming responsibility on behalf of the organization. The Allah Tigers, which took direct orders from Syed Ali Shah Geelani, carried out most of these murders in the name of JKLF.

Until the end of 1989, the murder of Hindu residents in Kashmir was selective. Following the foundation of Hizbul Mujahideen, however, hundreds of Hindus were killed, many brutally. Hizbul Mujahideen targeted residents without any association to political movements. Typical was the targeting of twenty-one-year-old Girija Kumari Tiku, which was covered in the local press. Tiku was a laboratory assistant at the Government High School in Trehgam. On June 11, 1990, after collecting her salary from her school, she was kidnapped by jihadis and taken to home of a Muslim friend, who was forced to watch as she was "stripped, gang-raped, placed on a mechanical saw, and chopped into two equal halves."[17]

Another target of Hizbul Mujahideen brutality was fifty-five-year-old-D.N. Chowdhary, a manager of the cement factory at Wuyan. On August 8, 1990, he was kidnapped from his office and murdered by Hizbul Mujahideen militants. According to one source, "his hands were broken with hammers and his tongue was chopped off. His whole face was mutilated and scarred by branding with a red-hot iron-press. His eyeballs were plucked out." On August 11,

1990, his body was dumped in a nearby village, Lethapora, on the Srinagar-Anantnag highway.[18]

Hizbul Mujahideen also continued their campaign of looting throughout the 1990s. Hindu homes were routinely burglarized with impunity, and the looted property of the Kashmiri Hindus soon formed an enormous underground economy, with stolen goods on sale in markets as far away as Bombay and Calcutta. They also destroyed a large number of temples and looted their property. Militants destroyed ninety-seven temples between 1990 and 1997.[19] According to the Panun Kashmir Movement, Hizbul Mujahideen also burned some 16,000 Hindu homes in Kashmir between the beginning of the insurgency and 1995.[20] Though many of their homes had historic value, Hindus began selling them and fleeing the valley, a fact that benefited Muslim real estate firms throughout the 1980s.[21] According to government sources, almost the entire Hindu population in the Valley of Kashmir, which numbered around 248,000, had shifted to refugee camps and elsewhere by October 1990.[22]

From the very beginning of the insurgency, the Islamist groups, particularly Hizbul Mujahideen and the Allah Tigers, have targeted what they deem "obscenities": cinemas, video stores, and bars. On July 20, 1989, the Khayyam Cinema was one of their first targets. There, a bomb was detonated in the women's bathroom. Following this opening salvo, they threatened further bombing of the cinemas— and the Islamic groups eventually succeeded in forcing the closure of all fifteen cinemas in the valley. It wasn't until June 1998 that cinemas began reopening.

When the Regal Cinema in Srinagar reopened in September 1999, jihadis threw two hand grenades into the theater after the conclusion of a Hindi film. The cinema had reopened only hours earlier.[23] Only one grenade exploded, though one person was killed and a dozen injured. The theater closed again. Later, Tehreekul Mujahideen claimed responsibility for the bombings.[24]

Another series of campaigns targeted women not wearing the veil. Again, it was an aim that the mujahideen pursued at the first opportunity: On July 29, 1989, a string of women were targeted. Fighters approached unveiled women in the street and threw acid on their faces. [25] Speaking about the attacks, one Hizbul Mujahideen leader said, "We will make their faces so ugly that they will wear the veil even when they sleep."[26] They also targeted women wearing makeup.

Many of the campaigns that targeted the Kashmiri public were claimed by front groups, who would spring up only to take credit for a single attack. This was particularly the case following a string of brutal attacks after 1999—at a time when Kashmiri society was beginning to open up. The previously unknown Lashkar-i-Jabbar, which was directly under the control of Syed Ali Shah Geelani, took credit for another acid attack on two unveiled women in Srinagar in 2001.[27] The group's spokesman telephoned a newspaper office and said the attack was just the beginning of a campaign to prevent "immodest dress among Kashmiri women." And the general public took such threats seriously—the local police had few resources to protect people. The veil campaign that Lashkar-i-Jabbar brought to Srinagar was already in motion in the rural areas of Kashmir, where residents could more easily be intimidated.[28]

When Lashkar-i-Jabbar set September 1, 2001, as a deadline to "adhere to the complete Islamic dress code," there was a noticeable increase in the number of women wearing veils in the streets of Srinagar.[29] The population had been threatened that "Following the expiry of the deadline, the cadres of the group will start targeting women without the veil under the new strategy."[30]

A group of conservative Islamic women, Dukhtaran-i-Millat (Daughters of the Nation) supported Lashkar-i-Jabbar position in a public message on August 28, 2001: The leader of the group, Asiya Andrabi, said, "We are indebted to these courageous men who have started a campaign for the veil in Kashmir and made us realize once again that we are Muslims." Two days later, on August 30, 2001, she urged Lashkar-i-Jabbar to extend its deadline "by at least ten more days" because women had not had enough time to obtain the veils. "It has been observed that due to heavy demand, tailors in Kashmir have not been able to cope with the rush. They will need more time to prepare veils and cloaks for the women."[31] Lashkar complied. On September 4, 2001, Syed Ali Shah Geelani also publicly supported Lashkar-i-Jabbar and asked Kashmiri Muslim women to "move about in veils or cloaks. The veil is a great thing provided by Islam to women."[32] One day before the new deadline, and encouraged by Asiya Andrabi's and Geelani's public support, Lashkar-i-Jabbar asked Hindu women to distinguish themselves from Muslim girls so that they would not be targeted in the *purdah* (veil) campaign, a tactic the Taliban would later borrow. They were asked to mark their foreheads, and Sikh women were to wear *kesari dupatta* (saffron-colored headdresses). In a statement, the Lashkar-i-Jabbar chief also asked non-Muslim girls to "show signs of decency in their dresses while moving about." The Lashkar-i-Jabbar quietly suspended its campaign in the aftermath of the September 11 terrorist attacks in the United States.

Lashkar-i-Jabbar restarted its veil campaign in 2002, setting another deadline for that April. Their 2002 statement read, "If our members see any boy or girl or any illegal couple doing acts of immorality they will be killed there and then." The statement also accused TV operators of showing "immoral and blue films" while claiming that hotel owners were allowing their premises to be used for "immoral and obscene" activities."[33] Three teenage girls were killed, two of them beheaded, on December 19, 2002, in Rajouri. Police later claimed they were killed because their fathers were Indian parliamentarians, though residents believed they were targeted because of their liberal dresses. Posters appeared in the third week of December 2002 in the name of al-Badr Mujahideen, warning of serious consequences for women not wearing burqas and men without beards. Newspapers reported on a rush to buy burqas in Rajouri in the wake of the killings.[34]

A previously unknown group calling itself Hai-e-Allal Fallah (Come Towards Virtue) targeted a cigarette seller, who they set on fire in Srinagar on December 23, 2002. The shopkeeper, Mohammad Shafi Teli, was hospitalized with burns over his entire body. In a faxed message to newspapers, the group's spokesman, who used the alias Mohammad bin Qasim, the first Muslim invader of India, said, "the shopkeepers selling cigarettes, tobacco, liquor and other such narcotics items should completely close down their business at once. Any shopkeeper or wholesale dealer found violating this dictate will end up like Mohammad Shafi Teli. Our aim is to cleanse the society of evils like cigarette smoking, drinking and use of narcotics."[35]

CHAPTER SIX

A CHANGE OF STRATEGY:
WAR IN THE OPEN

Plans for a Pakistani military invasion and reoccupation of the mountainous region in and around Drass and Kargil, tiny towns in the Kargil district of Indian-controlled Jammu and Kashmir, had been in play since the early 1980s. Such an operation had been a major tactical objective of the army since India took and occupied part of the region's Saichen Glacier in 1984.

A military takeover of the heights in Kargil was seen as a strategic step in any attempt to capture Kashmir. The top brass of the Pakistani army believed that by taking the strategic heights around the district they could choke off the Indian supply line—an Indian national highway, the NH1, which connects Srinagar to Leh cuts through Kargil—and penetrate Indian military outposts on the Siachen Glacier. Military logic also played a part: Drass and Kargil are some of the coldest inhabited places in the world, with temperatures dipping to near 50 degrees below zero, and they sit at 10,000 feet above sea level. Military officials believed that if the district could be occupied, it would be nearly immune to counterattack because of the complications of high-altitude warfare.

The Kargil district was also an appealing opening for Pakistani officials because the district's majority Muslim population. Most important, however, there was a diplomatic logic to a move on Kargil. A new operation in the region, and especially a military victory, would force the reopening of negotiations on Kashmir. Such an operation also had the potential to internationalize the conflict and force India back to a moderated negotiating table, a perennial obsession of the the military.

The conflict over the Siachen Glacier can be traced back to what is referred to as the Karachi Agreement, which had been signed by Pakistan and India in 1949 to demarcate a cease-fire line that would eventually become the Line of Control after the Simla Accord ended the war in Bangladesh in 1972. According to the Karachi Agreement, the border between the two occupied zones terminated in the Karakoram mountains in the Saltoro Range, at a point chosen for the sake of convenience. (The line formed the corner of a map square and was thus easier to identify.)

Beyond the mapped border, the agreement simply stipulates that India's territory extends "north to the glaciers."

The Siachen Glacier is the world's second-largest non-polar glacier, nearly forty miles wide, sitting 9,000 feet above sea level. Logically, India and Pakistan should have extended the cease-fire line to the commonly accepted northern limits of Kashmir on the frontier with China. However, the signatories to the Karachi Agreement did not foresee three decades of intricate dispute. (The agreement was further complicated over the meaning of the phrase "extending north": Did it mean exact magnetic north, or merely the region to the north?)

V. R. Raghavan, the former director general of Indian military operations, blames Pakistan for starting an armed conflict over Siachen by encouraging mountaineering expeditions to travel to the glacier in the 1970s, as part of a plan to extend the LoC to the Karakoram Pass. During the '70s, Pakistan went so far as to encourage climbers from the West and Japan to travel to the unexplored peaks in the region, even waiving fees for those who wanted to climb peaks in the western parts of the Karakorams. This in turn encouraged many, including Western journalists covering mountaineering, to think Pakistan held possession of the territory.

The journal *American Alpine* reported on expeditions to the Karakorams in 1981 and 1982. Pakistan cited these expeditions, and its sanctioning of them, as proof of its control over the region. According to Raghavan, India had long restricted mountaineering in the Karakorams, and thus India didn't consider this as signifying control: "The sensitivity of the region where the interests of India, China and

Pakistan are linked up was not regarded as an appropriate area to introduce either Indian or international climbers." In 1974, the U.S. Defense Mapping Agency's operational navigation chart showed an Air Defense Information Zone separating India and Pakistan in the Karakorams with a line drawn straight from the termination point of the cease-fire line to the Karakoram Pass. Other geographers followed this precedent.

The Pakistani army attempted a limited armed occupation of the passes west of the Siachen Glacier in September and October 1983. The attempt failed because of poor planning and logistical complications, although it was widely understood on both sides that if the attempt had succeeded it would have been impossible to evict the Pakistanis due to the location's altitude and the lack of military infrastructure. In January 1984, India learned through its intelligence agencies that Pakistan was purchasing large quantities of high-altitude equipment from the international markets, and this was interpreted as proof that there was another Pakistani operation planned to take Siachen. The Indian army responded by moving in to occupy the Saltoro Range west of the glacier, under a force commanded by Lieutenant General M. L. Chibber, in what was code-named operation Meghdoot. The Indian army went on to extend its military deployment on the Saltoro Range to encompass the range's entirety. Pakistan reacted to operation Meghdoot by launching its own offensive, called Operation Ababeel, "the swallows," a Koranic reference to Allah's sending swallows that carried small rocks in their claws, which they dropped on an army advancing toward Mecca, annihilating it.

Operation Ababeel was a dismal failure, as were subsequent Pakistani military efforts to occupy or dislodge the Indian army from the Saltoro Range. Beginning in 1984, the two countries established numerous military outposts in the region, though Pakistani soldiers were so far from the Siachen, according to V. R. Raghavan, that they could not even "get a glimpse of the glacier."

During the regime of General Zia-ul-Haq, plans for a military operation in Kargil were once again tabled. In one of the rare informed accounts the incident, former information secretary of Pakistan Altaf Gauhar writes that in 1987, General Zia-ul-Haq "authorized the preparation of a war plan to occupy several positions in the Kargil sector."

According to Gauhar's account, the plan was scrapped before it was approved because of critical flaws brought to Zia's attention by Lieutenant General Sahibzada Yaqub Khan, who was foreign minister at the time. At a final meeting meant to officially approve the plan, Khan, who had not previously been briefed, reminded the group that, though he was a foreign-affairs officer, he had been an army officer his entire life and thought the plan militarily inappropriate. According to Gauhar, he complained that "the posts which the Pakistani soldiers would occupy were totally covered by snow almost throughout the year. It was extremely difficult to maintain communications with the posts and meet the day-to-day requirements of the soldiers." He mentioned the case of some soldiers who had earlier occupied a similar post and been killed. Their bodies were still to be recovered. He added that, as foreign minister, "he would find it difficult to justify Pakistan's military action."[1] General Zia was so impressed with Gauhar's critique that he dropped the plan.

Corroborating this account, the writer Hassan Abbas further documents the existence of General Zia's plan, producing a verbatim transcript of the director general of military operations' failed defense of the plan at a meeting, likely the same meeting attended by Foreign Minister Khan. His source is a senior army officer also present at the meeting:

> Zia: When we take Kargil, what do you expect the Indians to do?...I mean, don't you think they will try to recapture it?
>
> DGMO: Yes, Sir, but we think that the position is impregnable and we can hold it against far superior forces.
>
> Zia: Now, that's very good, but in that case, don't you think the Indians will go for a limited offensive elsewhere along the Line of Control, take some of our territory, and use it as a bargaining chip?
>
> DGMO: Yes, Sir, this is possible, but...
>
> Zia: And if they are beaten back there also, don't you think they will attack across the international frontier, which may lead to a full-scale war?

DGMO: That's a possibility, Sir.

Zia: So in other words, you have prepared
a plan to lead us into a full-scale war with
India![2]

In the 1990s, Prime Minister Benazir Bhutto also twice rejected proposals for military operations in Kargil, which,
according to published accounts of military meetings, were
to be led by mujahideen forces, with only the minimal involvement of Pakistani regulars. As Bhutto later recalled,
"Plans were put up to me, where mujahideen activity could
have triggered desperation in India and led to them crossing
the LoC." Bhutto claimed to have vetoed the plan because
mujahideen activity posed a clear threat of all-out war: "I
said it's doable militarily. It is not doable politically."[3]

In 1990, Bhutto had been removed from office after a
series of corruption charges were leveled against her by
then-President Ghulam Ishaq Khan. She was succeeded, after an interim appointment, by Nawaz Sharif, a former
chief minister of the Punjab province. He had received the
post courtesy of Zia-ul-Haq, his political mentor. Sharif
was swept into office after vowing to form a conservative
government and to root out corruption. But President Ghulam Ishaq Khan turned on Sahrif as well, forcing him to
resign amidst corruption charges of his own in July 1993.
Bhutto was reelected prime minister that October.

Sharif, however, was reelected by a landslide in 1997.
He won nearly 90 percent of the ballots cast, the largest
mandate ever given to a Pakistani politician. He took office
for the second time on February 17, 1997.

In the wake of nearly fifty years of fighting over Kashmir, Sharif came into office with an eye to resolving the conflict. During his previous term, he had come to understand the delicate balance of power in Pakistan, with the army always lurking in the background, and, in many cases, holding the real levers of power. And the army would remain the power broker, in Sharif's estimation, as long as the Kashmir issue was live—it provided the army with a platform and a pretense under which to intervene in political matters. Sharif's preoccupation with army meddling led him to attempt to short-circuit the Kashmir issue by resolving it. He would seek peace with India.

Sensing Sharif's mood, Indian Prime Minister Atal Behari Vajpayee, who became prime minister for a second time in March 1998, started pushing for peace. Secret and not so secret diplomacy between the two prime ministers beginning in late 1998 led to peace talks, based on direct meetings, known as the "Lahore process." Early results were limited, though tangible: The two prime ministers decided to ease travel restrictions between India and Pakistan and start a Delhi-Lahore bus service. Prime Minister Vajpayee inaugurated the bus service in February 1999, riding the bus to Lahore, where he and Sharif signed the Lahore Declaration. The agreement stipulated that the two countries would "intensify their efforts to resolve all issues, including the issue of Jammu and Kashmir," as well as "affirm their condemnation of terrorism in all its forms" and "refrain from intervention and interference in each other's internal affairs."[4]

Pakistan and India had never been closer. Nervous and confused, the chief's of the armed forces, particularly the

Chief of the Army Staff General Pervez Musharraf, plainly kept their distance from the peace process.

On May 11 and 13, 1998, India detonated five nuclear fission devices. The detonations made headlines around the world, especially in the United States, where the state department had been attempting to discourage the tests for some time, fearing a nuclear arms race on the subcontinent. In Pakistan, agitation was widespread; Nawaz Sharif vowed that his country would give a suitable reply to the Indians.

On May 28, Pakistan's reply came in the form of a nuclear test of its own, just two weeks after the Indian tests. Pakistan also tested five devices, yielding nearly forty kilotons at the Chagai test site. International attention turned to India and Pakistan. United States President Bill Clinton complained that "by failing to exercise restraint in responding to the Indian tests, Pakistan lost a truly priceless opportunity to strengthen its own security, to improve its political standing in the eyes of the world. And although Pakistan was not the first to test, two wrongs don't make a right." International sanctions were applied to both countries.

The Indians had successfully tested a nuclear weapon more than ten years earlier, but Pakistan had finally caught up in the arms race, thanks to the work of A.Q. Khan, who had stolen nuclear secrets and worked since 1976 to develop a Pakistani bomb, and who was celebrated as national hero after the successful test. Much of the urgency put on exhibiting Pakistani nuclear technology was driven by the Pakistani army, which believed that if Pakistan could equal India's nuclear capabilities, it would enjoy a degree of immunity from Indian attack: Senior army officials believed that India would not risk a full-scale war with a nuclear Pakistan. It was in the context of a fevered war of words over the nuclear question that the Lahore process escalated, in a desperate attempt to ease tensions between the two countries.

By the time that the Lahore Declaration was signed, however, the army was already deeply involved in launching a new operation in Kargil. With the newfound confidence that followed Pakistan's successful nuclear test, the army again thought that a Kargil operation should be pushed forward, with senior members of the army, particularly Chief of Army Staff Pervez Musharraf, insisting that the risk of full-scale war was effectively neutralized.

General Musharraf was a lifelong military man, having entered the service in 1964 after studying at the Pakistan Military Academy, and, later, at London's Royal College of Defense Studies. He saw action in the 1965 Kashmir war and was promoted in 1991 to the rank of major general. He was eventually hand-picked by Sharif to take over as army chief of staff and chairman of the joint chiefs of staff. Musharraf's moves in Kargil, however, exposed a deep rift between the two and deeply undercut Sharif's public promise to promote peace with India. Also, in a major change in strategy, no longer would India be engaged by proxy forces. In Kargil, the army itself would launch an operation against India, a real war.

The Pakistani Army actually started their Kargil operation in the fall of 1998, nearly six months before the Indians discovered it in May 1999. The resulting conflict was rapidly played out, lasting only until July 1999. The body of the first documented casualty in the conflict, Haider Khan, was returned to his family in the village of Roushan in the Ghizer district of Pakistan in mid-October 1998. Khan was a soldier in the Nothern Light Infantry; he had died in an accident on October 13, 1998, in the Hamza-gun sector. The four soldiers who delivered his body to his family did not inform them about the circumstances or the place of his death, and his name was not publicly reported until June 1999, when the Pakistani army decided to acknowledge their direct involvement in the conflict. (The army took extensive measures to hide deaths in the Kargil conflict, delivering bodies to families before sunrise and forgoing military honors. Bodies were also delivered in civilian clothes.)[5] The operation was to be kept secret until the Pakistani forces had achieved their aims, occupying a long list of desired positions.

The infiltration was led by the elite Special Services Group, as well as by four to seven battalions of the North-ern Light Infantry, a paramilitary regiment not technically part of the Pakistani army at that time.

The Indian army discovered the presence of Pakistani regulars on May 7, 1999, when Indian units noticed that Pakistani forces had quietly occupied a series of vacated military posts formerly used by the Indian army. In the be-ginning, the Indian army thought that jihadis had occupied the posts, an impression that the Pakistani army encour-aged in an attempt to distance itself from the operation. The Indians responded with Operation Vijay, which called up 200,000 Indian troops, though just more than 20,000 were committed to the region owing to the difficulty of the terrain. The invasion force dwarfed the force of Pakistani regulars, which then numbered about 5,000 soldiers. The

Pakistani infiltrators had occupied pockets along a seventy-five mile-stretch of the LoC, nearly 15 percent of the total de facto border. The deepest intrusion was roughly a half mile into Indian-controlled territory, in Batalik, Drass, and Mushkoh.[6] According to Major General Rashid Qureshi, director general of Inter-Services Public Relations, the public office of the Pakistani military, early Indian attacks in these areas were rebuffed by the Pakistani army between early May and mid-July. Pakistani shelling of the highway also slowed India's momentum and threatened to cut off supplies from Leh. The Indians compensated by using a longer route called the Himachal Pradesh.

Because the Indians counterattacked any Pakistani encampment as soon as it was discovered, the Indian army was suffering heavy casualties, especially because of having underestimated the firepower of Pakistani encampments and because of poor strategic position. The Indians made use of some 250 artillery guns, especially the Bofors field howitzer, though their positions made use of artillery difficult.

After suffering heavy casualties for more than a month, India brought in its air power. Indian Air Force (IAF) attacks were of limited success: The IAF lost a MiG-27 jet, due, they claimed, to mechanical failure; the Pakistanis claimed it was a shoot-down. The Pakistanis also took out an MiG-21 fighter and a Mi-8 helicopter. By June 26, 1999, India claimed to have recaptured nine out of the twenty-nine peaks that had been occupied by Pakistani forces and to have cleared the heights thereby assuming command of the Srinagar–Leh highway.[7] By this time, India had confirmed that the occupants of the heights were indeed Pakistani regulars, and not jihadis, as was being claimed by Pakistan.[8] India claimed to have captured the 4,950-meter Tiger Hills after a fifteen-hour battle on July 4, 1999, which, if true, clearly showed that the Indian army was winning the battle. The Pakistani incursion seemed to have been a short-lived success.

The battle was short, but it was also deadly. Casualty estimates vary widely. Sharif later said that more than 4,000 Pakistani troops had been killed in the entire conflict, though at one time the Pakistani army claimed that only 187 Pakistani army personnel died between the start of the conflict and mid-July 1999.[9] The Pakistanis claimed that 1,700 Indian troops were killed during the same period, although most estimates put the number at closer to 850.

Throughout the conflict, India attempted to diffuse the situation and avoid total war. Prime Minister Vajpayee was ready to do whatever was possible, barring showing any signs of weakness. On June 21, 1999, he said that India would consider giving safe passage to fighters retreating to Pakistan: "If the infiltrators ask for safe passage to withdraw, the matter will be considered but there is no question of stopping the military action and allowing them to go without talks on the issue with Pakistan."[10]

It remains unclear, and a matter of great controversy in Pakistan, when and who formally approved a new operation in Kargil. The plan originated in, and was approved by, the Army General Headquarters, but it remains a puzzle whether Nawaz Sharif also approved it. According to a published account by Sharif, he was not consulted about the planning: "As prime minister I was not taken into confidence at all."

General Musharraf has claimed on a number of occasions that he informed Sharif of the operation, accusations that Sharif has repeatedly denied. At the time, Musharraf claimed that "Everyone was on board," adding that Sharif had also approved tactical questions and Army patrols into Indian-occupied Kashmir.[11] Later, according to Sharif's closest political lieutenant, Ishaq Dar, it was revealed that the army informed Nawaz Sharif about the Kargil operation only on May 17, 1999, though Dar admitted that there had been a strategic briefing on different locations, including Kargil, on January 29, 1999 in Skardu. However, there is no evidence that Sharif gave approval or was given information on the army's plans at the Skardu meeting. Sharif later admitted that he had been told about the operation in May 1999, some five months after fighting had begun.[12]

In his memoirs, Musharraf claims that the army "briefed the prime minister in Skardu on January 29, 1999; and in Kel on February 5, 1999. During these briefings, our defensive maneuver was explained as a response to all that was happening on the Indian side. Subsequently, the prime minister was also briefed on March 12 at the Directorate General Inter-Services Intelligence, which included a detailed survey of the situation inside Occupied Jammu and Kashmir and also along the LoC. As the operation developed, he was briefed in detail by the director general of military operations on May 17. Later, briefings were also arranged on June 2 and June 22."

Asked about the Kargil operation, Benazir Bhutto partly blamed Sharif for cheerleading on behalf of the operation, though she did not claim he had early knowledge of the campaign: "The people were euphoric. They were told we are shooting down Indian planes, the Indians were helpless, and they believed it."[13]

According to Sharif, the operation was only known to "Musharraf, Lieutenant Gen Aziz, then Chief of General Staff, General Mehmood, the Corps Commander of the area, and General Javed Hassan, the Divisional Commander of the Northern Areas. It was not in the knowledge of even any other corps commander. The Naval and Air Chiefs were also not informed. Just think, the prime minister was not informed, the Defense Minister and even the Defense Secretary were not informed... It was bound to fail."

One likely theory is that Sharif was promised, and approved, a far different operation than the one Musharraf carried out. Sharif may have been briefed on and approved an operation led by jihadi forces—even though the Kargil offensive was eventually launched as an army operation. Such a scenario would explain why General Musharraf and the army insist that they had briefed the prime minister, and why Sharif maintains that his government was not included in planning Kargil. It remains unlikely that a democratically elected Pakistani prime minister would make efforts to promote peace with India and sign the Lahore Declaration while also allowing the military operation to go forward.

By late June of 1999, the Pakistani army was badly hurt and retreating, looking for a face-saving formula to end the conflict. Around this time, it decided to induct jihadi forces into the operation and cut its losses.[14] Although it is still commonly believed that Kargil was from the beginning a joint operation of jihadi and Pakistani regulars, there is no evidence to support this. Musharraf and others have insisted on the point, despite the lack of any precise reports on militant operations during the early part of the Kargil conflict.

Militants found moving into the region amid heavy Indian fire difficult. And conflicts between the local population and the militants also developed. There was also extreme tension in the city of Skardu after the militants forcefully occupied a house and established an office there in July. (There was also tension between the civil administration and army officers. A local politician reportedly slapped a captain of the ISI, accusing him of favoring militants over the civilians.)[15]

Despite the obstacles, the militants claimed to have a string of successes. In an interview with the Associated Press of Pakistan, Lieutenant General Mujibur Rehman, who was Zia-ul-Haq's information minister, said that the mujahideen had seriously disrupted the communication lines of Indian forces stationed in Leh and Siachin, making it difficult for them to order supplies—and eventually forcing Indian forces to ration food and ammunition.[16] He said that the mujahideen had also inflicted heavy casualties.[17]

According to a former director general of the ISI Lieutenant General Javed Nasir, "The Mujahideen executed a brilliant plan. They did not believe in interdiction of Indian lines of communications by artillery fire only. They moved in physically... These mujahideen are different in many ways. They have shoulder-fired SAMs [surface-to-air missiles] and ATGMs [anti-tank guided missiles]. They have SPG-9s grenade launchers and MBRLs [multiple rocket launchers] gifted by the Afghan mujahideen. They now hold the first segment of the liberated territory after sacrificing over 20,000 shaheeds [martyrs] during the last ten years. They will not vacate it even if the Pakistan government asks them to do so."[18]

The plan to import additional militants was abandoned after Indian shelling devastated incoming fighters. Six mujahideen on a reconnaissance mission were killed on July 7, 1999, in the Mushkoh valley, and army officers took this as a signal that further movement of militants was impossible. These militants belonged to Tehreek-i-Jihad and al-Badr Mujahideen, although other militant groups were likely involved.[19]

Efforts eventually turned to a diplomatic solution, with Nawaz Sharif traveling to the United States to meet President Clinton in hopes of finding a formula to end the fighting. According to Sharif, he went to Washington only to save the honor of the army, after being encouraged by General Musharraf: "Kargil had the potential of full-scale nuclear catastrophe...therefore it was necessary to stop it immediately otherwise it could have resulted in the martyrdom of scores of our army officers." According to Sharif, the operation had gone so badly that Pakistan's Northern Light Infantry was wiped out completely during the Kargil fight. As the conflict continued, Pakistan was also losing more strategic positions, the most important being the Tiger Hills and what was referred to as Post 1514.[20]

According to an account that Clinton gave to the Pakistani press, Sharif "called and wanted to come and see me with a delegation on July 4, our independence day. I said...you have to know two things before you come. Do not come if you are not prepared for these two things. You cannot come for this emergency meeting unless you are prepared to withdraw Pakistani troops back over the Line of Control. And the second thing is you cannot expect me now to say I intend to mediate in this conflict because the Indians will not have it. So he, Sharif, said he understood it, he came to Washington...He tried to talk me out of my position and eventually I talked him back towards the phone conversation...And he withdrew back from the Line of Control."[21]

The joint declaration issued at the end of the meeting between Sharif and Clinton paved the way for a peaceful end to the conflict. Sharif agreed that it was vital that Pakistani troops retreat behind the Line of Control and respect it, according to the terms of the Simla Accord. Clinton said that if the border could be respected in the future, he would take a personal interest in the intensification of the bilateral peace talks that had been begun as part of the Lahore process.[22]

Pakistan's military operation in Kargil gave unearned publicity to the jihadis, both from Kashmir and Pakistan. For nearly two months, they claimed to be present and occupying part of Indian-controlled Jammu and Kashmir, and the media portrayed them as brave liberators of Kashmir and its people. Since any agreement would have deprived them of this newly gained fame, they rejected Sharif and Clinton's agreement. Syed Salahuddin, speaking their behalf, called the agreement "a stab in the back" and vowed to fight on. He added that the struggle in the Kargil-Drass sector would continue, and that the mujahideen would leave their positions only if the weather became intolerable or if their supplies were cut off. Salahuddin celebrated the mujahideen forces, which had helped seize more of the Kargil heights under a new strategy of area "occupation and domination," and this after more than ten years of hit-and-run tactics; he said that the same had to be done in other areas of Kashmir: "We will do it, Allah-willing, in eastern and southern regions of Kashmir."[23]

Upon Sharif's return from the United States, the Pakistani government formally appealed to the mujahideen on July 9 to draw down and withdraw from the Kargil sector. Immediately after a meeting of the Pakistan defense committee, Prime Minister Sharif met personally with eleven mujahideen leaders and requested their withdrawal from Kargil. Foreign Minister Sartaj Aziz announced that the fighters had started withdrawing from the Kaksar sector on July 10 and from the Mushkoh sector on July 11; the jihadis insisted that they were not retreating. In reaction to Foreign Minister Aziz's announcement, and what looked to be a face-saving formula, Salahuddin responded, on July 11: "We will not withdraw from Kargil but readjust positions due to strategic reasons."[24] Other jihadi commanders echoed his statement. However, the disengagement of forces was nearly complete by July 17, 1999.

In August 1999, a debate broke out in the Senate of Pakistan about the Kargil war and the secrecy and confusion that had clouded the operation. The retreat in Kargil had come so quickly, and the defeat seemed so total, that the politicians were at a losts to explain what had happened. There was also an intense controversy raging over why the army refused to recognize soldiers who had fought in the war.

Pakistan's policy of not recognizing the sacrifices of the army's Northern Light Infantry—instead accrediting all fighting to the jihadi forces—had sparked enormous resentment in the Northern Areas of Pakistan from the beginning, as the closely knit society there had known from the beginning of the conflict that Pakistani regulars were indeed fighting in the Kargil heights. Dead soldiers were being returned secretly, many of their bodies mutilated after heavy bombardment from the Indian Air Force. Other soldiers had died of hunger. Still, the government and the Pakistani army were praising only the jihadis, feeding resentment in Ghizer, Hunza, and Baltistan, where most of the NLI soldiers had come from.

Prime Minister Sharif tried to reconcile this situation by addressing the topic at the Skardu Military Hospital on June 24, 1999.[25] But it was too little and too late. On July 16, Sharif went further, announcing plans to give a house "in the city of their choice" and 500,000 rupees to legal heirs of soldiers killed in Kargil. He also promised to provide free education to their children and to give 500,000 rupees to disabled or wounded soldiers. But even this did not satisfy the people who wanted public recognition of the sacrifices that their family members had made. General Pervez Musharraf stepped in, honoring two casualties, Captain Karnal Sher Khan and Havaldar Lalak Jan, with the Nishan-i-Haider, the highest military medal. Twenty-six army personnel also received the Sitara-i-Jurat, another honor, and thirty-six more soldiers were also awarded.[26] Finally, cash payments were increased, with each bereaved family receiving 500,000 rupees out of the prime minister's package, as well as an additional 60,000 rupees from the army and 30,000 rupees from a fund set up personally by General Musharraf. Moreover, each family would receive between 200,000 rupees and 400,000 rupees in pension commutations, insurance, and other benefits.[27] Sharif also promised a housing initiative in the Northern Areas, including a plan to build 10,000 homes at a cost of 750 million rupees.[28]

The programs extended the cost of the conflict, which was already nearly $700 million.[29] In the Pakistani Senate, Senator Aitzaz Ahsan, leader of the Pakistan Peoples Party, demanded an explanation from Foreign Minister Sartaj Aziz: "Why are we burying our boys in so much secrecy? I have been to many of the burials where senior army officers told me about the valor of our young soldiers.... [but] the post mortems of these soldiers reveal that they were surviving on grass and dry *atta* [wheat flour]. They had no proper food because of bad planning."[30] Why, in other words, had so many soldiers died such painful deaths, and for what seemed like nothing?

Aziz responded simply: Kargil had been, more than anything, about "internationalizing" the conflict in Kashmir.

The internationalization of the Kashmir issue had, in fact, been a main objective of all the operations of the Pakistani army in Jammu and Kashmir from the time when tribal raiders were sent into Jammu and Kashmir in 1947. The military maneuvers have always been limited, even in Kargil, but each incursion was intended to recast the conflict and jump-start diplomacy. For this reason, despite the limited nature of the Kargil operation, there was euphoria in the army about the incursion. "Kargil was without doubt a very strong position to internationalize the Kashmir issue," according to a frank article by General Javed Nasir, a former ISI director general. [31] Nasir characterized the invasion, despite arguments to the contrary, as a "sane decision" and one that could easily have broadened Pakistani negotiating power.

General Musharraf has confirmed this on several occasions. In an interview with Indian NDTV, Musharraf said, "Let me tell you that before Kargil, Kashmir was a dead issue. To avoid Kargils, we need to resolve disputes and much depends on how we proceed on a peace track."[32] More recently, in his autobiography, Musharraf writes, "I would like to state emphatically that whatever movement has taken place so far in the direction of finding a solution to Kashmir is due considerably to the Kargil conflict."[33] Musharraf thought that Kargil had been "successful" in that it came near to forcing the Indians back to the negotiating table and reviving Pakistan's claims in the region.

According to one source, "General Musharraf told visibly restless audiences [at the end of the Kargil war] that the historic bravery shown by the mujahideen and the Pakistani army personnel in Kargil...had brought the Indian establishment to its knees and, in the first few weeks, Indian Prime Minister Atal Behari Vajpayee was forced to rush his emissary to Islamabad to seek an urgent solution." Present and former senior officials who had closely monitored the Kargil conflict "maintained a strikingly identical opinion that the Kargil operation had pushed Pakistan closest to a military victory against the Indian army in Kashmir....Intelligent use of the superior military position in the conflict could have transformed it into a situation where India had no choice but to come to the negotiating table for a final resolution of the Kashmir issue..."[34]

According to one officer, "Before the orders for retreat came, everyone from an ordinary soldier to a general officer was convinced that within the next six weeks, at least three divisions of the Indian army would surrender or abandon the territory up to the Siachen Glacier." He went on: "It was the biggest psychological blow to the troops...People in the Army thought that we were so close to settling the 1971 score with India."[35]

Despite a clear attempt to internationalize the conflict, the Kargil operation caused Pakistan to become totally isolated internationally. The United States and Europe clearly tilted in favor of India, outraged by Pakistani aggression so soon after the Lahore Declaration. They continued to press Pakistan to withdraw infiltrators from the Kargil heights and respect the Line of Control throughout the conflict. China, a longtime ally of Pakistan, also refused to take Pakistan's side.

Throughout the army, a popular anger was soon directed against Sharif's order to withdrawal from Kargil, though many suspected that Musharraf had concurred with the decision. Tension between the prime minister and General Musharraf reached a fever pitch. Instead of accepting the defeat and the flaws in planning the Kargil operation, the Pakistani army set out on a collision course with the democratic government. The ISI, which handles most of the fundamentalist rightist parties and jihadi organizations in Pakistan, unleashed them, one of the tactics the ISI has used since Zia-ul-Haq's days, to destabilize governments. Party members came into the streets and erupted against the Sharif government. Protestors reacted against the defeat and the slighting of soldiers who had fought in Kargil. There were countrywide strikes by traders, fermented in many cases by right-wing trade unions. Sectarian parties such as Sipah-i-Sahaba Pakistan (SSP) and Harakat-ul Jihad al-Islami (HUJI), Pakistani affiliates of al-Qaida (with their headquarters in then-Taliban-controlled Kabul) protested by instigating a killing spree, targeting Shia Muslims in Pakistan. At least forty-one died and scores were wounded in the anti-Shia violence.

Prime Minister Sharif heightened the animosity of his rivals by instigating a new diplomatic push in Afghanistan, an ally of many of his domestic enemies. He sent ISI chief Lieutenant Ziaud Din Butt to meet Taliban leader Mullah Omar, in Kandahar, Afghanistan, during the first week of October 1999. [36] General Butt was to express to Omar Pakistan's concern over the continued operation of militant training camps, arrests, and failed extradition of terrorists such as Riaz Basra, one of the most dreaded Sipah-i-Sahaba fighters, and Maulana Saifullah Akhtar, who heads one of the known Pakistani affiliates of al-Qaida, as well as some 150 other terrorists. (According to another account, Butt conveyed this message to Mullah Omar from Prime minister Sharif, and not from the ISI.[37]) Omar responded by promising to shut down all the training camps and turning over the requested suspects within ten days.[38] But, he never fulfilled his promise. On October 7, 1999, exasperated with the rising sectarian violence, Sharif publicly accused the

Taliban of running the militant training camps. "We have made it clear to the Taliban that this is not acceptable to Pakistan," Sharif said.[39] Then, accompanied by ISI Lieutenant Director General Butt, Sharif went to the UAE on October 11, 1999 to seek UAE President Sheikh Zayed bin Sultan Al-Nahyan's help in pressing the Taliban to close down the training camps.[40]

Exasperated with General Musharraf's efforts to destabilize his government, Prime Minister Sharif finally decided to oust General Musharraf on October 12. Musharraf was in the air, returning from Sri Lanka, when Sharif appointed Lieutenant General Butt as his replacement. But Sharif's move was too late. The Pakistani army generals rebelled and refused to accept Butt. When Musharraf reached Pakistan, he replaced Sharif as the chief executive in a bloodless coup, supported by the Pakistani generals. He dismissed the legislative assemblies and assumed the title of chief executive. According to some reports, Sharif had attempted to move against Musharraf—recommending a court-martial over his handling of Kargil. But there has never be an official inquiry into the matter.[41]

The Kargil operation was not planned to oust the elected government, but Prime Minister Sharif became its most important victim.

CHAPTER SEVEN

"IT WILL BE DONE BY THE MUJAHIDEEN"
JIHAD AND DIPLOMACY

The Kashmiri jihadis were jubilant over General Mushar-raf's military coup d'etat. Hizbul Mujahideen, in particular, welcomed the coup. A spokesman from the group said, "It is good to see military rule in Pakistan but the step is delayed. It should have come earlier at the time of the Kashmir [Kargil] war when Nawaz Sharif betrayed us."[1]

The jihadi response to Musharraf's rule was immediate: Recruitment camps sprung up all over the country. And fund-raising for jihadi groups accelerated. They put collection boxes on counters of big and small shops, and wherever else they thought people might donate money to the jihad. During the last months of 1999, there was great excitement throughout Pakistan; jihadis had never been more visible. A new "launching season" of fighting was planned for April 2000.

However, the South Asian visit of U.S. President Bill Clinton changed the situation considerably. In 1999, Clinton had announced a high-profile visit to India and Pakistan, set for the spring of 2000. He was expected to use his offices to help India and Pakistan resolve the Kashmir dispute. Clinton had said he would spend equal numbers of days in each country. The military coup, however, changed all of this. As it turned out, Clinton would reduce his visit to a quick stop.

On March 25, 2000, President Clinton landed in Pakistan at the Chaklala airbase in an unmarked Gulfstream IV; for security reasons, Air Force One was used as a decoy. At the airport, Pakistani troops were asked to stand by unarmed—an act that signaled great American distrust of Pakistani security officials. President Clinton spent only about six hours and twenty minutes in Pakistan. Of this time, nearly forty-five minutes were spent addressing the American community at the airport. The remainder of Clinton's time was spent meeting with Pakistani officials. There was a fifteen-minute protocol visit with President Rafiq Tarar. Later, accompanied by other officials, Clinton met with Musharraf for a little over an hour. The visit concluded with a twenty-minute discussion of economic affairs.

The public snub weakened Musharraf; for the first time since he had deposed Prime Minister Nawaz Sharif, he came under criticism from all sides. At home, he was accused of begging Clinton to visit Pakistan; abroad, he was accused of patronizing jihadis. Pakistan once again stood isolated in the world. Clinton had publicly made his anti-terror case to Pakistani people in a special article written exclusively for the Pakistani press. He wrote,

> The Pakistani people are our long-term friends. We want them to enjoy the benefits of democracy, to build a strong economy, to be free of terrorism and live in peace. Some say I should not go to Pakistan, because of the military coup that overthrew the democratically-elected Prime Minister, Nawaz Sharif. But engagement with Pakistan does not represent endorsement. Staying only away would strengthen hardliners in Pakistan who want their country to turn away from the world...I also believe that India and Pakistan will not achieve real security until they resume dialogue to resolve their tensions. I am not going to mediate the dispute between India and Pakistan. America cannot play that role unless both sides want it. But I will urge restraint, respect for the Line of Control in Kashmir, and renewed lines of communication. Both India and Pakistan have legitimate security concerns. But neither can achieve its aims in an escalating contest of inflicting and absorbing pain...Finally, I will speak directly to General Musharraf and to the Pakistani people about the steps we believe are important to building a hopeful future for Pakistan: an early return to democracy, a crackdown on terrorist groups, restraint

on nuclear and missile programs, and a real effort to create the conditions for dialogue with India. If Pakistan takes these steps, we can get back on the path of partnership.[2]

During his brief stay, Clinton also further elaborated U.S. policy in a live television address to the Pakistani nation. He minced no words about his disapproval of Pakistan's policy of using jihadi fighters as an instrument of foreign policy. He asked the Pakistani nation to abandon their support of extremism, saying:

If you choose this path, your friends in the United States will stand with you. There are obstacles to your progress, including violence and extremism. The Americans have also felt these evils. Surely, we have both suffered enough to know that no grievance, no cause, no system of belief can ever justify deliberate killing of innocents. Those who bomb bus stations, target embassies and kill those who uphold the law are not heroes. They are our common enemies, for their aim is to exploit painful problems, not to resolve them. Just as we have fought together to defeat those trafficking in narcotics, today I ask Pakistan to intensify its efforts to defeat those who inflict terror. I have listened carefully to General Musharraf and others. I understand your concerns about Kashmir. I share your conviction that Human Rights of all people must be respected. But a stark truth must also be faced—there is no military solution to Kashmir. International sympathy, support and intervention cannot be won by provoking a bigger, bloodier conflict. On the contrary, sympathy and support will be lost and no matter how great the grievance, it is wrong to support attacks against civilians across the Line of Control. I hope you will be able to meet the difficult challenges we have discussed today. If you do not, there is a danger that Pakistan may grow even more isolated, draining even more resources away from the need of the people, moving even closer to a conflict no one can win. But if you do meet these challenges, our full economic and political partnership can be restored for the benefit of the people of Pakistan.

Musharraf proved to be more susceptible to U.S. pressure than the jihadis ever expected, or at least it seemed so. Following Clinton's visit, an informal, unannounced peace process between India and Pakistan was put into motion. During a May 2000 visit to Islamabad by U.S. Under Secretary of State Thomas Pickering, the Musharraf regime agreed to a unilateral cease-fire along the Line of Control.

Pickering negotiated with a heavy hand in Islamabad, pressuring Pakistan to make a "detectable change" in its Kashmir policy. In good faith, India had released most members of the separatist parties it then held in its jails. But Pickering told the Pakistanis that further moves would be impossible without a similar good-faith effort from Pakistan. Pakistan finally agreed to stop firing artillery along the Line of Control, a practice which had long acted as a protective shield for infiltrating fighters moving across the LoC. Pakistan announced its move by sending Foreign

Minister Abdus Sattar to Washington in June, with the cease-fire coming into effect on June 25, 2000.[3] As soon as the artillery fire stopped, casualties among jihadi infiltrations increased dramatically.

The jihadi forces, too, would join this cease-fire in a way. In early 2000, "Brigadier Riaz" of the ISI Kashmir cell directed its jihadi groups to stop publicly claiming responsibility for bombings inside Kashmir. The ISI directed groups to form fronts to claim any attack instead, thus making it appear as if the traditional players in the jihad had slowed their assaults. On April 15, 2000, a large attack on the broadcast station Radio Kashmir was claimed by an unknown group, Hizb-e-Tawheed. There had been several attacks on the radio station in the past: In March, militants had attacked the adjacent TV center with grenades.

The ISI also approached the leaders of Jamat-i-Islami and Hizbul Mujahideen fighters about the possibility of a temporary cease-fire. The ISI argued that such a gesture would help Pakistani negotiating efforts and increase international support for their cause. Furthermore, since India would not reciprocate and pull their forces, the ISI argued, a cease-fire would add the appearance of Pakistani goodwill. The jihadis generally disapproved of the scheme. Chief Hizbul Mujahideen Operational Commander Abdul Majeed Dar, in particular, disagreed with the ISI plot and broke off meetings in July, traveling from Pakistan to Srinagar via Dubai.[4]

On July 24, 2000, however, in an about-face Dar appeared at a press conference in Srinagar—held at a secret location—to announce a three-month unilateral cease-fire.

At the press conference Dar was flanked by all the senior Hizbul Mujahideen commanders, demonstrating that his cease-fire enjoyed the legitimate support of the jihadi forces.[5] Dar said, "We want to show the world that we are not hard-liners and we are flexible in the search for a solution.... There should be no use of force against Mujahideen and no excesses carried out on the Kashmiri people." Dar added that if the Indian authorities failed to respond appropriately to the cease-fire announcement "then we will once again go on the supreme offensive."[6]

Hizbul Mujahideen commander Syed Salahuddin had discussed and approved the cease-fire plan before Dar left for Srinagar, but the timing of the message caught him off guard. He learned of the announcement only after the fact.[7] He had not had a chance to brief his contacts in the ISI on the specifics, nor to discuss the cease-fire with the leaders of the Jamat-i-Islami of Pakistan. For a time, Salahuddin turned off his mobile phone, disappeared from public sight, and met with ISI and Jamat-i-Islami officials, explaining their decision to go forward with a cease-fire.

At a press conference at the Holiday Inn in Islamabad, Syed Salahuddin publicly confirmed the authenticity of Dar's cease-fire offer, saying that the cease-fire was intended to dispel Indian propaganda that claimed the Kashmiri fighters were the only obstacle in the way of a peaceful resolution of the Kashmir conflict. He asked India to initiate dialogue with Pakistan, and he designated the Hurryyat Conference, an alliance of twenty-six political, social, and religious organizations in Kashmir, including the JKLF and Jamat-i-Islami, as the proper negotiating partner for a final settlement of the Kashmir issue. He warned that Hizbul Mujahideen would resume its militant activities if India did not show a positive response, and he further threatened that, if a favorable agreement could not be reached, its fighters might not remain restricted to the state of Jammu and Kashmir. India could be targeted next.

Dar's cease-fire was a shock for the leaders of the Jamat-i-Islami of Pakistan and other jihadi organizations. On July 26, 2000, the United Jihad Council (UJC), a coalition of jihadi groups, condemned the cease-fire, expelled Salahuddin from its organization, and suspended the membership of Hizbul Mujahideen.[8] A still stronger reaction came from the amir of the Jamat-i-Islami of Pakistan, Qazi Hussain Ahmed. The amir, who was on a high-profile tour of the U.S., rejected the cease-fire offer, saying in an address in New York, "no individual can impose cease-fire after millions of people have laid down their lives to achieve freedom."[9] He called a meeting in Lahore of the majlis-i-shoura of the Jamat-i-Islami of Pakistan to discuss the situation, and he cut his U.S. visit short, returning to Pakistan on July 27.

Qazi Hussain Ahmed had addressed the cease-fire in the United States because there was an impression in Pakistan that the cease-fire had been the result of a Jamat-i-Islami deal with the United States. The accusation seemed particularly credible because Ahmed's United States visit had been partly arranged by the Pakistani embassy, and because Ahmed met Pakistani ambassador Maleeha Lodhi in the U.S. He had also met with numerous U.S. officials, including a five-hour meeting at the State Department, as well as meetings with Assistant Secretary of State for South Asia Karl Inderfurth, chief of the U.S. Task Force on Terrorism

Michael Sheehan, Assistant Secretary for Democracy and Human Rights Harold Koh, and numerous senators and congressmen. A rival of Ahmed's, Maulana Fazlur Rehman, responded by saying that the cease-fire had "been a far greater debacle than the withdrawal of mujahideen from Kargil by Nawaz Sharif, and the military rulers must dispel the impression Qazi's visit was government sponsored."[10]

On July 28, a senior Indian army officer said that India had suspended its offensive against the Kashmiri fighters, and he asked Hizbul Mujahideen to establish contact with its officials. Indian Major General Basant Singh confirmed this, saying "We have stopped operations against the mujahideen locally." He added that his troops had not carried out a single operation against the separatists since the cease-fire announcement: "There will be no deliberate attempt against the militants on our part. We have issued instructions to all our field commanders to stop these offensive operations." Explaining the subtleties of the truce, he added, "It is very difficult to identify which militant is of Hizbul Mujahideen or another outfit." This was the first time in eleven years that India had stopped military operations against the fighters.

During Jamat-i-Islami of Pakistan meetings about the cease-fire, Qazi Hussain Ahmed speculated that it was really part of the power struggle developing between Syed Salahuddin and Abdul Majeed Dar. Another senior Jamat-i-Islami leader speculated that Dar had acted on behalf of the ISI.[11] Qazi Hussain Ahmed was able to offer some evidence of government intervention, but there was little consensus how to proceed.[12] The group panicked, seeing that its jihad was at risk of slipping away. Eventually, in a large meeting on July 30, the Jamat-i-Islami of Pakistan responded by pressing Syed Salahuddin to withdraw the cease-fire order and to blame the incident on the intervention of the Pakistani government. On July 31, the group went public with its message in a press conference in which it asked Syed Salahuddin to retract the cease-fire order. Qazi Hussain Ahmed also publicly claimed that the government was behind the cease-fire plan.

But by July 31, Dar had contacted Fazul Haq Qureshi, the fifty-six-year-old chairman of the Peoples Political Front, to be its emissary in talks with India. Qureshi accepted. On August 1, the Indian government also accepted Qureshi's appointment and contacted him to schedule a meeting; Qureshi asked that no preconditions be imposed on their meetings.

By this point, it had become clear that there was indeed a deep, public split between two camps within Hizbul Mujahideen, one led by Dar and the other led by Salahuddin. While Salahuddin appeared to be supporting Dar's work on a cease-fire, telling reporters, "There should be no ambiguity regarding our stand. We want unconditional and tripartite talks so that the festering Kashmir problem is resolved at the earliest time in accordance with the wishes and aspirations of the people of the disputed state," he also attempted without success to join the process. According to a spokesman, he requested that a three-member team be added to the talks, a request that he had to withdraw the next day: "We have created a peaceful atmosphere for the Kashmiri leadership and the world to use their influence for talks. Hizbul Mujahideen will only want to play a role of monitor."[13]

Seeing an impasse, elements of Jamat-i-Islami and Hizbul Mujahideen that opposed the cease-fire attempted to wreck the process through violence. On August 1, a series of militant attacks in Kashmir claimed nearly one hundred lives. President Clinton himself intervened to stop the escalating violence and get peace talks back on track. Clinton called Indian Prime Minister Vajpayee the following day and expressed his sympathy for the recent militant attacks.[14] Later, he wrote a letter directly to Musharraf to express his dissatisfaction over the August attacks.

In early August, Vajpayee traveled to Kashmir, where he announced that talks with Hizbul Mujahideen would indeed take place, though he insisted that the talks were *insaniat*, done for the sake of humanity, and thus technically outside the law of the Indian constitution. On August 3, formal talks began between Hizbul Mujahideen and high-level Indian government officials. The two sides agreed to work in six-member negotiating teams, and to first tackle the terms of the cease-fire. Early in the process there was great optimism, with Indian Home Secretary Kamal Pande saying that "the members of the two committees will work in a spirit of cooperation and understanding and finalize the modalities for effective implementation of the [cease-fire] ground rules."[15] The Hizbul Mujahideen delegation included the commanders Riaz Rasool and Masood Ahmed.

Hizbul Mujahideen forwarded a list of twelve demands to the Indian team: (1) that the region's designation as a "disturbed area" be removed; (2) that the special powers of the police forces be withdrawn; (3) that bunkers be removed from civilian areas; (4) for police crackdowns and intrusive searches be given up; (5) that political activities by all their parties be allowed; (6) that harassment of the political workers be stopped; (7) that Indian human right violations be halted; (8) that current cases against mujahideen be withdrawn; (9) that all detainees and political prisoners be released; (10) that harassment of released and ex-mujahideen be stopped; (11) that police seizure of vehicles be stopped; and (12) that all active Mujahideen forces be involved in the peace process.

It was an extensive list, but the Indians did not balk; Prime Minister Vajpayee invited all fighters to the talks. "It is futile for them to continue on the path of violence. They should come forward for talks with the government for redress of their grievances," he said.[16]

However, the talks stalled when Hizbul Mujahideen insisted on tripartite peace talks, with Hizbul Mujahideen's Masood Ahmed demanding that "Pakistan has to be involved...a permanent solution of Kashmir cannot be achieved without Pakistan's participation."[17] Salahuddin also used the issue to stall the talks. On August 5, 2000, under the pressure of the Jamat-i-Islami, he intervened by announcing that if India did not agree to tripartite talks, he would cancel the cease-fire. He set a deadline for 5:00 p.m. on August 8: If the Indians hadn't agreed to bring the Pakistanis into the talks by then, Salahuddin would withdraw the cease-fire and begin attacks.

India could not accept this condition, and Salahuddin proceeded with the cancellation of the cease-fire on deadline. "Indian leadership has failed to respond to our icebreaking move which could have become productive and meaningful if New Delhi had accepted unconditional tripartite talks between India, Pakistan and Kashmiris... We direct all the commanders with the Mujahideen in the field to break the cease-fire and go ahead with all target-oriented missions," said Salahuddin. On the same day, the Pakistani foreign office hastily accused India of destroying the possibility of a peace process. A foreign office spokesman said, "India demanded that the freedom fighters should accept talks within the Indian constitution, which would have negated the very purpose of more than half-a-century-old Kashmiri struggle for self-determination."[18]

The withdrawal of the cease-fire by Syed Salahuddin had once again brought the conflict between Salahuddin's and Dar's factions out into the open. For a while, the two kept issuing statements contradicting each other.

On August 22, Dar told the press, "I hope that a new cease-fire will take place in the next two months because of the efforts at the international level to break the deadlock. To end the deadlock, people at the international level are active and the talks between Hizbul Mujahideen and the Indian authorities will start again." Though he was eager to get the process back on track, Dar also confirmed that only tripartite dialogue could resolve the Kashmir problem. And, in an attempt to minimize confusion, he claimed he was in contact with Salahuddin on a daily basis.[19]

Salahuddin reacted to Dar's statement on August 23 by saying, "The cease-fire will be resumed only after India accepts our basic demands, whether in two days, two months, or in ten years." On August 24, Dar chimed in again, telling the BBC, "The talks will begin after two months. We hope that matters will be clear in two months whether or not the talks could begin. We have kept our doors open. We are ready to cooperate for any peaceful settlement."[20]

Salahuddin also told a press conference in Islamabad that he had sent a letter to President Clinton through Mansoor Ijaz, a prominent Pakistani-American businessman who Salahuddin believed was in close contact with the CIA and the State Department. He had asked Clinton to coax India into tripartite talks, making it clear there would be no second cease-fire without such talks.[21]

On November 17, 2000, Salahuddin admitted to the BBC that, since Hizbul Mujahideen had first broken away from its talks with the Indians, it had not had further meetings. The process appeared stalled permanently.

With the peace process stalled, Salahuddin called a meeting of the majlis-i-shoura of Hizbul Mujahideen. His goal was to expel the followers of Abdul Majeed Dar. Dar had become too towering a figure in the organization, and he had become Salahuddin's rival. Salahuddin had cleansed his organization many times before, and he didn't think ridding Hizbul Mujahideen of Abdul Majeed Dar would be any different.

But Hizbul Mujahideen was in the midst of a crisis. Salahuddin knew that the Jamat-i-Islami of Pakistan was considering replacing him; they had been greatly angered that Salahuddin had confirmed Dar's cease-fire announcement against their wishes.

But there was something else: According to two sources, Salahuddin lied to leaders of Hizbul Mujahideen. Salahuddin claimed that he been had asked, by the Jihad-i-Kashmir

Committee, to "disown" Dar's cease-fire. According to the sources, however, the Jihad-i-Kashmir committee had actually asked him to stay silent on the matter.

As it turned out, Salahuddin was attempting to conceal something more significant: The ISI indeed had leaned on him to accept the cease-fire and thus preserve the unity of Hizbul Mujahideen.[22]

Despite the impasse with Hizbul Mujahideen and the rhetoric from the Pakistanis, both India and Pakistan attempted to continue the formal peace process that had been inaugurated by President Clinton's visit. In an interview with London-based *Al-Hayyat* on July 31, 2000, Musharraf had vowed to sign a formal agreement with India to prevent war. He repeated this offer to India in his speech at the UN General Assembly on September 6, 2000. He had also made this offer once before, in a public forum:

> Pakistan stands for peace and is prepared to take bold initiative to change the status quo through a dialogue with India at any level, at any time and anywhere. Let me commit at this world forum that we desire a no-war pact; we are ready for a mutual reduction of forces; and we also seek a South Asia free from all nuclear weapons. Pakistan shall not be drawn into an arms race, nuclear or conventional, irrespective of provocation.[23]

Further steps for the continuation of the peace process were taken during a three-day biannual meeting in Lahore on November 23, 2000, where officials of the Indian Border

Security Force and Rangers agreed to stop unprovoked cross-border shelling.[24] Soon thereafter, India also offered a new cease-fire offer, to begin on the first day of Ramadan, November 28, 2000. Prime Minister Vajpayee said,

> The holy month of Ramadan during which Prophet Mohammad exhorted one and all to live in peace and harmony, is soon approaching...The government has therefore instructed [Indian] security forces not to initiate combat operations against the militants in Kashmir during this most pious month in the Islamic calendar.... We have continued our efforts to normalize the situation in the state and to hold talks with all those who are prepared for a dialogue.[25]

Imam Bokhari of the Jama Masjid, the principal mosque in Delhi, called Salahuddin and requested that he observe the cease-fire, but Salahuddin was in no mood to oblige.[26] Hizbul Mujahideen spokesman Saleem Hashmi said the Hizbul Mujahideen would only react positively to the short-term cease-fire announcement provided that India agree to tripartite negotiations.[27]

Despite the seeming impasse, Pakistan made other moves in an attempt to push the peace process forward. On December 20, a military official announced that Pakistan would proceed with a unilateral withdrawal of a portion of its troops deployed along the Line of Control. According to the government, this was the fourth concrete step the Musharraf government had taken to reduce tension along the LoC since October 1999. In 1999, the Musharraf regime had reduced the number of forces along the LoC, though where exactly that had occurred remained classified. And earlier in December 2000, Pakistan had also announced a policy of maximum restraint along the LoC. At around the same time, both Pakistan and India started observing the cease-fire in Siachin.[28]

India responded to Pakistani moves by extending another month of cease-fire to Hizbul Mujahideen. Prime Minister A.B. Vajpayee personally announced the decision to the Indian parliament: "After careful considerations of all aspects, the government has taken a decision to extend the period of no-initiation of combat operations by another month."[29]

The continuing peace process angered many in Pakistan, particularly the ISI and the jihadis. On December 22, 2000, in an attempt to sabotage the peace process, two militants from the jihadi group Lashkar-i-Taiba managed to enter the Red Fort, a historic fort located on the edge of the old city in Delhi and a popular tourist attraction, and killed one soldier and two civilians. A spokesman for Lashkar-i-Taiba threatened more such attacks inside India. He told the Reuters wire service, "This is our first operation against an Indian military installation inside India.... By attacking the Red Fort, we want to stress that India should stop this drama of cease-fire and talks; it should pull out its forces from Kashmir so that the valley's people could get their fundamental rights."[30]

Unexpectedly, the attack on the Red Fort did not derail the peace process. India, it seemed, desperately wanted talks with Hizbul Mujahideen. It extended the cease-fire for another month and then for a further three months. Pakistan's interior minister, Lieutenant General Moeenud

Deen Haider, also repeatedly pledged to curb the activities of jihadis during the following months.

Syed Salahuddin had been unhappy with the United Jihad Council and the existence of other jihadi groups for a long time. He had been considering founding a new organization. He wanted loyal jihadi groups to merge into a new group, the Kashmir Liberation Army, which would be under his direct command. Though the cease-fire period was politically sensitive, Salahuddin proposed the idea. The merits of such a plan were obvious to Salahuddin's patrons in the government: The organization would strengthen Hizbul Mujahideen and weaken or eliminate rival jihadi organizations.

But there was another side to the plan. By eliminating Salahuddin's rivals the Pakistanis could also claim to be combating terror groups and win points with the Americans. General Musharraf supported the plan, and the ISI took little time to implement it. On February 19, 2001, the Azad Kashmir government shut down the offices of four insignificant jihadi groups that they opposed: the Mujahideen-i-Jammu and Kashmir, Karwan-i-Khalid, Zarbe Momin, and Zarbe Islami. The groups were Shia and Barelvi jihadi groups, which the ISI never supported. But many of the small groups pushed back, and the plan was eventually abandoned.

Though ultimately unsuccessful, the plan was a sophisticated example of Pakistani duplicity.

After more than a year of negotiations on Kashmir, India and Pakistan moved to hold a summit. India had decided not to renew its six-month-old cease-fire, but, on May 23,

2001, Indian Prime Minister Vajpayee invited Musharraf to India for peace talks. India was desperate to restart the process.

Vajpayee's letter read in part, "We have to pick up the threads again including renewing the composite dialogue so that we can put in place a composite structure of cooperation and address all outstanding issues including Jammu and Kashmir."[31] Musharraf accepted the invitation, acknowledging that "The root cause of tension between our two countries is the unresolved Jammu and Kashmir dispute.... We are ready to discuss all other outstanding issues between our two countries as well."[32]

In the period before the summit, Musharraf made a number of public denouncings of Islamists and jihadis, and he stepped up his statements on 'Id Miladun Nabi, June 5, 2001. He criticized public jihadi threats against India, saying that such rhetoric causes "suffering among the Indian Muslims and, as a result, Pakistan is being dubbed as a terrorist state." Vajpayee welcomed these statements, thanking Musharraf and saying that "India has always been asking for an end to the propaganda war between the two countries. This is the first step in the direction of lasting friendship between the two countries."[33]

Setting the agenda for the summit, Musharraf also again openly discussed a "no-war" pact, which had been a Pakistani foreign-policy goal since the early 1980s. The Pakistanis had been pursuing such a pact in hope of permanently avoiding the possibility that the Kashmir dispute would erupt into full-scale war. Musharraf also mentioned the proposal in a July 5 interview with the *Times of India*.

As Musharraf prepared to travel to India for the summit, a sense of euphoria spread in India and Pakistan—

and many believed that a peace treaty was imminent. The
jihadis, however, were nervous in the weeks preceding the
summit. They feared the unknown. And Musharraf drew
harsh criticism from jihadi leaders in Indian-controlled
Jammu and Kashmir. Dukhtaran-i-Millat leader Aasya Andrabi spoke for hard-line jihadis:

> the General's assertion that religion should be kept
> at a distance from politics makes its clear that he
> is ignorant about real Islam...General Musharraf
> should know that the Kashmir issue is also a reli-
> gious one as people of Kashmir want to accede to
> Pakistan on the grounds that it is an Islamic na-
> tion...By making statements against those involved
> in jihad in Kashmir, Musharraf may have won ap-
> preciation from New Delhi, but he should know
> that the Islamic flag will not be hoisted on New
> Delhi at his orders. It will be done by the muja-
> hideen some day.[34]

In July 2001, General Musharraf went to India to meet Indian Prime Minister Vajpayee in the historic city of Agra,
in what would be known as the Agra Summit.

Though many predicted that Musharraf would hammer
out an agreement—as leader of the military and the government, he was answerable to no one and had great flexibility
to come to terms—the summit was unproductive. The two
countries could not even agree on the text of the joint communiqué, and Musharraf returned to Pakistan.

Jihadis received the news about the failure of the Agra summit with jubilation. They gave a hero's welcome to General Musharraf when he returned from Agra. And they renewed their mission with a new zeal, vowing to take the jihad to new heights. At a July 18, 2001, press conference in Peshawar, Bakht Zameen of al-Badr Mujahideen said that the aborted negotiations had shown that jihad against the Indian government was the only way to liberate the Muslims of Kashmir. He vowed that al-Badr Mujahideen would carry out operations against the Indian army inside India, which, he claimed, had become easier than fighting inside Indian-controlled Kashmir. In a speech in Peshawar, another jihadi from the Hizbul Mujahideen, Javed Qasuri, also threatened to take the jihad into India.[35]

Soon after General Musharraf's return from India, though, the security agencies began arresting jihadis. And on August 22, 2001, in what was the most important action against the jihadi groups to date, the Sindh police arrested some 200 fighters in Karachi, members of such groups as Lashkar-i-Taiba, Harakatul Mujahideen, and al-Badr. The police also closed their offices, justifying the crackdown by saying that these groups had defied a ban on publicly raising funds for jihad by displaying banners advertising their cause. Karachi southern district police chief Majeed Dasti said, "We have removed signboards from the offices of the Al-Badr, Harakatul Mujahideen...while more will be removed later today."[36] The raids, however, were meant only to be a show for the international community, and the Sindh government had gone too far. Musharraf's government intervened; the Sindh government had apparantly misunderstood General Musharraf's intentions.

The federal government ordered the Sindh government to freeze police action against the jihadi groups within a few hours, and the police released all the arrested jihadis before midnight.[37] Home Secretary Sindh Brig Mukhtar Ahmed also said that the Sindh government had no intention of banning the jihadi groups: "There is no such intention. This is not a ban. If somebody wants to give a donation, he can give it to their organizations." The government said the groups had simply gone too far with their fund-raising efforts, placing collection boxes in shops, roads, and kiosks. "We have said that this is not correct, if somebody wants to give donation, he should give it but it is not correct to run house to house and shop to shop campaigning for funds."[38]

In the aftermath of the September 11, 2001 terrorist attacks on the United States, the peace process broke down further. After a year and a half of negotiations, both India and Pakistan broke away from the process completely and scrambled to find a place in the American-led coalition response to September 11. Both countries stepped up, offering resources and logistical aid to any American response. But these moves again heated the war of words between India and Pakistan.

In a September 19 televised address to the Pakistani people, meant to justify his decision to join the U.S.-led coalition, Musharraf said,

Let us now take a look at the designs of our neighboring country. They offered all their military facilities to the United States. They have offered without hesitation, all their facilities, all their bases and full logistic support. They want to enter into any alliance with the United States and get Pakistan declared a terrorist. They want to harm our strategic assets and the Kashmir cause.... What do the Indians want? They do not have common border with Afghanistan anywhere.... In my view, it is not surprising that the Indians want to ensure that if and when the government in Afghanistan changes, it shall be an anti-Pakistan government.... If you watch their television, you will find them dishing out propaganda against Pakistan, day in and day out. I would like to tell India "lay off."[39]

India's minister for external affairs, Jaswant Singh, responded the next day:

Pakistan's subtle conversion and its arrival into a concert of nations is a development which we should encourage. But that development is a development that remains at the level of declaration alone. It must convert itself into action and not simply remain a declaration of intent. Has it stopped being a promoter of cross-border terrorism? Or terrorism of other varieties? Most regrettably no.

Tension between the two countries remained high, peaking on the eve of United States Secretary of State Colin Powell's visit to South Asia. Indian defense sources claimed that their gunners had attacked eleven Pakistani posts across the borders of Jammu and Kashmir. The Indian military commander in Kashmir, Brigadier P.C. Das, said that the action was "punitive," meant to punish the Pakistanis for "arming and funding militants in Kashmir... to tell them that they cannot go on with this any more." Pakistan said that twenty-five people were wounded, and one killed, when the Indian army fired across the LoC.[40] Indian and Pakistani troops also exchanged fire on a second occasion. In another separate incident, a teenager in Pakistani-controlled Kashmir also died from Indian fire.[41]

In hopes of putting a stop to the violence, President George W. Bush intervened publicly: "It is very important that India and Pakistan stand down during our activities in Afghanistan, for that matter for ever," he said.[42]

Just before noon on December 13, 2001, five gunmen wearing commando outfits drove into the Indian parliament complex in New Delhi in an official-looking white car, with fake security stickers and sirens blaring. The car entered the complex in a lane used exclusively by Indian Vice President Krishan Kant, a fact that roused the suspicions of a police officer. When the officer approached the car, its driver reversed and slammed into the vice president's car. Moments later, the five commandos got out of their vehicle, carrying AK-47 rifles and grenades. They moved toward the parliament building, but they quickly panicked and started shooting. Forty minutes later, the gunmen were all dead—along with seven others.

It had been the most direct assault on the Indian government since the 1991 assassination of Prime Minister Rajiv Gandhi. But it could have been much worse: Nearly 300 ministers and members of parliament were in the parliament building at the time.

The attackers had been jihadis. The Indian government blamed the attacks on Lashkar-i-Taiba and Jaish-i-Mohammad. The Kashmir connection again brought India and Pakistan to the brink of war. The two countries expelled each other's diplomats, and India broke all communications with Pakistan on December 31. Their last communication had been a demand that Pakistan extradite twenty known terrorists, including the heads of three top jihadi organizations: Syed Salahuddin of the Hizbul Mujahideen, Maulana Masood Azhar of the Jaish-i-Mohammad, and Hafiz Saeed of Lashkar-i-Taiba. They also requested extradition of the hijackers of an Indian airplane that had been hijacked and taken to Afghanistan in 1999.[43] Finally, the Indians demanded the extradition of a group of Indian terrorists believed to be in Pakistan.[44]

Fearing that the situation would get out of control, the U.S. brought unprecedented pressure on Pakistan to take tangible measures to demonstrate that it was serious about dismantling terrorist infrastructure on its soil. Musharraf responded that he would address the issue in a speech, wherein he was widely expected to announce steps to rein in the Kashmiri jihadi networks. In Washington, the speech was eagerly anticipated. On January 10, 2002, Secretary of State Powell said, "We are looking forward to the speech he will be giving later this week, which I think will be a powerful signal to his nation and to India and the rest of the world."[45] On January 12, White House Press Secretary

Ari Fleischer reported that "It will be an important speech, and the president looks forward to hearing it."

On January 12, in his now famous speech, General Mushar-raf announced that he would ban five more jihadi and sec-tarian organizations: Lashkar-i-Taiba, Jaish-i-Mohammad, Sipah-i-Sahaba Pakistan, Tehreek-i-Jafria Pakistan, and Tehreek-i-Nifaz-i-Shariat-i-Mohammadi. Two other orga-nizations had already been banned, and this brought the list to seven targeted groups—though Hizbul Mujahideen was still not on the list. The speech turned General Musharraf into a kind of hero in the United States. Officials had asked him to do what seemed an impossible political task, and he had complied. Unfortunately, few of Musharraf's actions would turn out to be significant.

Soon after Musharraf's speech, the security forces start-ed cracking down on the banned groups.[46] Over the next two weeks, according to the figures of the Punjab Home Department, the security agencies arrested 2,010 militants and closed 624 offices operated by the banned groups. The security agencies also arrested 130 militants and closed down 181 offices connected to Jaish-i-Mohammad. Lashkar-i-Taiba was also targeted: 203 militants were arrested and 187 offices were closed.[47] Other groups were also raided, but beginning on January 24, 2002, the government started releasing the arrested militants, citing "lack of evidence." By March, the federal government stepped in, asking the provincial governments to release jailed jihadis who agreed to dissociate themselves from the jihadi groups.[48]

Strangely, but not unexpectedly, the arrested militants still did not include members of Hizbul Mujahideen.

In the post–9/11 period, particularly after the attack on the Indian Parliament, the Kashmir cell of ISI focused almost exclusively on reviving and protecting the jihad. In particular, the ISI devised a new code of conduct for jihadis, both Kashmiris and Pakistanis. Among the new directives, jihadis were told to strictly avoid media attention and to stop making inflammatory statements against the West, particularly the United States. Kashmiri jihadi operations were told to move their offices from Islamabad to Pakistani-controlled Jammu and Kashmir, and to remove signs from any office they needed to maintain in Islamabad. They were also told to stop holding rallies in Pakistan and to tone down their imagery: Advertisements depicting Kalashnikov rifles soon started disappearing from Pakistani streets. The government eventually also asked the jihadi organizations to shutter their offices in Pakistani-controlled Kashmir, setting a deadline of May 31, 2003.

The ISI also asked fighters to stop wearing fatigues, and to stop adopting *kunyat*, the Arabic style of nickname (Abu Jundal, for example), which seemed, in light of the 9/11 attacks, to connect the fighters to al-Qaeda. It also attempted to have some organizations renamed, asking that the words *lashkar* (militia), *jaish* (army), *sipah* (army or militia) or *hizb* (party) not be used—a fact that would make it easier for the ISI to claim that the jihadi groups were actually political organizations. It also asked them to cease claiming responsibility for terrorist attacks inside Indian-controlled Jammu and Kashmir.

The ISI also changed its own tactics. It started sending smaller groups of fighters into Indian-controlled Kashmir in an attempt to keep new operations secret. It also become more selective, sending only fighters it trusted. A new system of meeting with jihadi operatives was also developed: No longer would jihadis visit ISI offices. And cells were now briefed individually, to keep cells from knowing about one another's identities.[49]

There was also another concerted attempt to merge some jihadi organizations: Al-Jihad, al-Umar, and Lashkar-i-Taiba were asked to work as one group. Hizbul Momineen and Harakat-al-Jihad-al-Islami were regrouped into a single organization. And in early 2003, many jihadi organizations were merged into the newly created fronts Freedom Fighters of Kashmir (FFK) and the Kashmir Resistance Force (KRF). In 2004, another unsuccessful attempt was made to group jihadi organizations into six smaller alliances. Here the ISI was hoping to hide Pakistani fighters behind Kashmiri organizations and make the militancy appear indigenous.[50]

During a two-day tour of Jammu and Kashmir in mid-April 2003, Prime Minister Vajpayee made a surprising move: he again offered to open peace talks with Pakistan. "We should resolve issues through talks. All issues can be resolved through talks, nothing can be solved through war," he said. And the following day, he repeated his offer of conditional talks: "If Pakistan says tomorrow that it will close down the

terrorist camps in Pakistan, if it says this today, I will send a
top foreign ministry official to Islamabad tomorrow to draw
up a schedule for talks. Cross-border terrorism should end.
Then the path of talks can open. We are ready for talks on
all issues including Jammu and Kashmir."

On April 28, 2003, Pakistani Prime Minister Zafarullah Khan Jamali telephoned Prime Minister Vajpayee and
agreed to visit India for the sake of peace and stability. In a
thirty-minute talk with Vajpayee, he discussed ways to increase economic, cultural, and sports cooperation between
the two countries. Vajpayee also took steps to normalize
relations, easing economic and travel restrictions. To step
up pressure on the Pakistanis to make real moves on terrorism, the United States added Hizbul Mujahideen to a terror
watch list on April 30, 2003.[51]

On May 2, 2003 Vajpayee spoke to the Indian parliament, making it clear that this peace salvo would be his
last: "How long will we keep fighting with Pakistan? We
want to give Pakistan one more chance, not out of weakness but out of self-confidence. The third attempt will be
decisive and will be the last in my lifetime."

On the eve of the talks, the Americans worried that General Musharraf might not be able to live up to any agreement he reached with the Indians. And it seemed apparent
that any agreement wouldn't last if the jihadi infrastructure
in Pakistan couldn't be dismantled. U.S. Deputy Secretary
of State Richard Armitage came to seek assurances that the
Pakistanis would indeed disable militant training camps in
Pakistan and the Pakistani-controlled Kashmir. On May 9,
2003, after meeting with General Musharraf, Armitage reported that Musharraf had promised that "nothing is hap-

pening at the Line of Control. He said that there are no training camps in Azad Kashmir and if there are, they will be gone by tomorrow."

In a televised address on November 23, 2003, Pakistani Prime Minister Zafarullah Khan Jamali added to the momentum surrounding the new round of talks by announcing a complete unilateral cease-fire on the LoC effective on 'Id, which fell on November 26, 2003. He hoped the Indians would reciprocate. Jamali also announced a slew of other good faith efforts.

India responded by agreeing to the cease-fire, and in one of the more important announcements in the ongoing negotiations, General Musharraf also offered to abandon a handful of historic Pakistani demands. Pakistan would no longer insist that the Kashmir dispute be resolved under existing UN resolutions. In a press interview, Musharraf also offered to drop the fifty-year-old Pakistani demand for a plebiscite in Jammu and Kashmir: "If we want to resolve this issue, both sides need to talk to each other with flexibility, coming beyond stated positions, meeting halfway somewhere. We are prepared to rise to the occasion, India has to be flexible also."[52]

In a later dialogue between General Musharraf and Prime Minister Vajpayee on January 4, 2004, plans were set to start a formal dialogue in February to resolve all bilateral issues, including Kashmir. A joint press statement issued on January 6 read,

> To carry the process of normalization forward the president of Pakistan and the prime minister of India agreed to commence the process of compos-

ite dialogue in February 2004...The two leaders
agreed that constructive dialogue would promote
progress towards the common objective of peace,
security and economic development for our people
and the future generations.

Some results were immediate: Visas to visit India and Pakistan, which had decreased dramatically after Kargil, were increased.[53]

Jihadi infrastructure in Pakistan and Pakistani-controlled Kashmir, however, had still not been dismantled, and this delayed significant progress. Addressing a July 14 news conference in New Delhi, Armitage confirmed this, saying, "Clearly all infrastructure has not been dismantled.... Some have been dismantled as you know...[but] any level of infiltration is too much."[54] Armitage, still fearful that the training camps would derail the peace process, returned to Islamabad, where he again pressed General Musharraf to fully dismantle the militant infrastructure. The Indians had also confirmed that this infrastructure remained mostly intact. A senior BSF officer noted in November that "the number of militancy-related incidents came down by 1,500" from the year before, but Indian intelligence estimates still showed that 370 militants had crossed into Indian-controlled Kashmir from the Pakistani side, though this number was down as well, by about 1,200, during the first ten months of 2003.[55] Indian General Nirmal Chandra Vij noted in November that "the internal offensive against militants has brought down the number of militants by half—from 3,500 to around 1,800 inside Jammu and Kashmir."[56] But many fighters were still active.

Without definitive Pakistani moves, the Indians proceeded cautiously, only agreeing to withdraw an "unspecified number of troops" from Jammu and Kashmir. The first contingent of Indian soldiers, which numbered at least 1,000, left Jammu and Kashmir on November 17, 2004. But the withdrawal was only marginally significant.[57]

In a devastating blow to Pakistan and the United States, the peace process between India and Pakistan eventually slowed, and then stalled completely with the installation of a new Indian government. The new prime minister, Manmohan Singh, told reporters in Srinagar on November 17 that he was suspending peace efforts until the Pakistanis made more significant moves. He also seemed to dismiss the process out of hand: "I have made it clear to President Musharraf that any redrawing of the international border is not acceptable to us. Any proposal that smacks of further division is not going to be acceptable to us."[58]

It had been more than four years since Bill Clinton had traveled to India and Pakistan and inaugurated the new peace process, but the process had finally died.

In October 2001, Syed Salahuddin finally removed Abdul Majeed Dar as the chief operational commander of Hizbul Mujahideen. Elements within Hizbul Mujahideen protested strongly against the dismissal. Salahuddin responded, the following May, by completely expelling Dar and his supporters, claiming that they were working for the Indian secret service. When senior commanders asked for some evidence of Dar's Indian connections, they too were expelled.

Indeed, Salahuddin moved to remove any commander sympathizing with Dar.[59]

Dar's exiled supporters, however, constituted a powerful faction of Hizbul Mujahideen. And they were joined by more of the group's senior commanders. Dar had many powerful allegiances. As a result, the new faction did not disappear from the scene. They regrouped and organized. In November 2002, when Salahuddin's forces attacked one of Dar's camps in Taxila, Pakistan, near Islamabad, the rift between the two camps broke open. In order to put an end to infighting, the Kashmir cell of the ISI moved to reorganize Dar's wing of Hizbul Mujahideen as a separate group at the end of January 2003. Salahuddin, however, strongly opposed the move, believing that Dar would eventually topple his command of Hizbul Mujahideen.

As it turned out, Dar wouldn't have the chance to reorganize. In March 2003, Hizbul Mujahideen gunmen assassinated Dar as he was saying good-bye to his family, just in advance of a trip to Pakistan. Dar's funeral grew into an extension of the fighting. Salahuddin threatened those planning to attend—and Dar's funeral procession in Muzaffarabad climaxed in a huge, anti-Salahuddin rally.[60]

But Dar's death didn't put an end to the fighting between the two factions. Dar's wing nominated Dr. Asad Yazdani to lead the group, and he traveled to Pakistan on April 9, 2003, on a forged Indian passport.[61] In a statement in Pakistan, Yazdani emphasized the political role his new organization could play: "We will continue our militancy. But, we will hold consultations and create coordination with the political leadership of Jammu and Kashmir all over the world." [62] The rivalry between the two groups, however, again turned violent on April 27, 2003, when Yazdani's group of Hizbul Mujahideen raided and occupied Salahuddin's offices near the Khannakak Bridge in Islamabad. When Salahuddin's men opened fire on the office in an attempt to expel the rival fighters, using machine guns and grenades, the army was called in to stop the fighting. Two days later, Salahuddin's forces retaliated, attacking Yazdani's group at their offices in Muzaffarabad.

The ISI was again drawn into the conflict, with officials deciding that they needed to put a permanent end to the infighting between the groups. The ISI first moved to arrest almost the entire leadership of Salahuddin's faction of Hizbul Mujahideen, with the exception of Salahuddin himself and a few others. The ISI interrogated the fighters in an attempt to find out who was most responsible for the rift.

The ISI's Kashmir cell expanded their investigation into a large search to understand the massive rift that had formed in Hizbul Mujahideen.[63] Led by a four-member investigating team, the ISI eventually took dozens of fighters from Dar's group into custody as well, keeping them in a safe house in Islamabad.[64] The ISI questioned members and held the entire group for nearly three weeks. At the end of the investigation, Dar's comrades were told that the ISI could no longer tolerate attacks on Syed Salahuddin. Most fighters from Dar's group were eventually released, but only after they signed a declaration stipulating that they would not carry out any organizational or jihadi activities in the future. Dar's old faction was also completely cut off from ISI funds and was asked to return nearly 1.5 million rupees it had taken from Hizbul Mujahideen.[65]

Salahuddin's faction was also ordered to pay blood money to Dar's group as payment for its attack on its compound, though it remains unclear if such a payment was ever made. Indeed, many of the ISI orders relating to the investigation were not carried out.

After ISI intervention, Salahuddin remained very much in charge of Hizbul Mujahideen, though he was increasingly nervous about the confidence of his supporters in the ISI, in the wake of 9/11, and in Jamat-i-Islami. Salahuddin also remained obsessed with clearing the Hizbul Mujahideen ranks of dissenters. He began sending senior commanders who had fallen out of his favor across the Line of Control without proper training, where Indian forces eventually targeted them. Typical was Salahuddin's replacement of Ghulam Rasool Dar, his new chief operational commander. Salahuddin wanted him out because of his growing religious stature, and he was sent across the LoC in August 2003.[66] His family received news of his death in January of 2004.[67] His replacement, Abdur Rashid, was killed in the same way, sent to Indian-controlled Kashmir and killed in May 2004.[68]

CHAPTER EIGHT

A POLITICAL FACE
"A MOVEMENT OF KASHMIR'S PEOPLE"

While planning the jihad, the ISI had envisaged a very limited role for political parties. There were of course a multitude of political actors on the scene in Kashmir and Pakistan. But the ISI had only a specific use for the Jamat-i-Islami of Indian-controlled Kashmir. This had an unintended consequence: By early 1990, the Indian authorities were intensely focused on the party, which had by that time become fully, though secretly, involved with the militancy. The ISI desperately wanted Jamat-i-Islami to be able to satisfactorily respond to Indian allegations of its involvement in the jihad, as well as to allegations of a special relationship with the ISI.

ISI officials thought that the best way to proceed was to give a number of political parties a limited but well-defined role in the jihad. Instead of having the parties deny any involvement with the militants, the ISI would now instruct the parties to advocate for a political solution. The parties would thus give a political facade to the jihad. The ISI also thought that a vocal coaltion of political parties in Kashmir would alleviate many of the problems of Jamat-i-Islami of Indian-controlled Kashmir, taking focus off the group and allowing it to enter the political scene in a limited way.

It was in this context that the ISI asked pro-Pakistan political parties in Kashmir to set up Tehreek-i-Hurryyat-i-Kashmir (the Movement for the Freedom of Kashmir) in March 1990. Mian Abdul Qayyum, the president of the Kashmir Bar Association, who was known to be affiliated with Jamat-i-Islami, became its first president; Ashraf Sehrai, another follower of Jamat-i-Islami, its first secretary general. It would be a wide coalition, containing the most important political players: Jamat-i-Islami, Jamiat Ahle Hadith, the Muslim Conference, Mahaz-i-Azadi, the Peoples League, the Islamic Students League, the Muslim League, the Islamic Study Circle, Mahaz-i-Islami, Dukhtaran-i-Millat, and the Kashmir Bar Association.

On March 31, 1992, Tehreek-i-Hurryyat-i-Kashmir opened its first chapter in Pakistani-controlled Kashmir.[1] Although a branch in Indian-controlled Kashmir was also established, it had little room to maneuver because of the ongoing violence. Tehreek-i-Hurryyat-i-Kashmir's Muzaffarabad office, however, immediately put staff to work publishing propaganda material, particularly *Kashmir Update*, which was sent to foreign diplomats, politicians, and journalists in North America, Europe, and the Middle East. There was initial interest in expanding the organization, but Major General Iftikhar Shah of the ISI Kashmir cell intervened, saying he wanted the activities of the new group to remain limited.[2] In 1993, however, when the United States appeared ready to designate Pakistan a state sponsor of terrorism, this opinion was revised.

At the end of his term, which ended in 1991, Pakistani Chief of the Army Staff General Mirza Aslam Beg had admitted that Pakistan had helped train thousands of Kashmiri militants. Beg had reportedly told then–CIA chief Robert Gates, who was on a secret mission to Pakistan, that there had been thirty-seven training camps built for Kashmiris on Pakistani soil, though all had been shut down. In late 1993, Pakistan had also ignored several messages from the United States, causing the Americans to send Robert Oakley, a former U.S. Ambassador to Pakistan, to Islamabad. Oakley arrived on December 10, 1993, with a secret message: Pakistan needed to convince Washington that it had stopped supporting the Kashmiri militants. The message, however, came at a moment of great tension, when Pakistan had also refused to stop development of its nuclear program. The ISI-backed jihadi groups and Jamat-i-Islami had also become active in militant operations outside Kashmir, alarming American officials. In addition to Afghanistan, the ISI-backed Jamat-i-Islami of Pakistan had become involved in military actions in several Central Asian states during the early 1990s. Uzbekistan and Tajikistan accused the Islamabad government of doing nothing to stop what they called "Pakistani interference."[3] The ISI was also supporting the Chinese Muslim separatists in the Xinjiang Province, jihadi Muslim groups in the Philippines, and other jihadi groups in Central Asia.[4]

Pakistan had once before avoided being labeled a terrorist state, in December 1992. It had, however, been placed on a U.S. terrorist watch list for six months (the designation expired in June 1993). In December 1992, in an attempt to please the Americans, the Pakistani government had ordered all the remaining Afghan mujahideen groups and Islamic charities operating within Pakistani borders to close down by December 31. Between October 1992 and July 1993, the police and security agencies also arrested some 300 Arab mujahideen who were working as aid workers in Peshawar. Most were interrogated and then released. These Arabs had traveled to Afghanistan to support the jihad and eventually made their way to Pakistan to support veterans of the Afghan campaign. At the time, an estimated 600 Arab aid workers resided in Peshawar, running seventeen known relief agencies.[5] Abdullah Azzaam's Afghan Services Bureau, co-founded by Osama bin Laden, remained in operation until August 1993. Shuttering these operations was an attempt to win back American trust.

In April 1993, after the Sharif government was ousted for the first time, an interim government replaced ISI chief Lt. General Javed Nasir with the moderate-seeming Javed Ashraf Qazi, who was tasked with further improving Pakistan's image for the Americans—an issue that revolved around Kashmir. The new ISI chief decided to pick up the political project that had been inaugurated with Tehreek-i-Hurryyat-i-Kashmir: Instead of shutting down the Kashmiri groups, he would again attempt to raise the profile of active political parties and hide jihadi organizations behind them. He began by dissolving the ineffective Tehreek-i-Hurryyat-i-Kashmir.

The ISI initially discouraged the formation of the group that would replace it: the Hurryyat Conference, founded by Mirwaiz Umar Farooq, who had been working on erecting such an alliance since the fall of 1992.[6] The group was announced in September 1993, under the name of All Parties Hurryyat Conference (APHC); it is commonly known as "Hurryyat."[7] The militant groups, particularly Hizbul Mujahideen, opposed the formation of Hurryyat because they perceived it as a potential rival, but Farooq held an important meeting of political leaders on March 8, 1993, in which they solidified the new group and constituted a seven-member committee to draft a constitution for the new alliance.

The ISI, also, asked militant organizations to support the political initiative. A group of seven such organizations eventually offered a hesitating appeal for their constituents to extend support and cooperation to the Hurryyat Conference.[8] The ISI's ruse was temporarily effective; it shielded the jihadi groups from some scrutiny, and it allowed the ISI to continue to partially conceal its open support of militant groups.

The Hurryyat Conference was, however, a precarious organization, especially susceptible to political infighting because of its coalition structure. And there were numerous questions about who would control it. Jamat-i-Islami, for instance, almost refused membership in Hurryyat. Syed

Ali Shah Geelani, who boycotted the group's first meeting, thought he had the right to lead it, given Jamat-i-Islami's long association with the Kashmir struggle. In a compromise, Jamat-i-Islami accepted the choice of Mirwaiz Umar Farooq as head of the Hurryyat Conference "in the larger interest of unity," and on the condition that "the moment we feel that it is going in the wrong direction we will withdraw."[9]

The coalition held, however, and two years later, Mirwaiz Umar Farooq was able to claim success for his organization, explaining that "the Hurryyat Conference has played a major role in dispelling the impression that the present uprising is a fundamentalist movement, or that those involved in it are fanatics.... This is not an Islamic movement, but a movement of Kashmir's people."[10] The jihad had successfully been given a political face.

The most important task the Hurryyat Conference leaders undertook was to internationalize the Kashmir issue: From the very beginning, Hurryyat had called for international, particularly American, mediation. And from its founding to the time of this writing, Hurryyat leaders have been meeting diplomats and world leaders at international conferences. They have also courted diplomats in New Delhi.

The ISI closely supported this work, sending Hurryyat delegations to United Nations conferences, particularly those on human rights. Beginning in September 1995 with a trip to Switzerland to participate in a UN Sub-Commission on Prevention of Discrimination conference, two Hurryyat members, Jaleel Andrabi, chairman of the Kashmir Commission of Jurists, and Ghulam Mohammad Bhat, chairman of the Institute of Kashmir Studies, were particularly active and influential.[11] The ISI also encouraged the Hurryyat Conference to attend meetings of the Organization of Islamic Countries (OIC) to highlight the Kashmir dispute and win political, diplomatic, and financial support from the Muslim world. India, however, intervened on numerous occasions, barring Hurryyat members from leaving Indian-controlled Kashmir to attend international meetings. A four-member Hurryyat delegation was refused exit for a December 1997 OIC summit in Tehran because Pakistan had reportedly planned to table two resolutions on the Kashmir issue. Hurryyat leaders would assumably have helped Pakistan gather support for the resolutions. India again refused to allow a Hurryyat delegation to leave to attend the OIC Ministerial Conference at Doha in Qatar in March 1998.

The Hurryyat Conference also worked to develop communication channels with Indian political parties, intellectuals, human rights activists, and the press. On November 5, 1995, Hurryyat opened an "awareness office" in New Delhi, which was first headed by Firdous Asmi and then by Abdul Majeed Bandey. The office disseminates information about Hurryyat policy and aims throughout India.

In Indian-controlled Kashmir, Hurryyat makes frequent use of *hartals*, or strikes. Critics of the group accuse them of using the tactic too often, so much so that its detractors, both the militant organizations and pro-Indian politicians such as Kashmir Chief Minister Farooq Abdullah, have nicknamed it "the Hartali Conference." In the late 1990s, the Hurryyat Conference would call for strikes on most days of political significance, leading critics to accuse the group of wreaking a kind of economic terrorism on the valley. According to a government statement, "The hartal is the lone weapon in the APHC arsenal which has brought havoc to the Kashmir economy and made the position of the APHC ridiculous."

Not surprisingly, the militant groups never truly accepted the Hurryyat Conference as a useful alliance. Abdur Rafey, the acting amir of Jamiatul Mujahideen, spoke for most jihadis when he claimed that the "Hurryyat Conference is the biggest threat to militant groups...[it] will be the biggest obstacle in the implementation of Islamic laws after the liberation of Jammu and Kashmir."[12]

Because the militants generally believe that Hurryyat has weakened the militancy, they frequently clash with it. The fact that the group's membership contains many former militants is particularly galling. Militants have also threatened Hurryyat members. In February 1995, Ikhwanul Muslimeen accused a Hurryyat member of sabotaging the freedom struggle and issued a death warrant against him when he attended a meeting in New Delhi to discuss solutions to the Kashmir problem.[13]

The militants also publicly clash with Hurryyat over contentious issues. In October 1995, a Hizbullah spokesman criticized Hurryyat's strike policies. In September 1999, Hurryyat's Mirwaiz Umar Farooq condemned Hizbul Mujahideen for demanding an end to cable television in Jammu and Kashmir, arguing that not all TV broadcasts were un-Islamic. Hizbul Mujahideen issued press releases asking Farooq not to speak further on the subject. Farooq remained quiet after Hizbul Mujahideen killed four cable-network operators in Srinagar.[14] In a press conference on March 5, 1997 Asiya Andrabi described the Hurryyat leaders as "apostates and renegades" and criticized them for reducing the Kashmir issue to one of secular politics."[15]

Despite the ongoing conflict between the militants and the political leaders, the ISI's political intervention appeared to be effective by November 1997, when Jamat-i-Islami of Indian-controlled Jammu and Kashmir could claim, in a major announcement, to be abandoning the culture of violence. The creation of the Hurryyat Conference had changed the terms of the debate, and Jamat-i-Islami of Indian-controlled Kashmir could slowly inch away from the militancy. Its amir, Ghulam Mohammad Bhat, said he considered the armed struggle a legitimate movement, but that it had served its purpose, and that it was now time for political dialogue.

But Jamat-i-Islami of Indian-controlled Jammu and Kahsmir would also move to take the reins of what was becoming an increasingly mainstream and accepted Hurryyat Conference. On April 24, 1998, Jamat-i-Islami's Syed Ali Shah Geelani replaced the Mirwaiz, whose term had expired, as chairman.

From the very beginning, the Hurryyat Conference has refused to hold direct, bilateral talks with Indian Union leaders, saying that such talks would define the Kashmir issue as a domestic affair. It has rejected whatever overtures the

Indian government has made, and it has insisted on participating only in trilateral talks in which Pakistan, India, and the people of Jammu and Kashmir—meaning the Hurryyat Conference—were included. In early July 1995, Hurryyat even refused to meet a high-level delegation, headed by Bhuvnesh Chaturvedi, from the Indian prime minister's office, that had been established to hold talks with Kashmiri leaders.[16]

However, some of the moderate Hurryyat leaders, such as Abdul Ghani Lone and Mirwaiz Umar Farooq, had a change of heart in the aftermath of the Kargil conflict. There was a feeling that Pakistan might not continue to support Hurryyat in the future. A pro-negotiation group started testing India to see if it might engage in a dialogue. Lone asked Indian officials if they would be willing to talk with the Kashmiris, since "only this will enable us to prevail upon outsiders to keep off Kashmir."[17] A couple of weeks later, the Mirwaiz also showed his readiness to hold direct dialogue with India and invite Pakistan later, a significant concession. Pro-Pakistani members of the General Council accused the Mirwaiz of treachery.

As Pakistan and India started their own dialogue after President Clinton's 2000 visit to the subcontinent, several Hurryyat leaders considered their situation more closely. Partly afraid of being abandoned by Pakistan, and partly afraid of losing a seat at the negotiating table, these leaders moved to participate in whatever negotiations might take place. On May 7, 2000, the Mirwaiz expressed the feelings of several Hurryyat leaders when he said, "There is a great deal of mistrust between Pakistan and India. Both are unwilling to sit together. In this scenario, the Hurryyat

Conference can break the ice between the two.... We are willing to go to Islamabad, Muzaffarabad, and New Delhi to break the ice; we can play the role of a broker and bring this crisis to an end."[18]

After meeting General Musharraf on the sidelines of the OIC summit in Doha, which ended on November 13, 2000, the Mirwaiz told the Gulf News,

> There is a shift in Pakistan's position. Musharraf's stand [on Kashmir] is very flexible. It is change from the position held by Pakistan in the past where they have always insisted on a solution based on the implementation of UN resolutions that call for a plebiscite... Musharraf seems agreeable to a negotiated settlement. He wants to have a dialogue with us to reach a solution that is agreeable to us, the people of Kashmir.[19]

The political leaders of the Hurryyat Conference thus involved themselves in the peace process that had been inaugurated by President Clinton's visit. After the July 2000 Hizbul Mujahideen cease-fire, which pointed to Hurryyat as a key negotiating partner, the process accelerated. Though the negotiations overlapped with those extended to Hizbul Mujahideen, they were part of a separate process.

The possibility of a brokered agreement divided the Hurryyat Conference into two groups: moderates, who favored some form of negotiations, and hard-liners, who were deeply pro-Pakistan and skeptical that negotiations would lead to a favorable resolution to the dispute. The moderate group started inching toward talks. But the Kashmiris continued to stress that the talks should be tripartite and without any preconditions; but by this time India was refusing to hold talks with Pakistan until it stopped cross-border terrorism.

Against this backdrop, Abdul Ghani Lone, one of the moderate Hurryyat leaders, arrived in Islamabad on November 16, 2000, to participate in his son's marriage. During his stay in Pakistan, Lone did not hesitate to criticize Pakistani policies and the role of Pakistani jihadis in Jammu and Kashmir. In one interview he said, "Any talks on Kashmir should consider all the options." Regarding foreign fighters, he said,

> Pakistani mujahideen come to Kashmir, and we thank them for their struggle and sacrifices. We expect that they should be part of our struggle and support it. But they should not have their own agenda. They are great sympathizers, but they should confine their role to support only... The Indian ploy is to portray Kashmir's freedom struggle as one sponsored and fought by non-Kashmiris. But this is wrong. The ratio of Pakistani fighters is not more than 20 percent. Non-Kashmiris cannot come and fight without help and support from the local population. India says that 80 percent are non-Kashmiri fighters, but casualty figures show that 80 percent who die are Kashmiris.[20]

By the end of 2000, moderates in the Hurryyat Conference had asked the Indian government to allow them to travel to Pakistan. They intended to ask the jihadis to end their militancy and look for a negotiated settlement of the Kashmir dispute. It was a key demand, since Hurryyat could not broker peace without support from the jihadis. The group asked the Indian government to issue travel documents to all the members of the Hurryyat Conference Executive Council so that they could go to Pakistan for talks with jihadis before January 15, 2001. The Indian government gave clearance to four moderate Hurryyat leaders, but it refused to allow the three other pro-Pakistani leaders, including Syed Ali Shah Geelani, to travel.

The possibility of a selected delegation made both the ISI and the jihadis nervous because any appeal by Hurryyat to end the militancy would deprive the jihadis of any legitimacy they enjoyed. Asiya Andrabi spoke for both the ISI and jihadis when she said, "The Hurryyat leaders are going [to Pakistan] with an agenda prepared by the government of India, and the only motive of their visit is to persuade mujahideen groups for a cease-fire." She advised them not to visit Pakistan because they would not be able to persuade groups like Lashkar-i-Taiba, Jaish-i-Mohammad, and al-Badr. "The role of Hizbul Mujahideen is doubtful and it seems Abdul Majeed Dar is playing into the Indian hands," she said.[21]

On January 11, 2001, Hurryyat named a five-member delegation that it wanted to send to Pakistan along with those who had been cleared by the Indians. The list included Abdul Ghani Lone and Umar Farooq, who preferred independence, but it also included Syed Ali Shah Geelani and Abdul Aziz, who supported Kashmir's accession to Pakistan, as well as Abbass Ansari, whose position was between the two extremes. Despite the attempt at balance, only Abdul Ghani Lone and Umar Farooq received travel documents. As a result, they declined to travel to Pakistan.

On April 15, 2001, the Indian government began preparing their dialogue with Kashmiri leaders. Surprisingly, Krishna Chandra Pant, India's chief negotiator, invited not only the Hurryyat Conference but many other Kashmiri groups as well. The talks were to be held at Pant's New Delhi residence. Hurryyat's Abdul Ghani Bhat accused Pant of turning the Kashmir dispute into an open "fish market," where any group, no matter how insignificant, "could come along and negotiate.... For me, the main parties to the talks are only India, Pakistan, and the Hurryyat Conference."[22]

Some jihadi groups also reacted negatively: Jamiatul Mujahideen threatened Hurryyat not to engage in the talks. In a press release, the group stated that "All mediators will be dubbed traitors and will only receive alienation and humiliation from the Kashmiri masses. Jihad is the only way to achieve the freedom of Kashmir." Al-Umar Mujahideeen issued a similar warning: "The traitors will have to face death in Kashmir."[23] Just after noon on April 23, unknown militants threw a grenade into the offices of the Hurryyat Conference in Srinagar, injuring four. Al-Qasas and Mujahideen-i-Haq, two previously unknown militant organizations, claimed responsibility.[24] The Al-Qasas spokesman said before taking any decision the Hurryyat Conference should take militants into the discussion.[25] Salahuddin described the offer of talks as "a farce and deceptive" and warned Hurryyat against betraying the aspirations of the Kashmiri people. He insisted that only tripartite talks could lead to the resolution of the Kashmir dispute.[26]

The continued threats from militants proved effective and, after dragging its feet for several days, the Hurryyat Conference rejected the Indian government's offer of peace talks on April 26, 2001. In rejecting the talks, Abdul Ghani Bhat connected the decision with not being able to travel to Pakistan to consult the mujahideen: "The Pakistan tour... has to materialize. If we visit Pakistan, we will be talking to the mujahideen leadership and Pakistani officials. On our return we will talk to the people in New Delhi."[27]

Another Kashmiri political group, the Jammu and Kashmir Democratic Freedom Party, however, continued considering India's invitation to meet. Their leader, Shabbir Shah, sent a letter to the Indian negotiating team asking for clarification on the proposed process. He also criticized Hurryyat representatives for rejecting talks outright:

> They should have gone to the table and told Pant to his face what lacks in the offer... I am well aware of the Indian tricks. They want to show to the world that they are ready but Kashmiris are not coming forward for the talks to settle the issue. I want to show to the world that Kashmiris are ready for talks, provided they give us what we have been demanding and struggling for over last fifty years.[28]

In a reply to Shabbir, delivered on May 15, 2001, Pant said that New Delhi was "not averse to engage Pakistan in meaningful talks on Jammu and Kashmir and is hopeful that Pakistan will cooperate with India and initiate measures that would facilitate the process."[29]

Shah responded on May 19, 2001 that he would indeed hold talks with Pant, but not until Pant visited Kashmir. Nine days later, Pant arrived for a six-day visit. Upon arrival, he announced: "I want to see how we can make progress to write a new chapter and move toward a restoration of peace which is necessary for a political settlement of the Kashmir problem." Shah justified his decision to meet Pant by saying, "We had stressed that Pakistan's involvement is mandatory." Referencing the upcoming Agra summit, Shah added "Vajpayee has given a practical shape to it by inviting General Musharraf for talks." Shah's office was attacked twice amid continued militant threats against the negotiations. His eventual talks with Pant were inconclusive.[30]

As Pakistan and India moved closer to formal talks, in the period before the Agra Summit, Hurryyat Conference members increasingly lashed out at Pakistan's failure to include Hurryyat political leaders in their process. Kashmiris had held out for, and in fact insisted on, Pakistani participation in any formal talks. But now the Pakistanis seemed to be moving into negotiations with the Indians without any Kashmiri participation. In an attempt to appease Hurryyat members, General Musharraf told foreign journalists on June 28, 2001, that he would like to see Kashmiri representatives, particularly the Hurryyat Conference, "coming on board at some stage. However, before that, since it is the Indian stance that they would not like to talk to the APHC and they only want to talk to Pakistan, we show flexibility."

After the disappointment of the Agra summit, the moderate leaders of the Hurryyat Conference again moved to hold talks with their Indian interlocutors. They also reversed course and expressed a willingness to hold talks with K.C. Pant. The group was unable to understand why they could not hold talks with the Indian leaders if the Pakistanis could.

. But again the jihadis decided to threaten the process and use violence to stop any meeting between the moderate leaders of Hurryyat and the Indian government. Abdul Ghani Lone was threatened by al-Barq, once an armed wing of his own party, and accused of "usurping its assets." On November 2, 2001, Lone escaped a late-night attempt on his life by armed militants. Lone reported that he and other Hurryyat leaders had been receiving a steady stream of threatening letters from militant groups. He also claimed that three attempts on his life had been made by the Indian agencies.[31]

The moderates pushing for negotiation couldn't be silenced this time. On November 12, 2001, Abdul Ghani Bhat confirmed the group's desire to proceed with talks: "We propose that India, Pakistan, the APHC, and other parties concerned call for a cease-fire . . . The APHC proposes that India, Pakistan and the APHC initiate negotiations with the seriousness and purpose to move forward. All parties [should] come forward and resolve the issue of Kashmir per the wishes of the people of the troubled state."[32]

But the continued drive for peace talks was too much for pro-Pakistani hard-liners, and there were defections from the Hurryyat Conference: On November 14, 2001, even Geelani, the Hurryyat chairman, dissociated himself from the current proposal, saying he had not been consulted and did not agree with the decision to go forward with talks.

In April 2002, without the sanction of the senior members of the Hurryyat Conference, Abdul Ghani Lone and Mirwaiz Umar Farooq met in Dubai with a small group of Kashmiri leaders. The group included former president and prime minister of Pakistani-controlled Kashmir Sardar Abdul Qayyum Khan and a handful of Kashmiri expatriates. The meeting remains shrouded in mystery, though participants later said that it concerned ways to put an end to the violence in Kashmir and resolve issues politically.[33] The unauthorized meeting was a bold move, and it infuriated the Hurryyat hard-liners, especially Syed Ali Shah Geelani, as well as the other excluded Kashmiri leaders. Geelani claimed that he had not been consulted about the meeting—and that the jihad would continue.

The meeting and Geelani's response to it exacerbated the rift in the Hurryyat Conference. Jamat-i-Islami of Indian-controlled Kashmir, desperately wanting to distance itself from the jihad, issued a statement rejecting Geelani's vow to continue the jihad, saying that the remark was made "in his personal capacity. Jamat-i-Islami believes in peaceful tripartite talks for the resolution of the Kashmir issue."[34]

But the feud escalated further. On May 21, 2002, Abdul Ghani Lone was killed while walking to his car when an unidentified gunman opened fire with an automatic rifle. His elder son, Sajjad Lone, blamed a coalition of forces that had been working against continued talks with India, naming in particular "the ISI, Pakistan, and Geelani." Until just before his death, Lone had been guarded by twelve state-supplied personal security officers. But the government had begun removing the officers slowly, in seeming ratio to the number of attempts made on his life. When he was finally murdered, he had only two guards.[35]

Later that year, Ram Jethmalani, India's former law minister, attempted to salvage the peace process by launching a seven-member "Kashmir Committee," made up of prominent lawyers and journalists, including the ediors of the *Times of India* and *Asian Age*.[36] Jethmalani immediately initiated a dialogue with the Hurryyat Conference, which not only approved of the initiative but encouraged it. On August 17, 2002, the committee met with the Hurryyat members in Srinagar. The two groups reported a "fruitful first step," and Jethmalani also delivered an invitation to the Hurryyat Conference from Prime Minister Vajpayee, an appeal for direct talks. Though a direct meeting wouldn't happen for a year, the move was considered a significant step. Later talks between the Kashmir committee and Hurryyat took place in Delhi in Septermber 2002.[37]

In February 2003, India appointed former Home Secretary N.N. Vohra as its main interlocutor in Kashmir, and, in an attempt not to interfere, the independent Kashmir Committee suspended its work.[38]

The infighting within the Hurryyat Conference reached a fever pitch during the fall of 2002. The jihadis had targeted Sajjad Lone, the elder son of Abdul Ghani Lone, calling him "a puppet of Indian intelligence agencies." Lone in return had called the jihadi commanders "escapists, who do not represent the Kashmiri people, their interests or aspirations." And he had continued to blame hard-liners within Hurryyat for the death of his father. The jihadis demanded that Sajjad Lone be expelled from the Hurryyat Conference executive council.[39]

When Syed Ali Shah Geelani started boycotting Hurryyat conference meetings, over the conflict with Lone and a slew of factional disputes, Jamat-i-Islami of Indian-controlled Jammu and Kashmir moved to remove him as their representative on the Hurryyat executive council. Shaikh Ali Mohammad a junior Jamat-i-Islami member, was appointed to replace him. But there was major protest over Geelani's removal. Jamat-i-Islami of Indian-controlled Jammu and Kashmir tried to backtrack, saying they had removed Geelani because he was sick. But the damage was already done.

On May 28, 2003, Salahuddin, in an extraordinary meeting of the United Jihad Council, urged Jamat-i-Islami to reappoint Geelani as its representative on the Hurryyat Conference executive council. Salahuddin lashed out at Jamat-i-Islami's attempt to to sideline Geelani. Under intense and growing pressure from the militants, a Jamat-i-Islami majlis-i-shoura withdrew its earlier decision and decided to retain Geelani. However, Geelani defied orders from Jamat-i-Islami and boycotted further Hurryyat meetings. Geelani said that he would not attend the meetings until action was taken against the Peoples Conference, which had participated in recent elections. In July, Geelani also threatened to set up his own party unless his demands were met: "There is a need to set up a party . . . whose foundation should be the cadres of Jamat-i-Islami. We should also involve those people who do not accept Jamat's constitution to the greater extent, but want to play their role in resolving the issue of Kashmir."[40]

On July 12, 2003, the dispute between the two Hurryyat factions was exacerbated again when the Hurryyat executive council elected Abbass Ansari as its new chairman. For the first time, the ISI had no role in Hurryyat's election of a chairman. Ansari was a shia and a kind of moderate, but he had views the Pakistanis vehemently disagreed with. For instance, he opposed mediation by the United States in Kashmir, a cornerstone of Pakistan's foreign policy. Ansari said,

> I am dead against mediation by the United States between India and Pakistan in getting the issue of Kashmir resolved. And if the United States gives a roadmap to resolve the Kashmir issue, it will not be good for India, Pakistan and the people of held Kashmir....I am very much optimistic if we...India, Pakistan, and Kashmiris, sit to discuss the issue, we will definitely negotiate a solution. Even if the United States intervenes, we will have to sit and talk. So let's do it ourselves.[41]

In one of his first statements, Ansari made it clear that Hurryyat would work for peace under his leadership. Talking to the BBC on July 17, 2003, Ansari appealed to the mujahideen and India to announce a cease-fire to create a conducive environment for India-Pakistan talks. He repeated the statement a week later.

On August 20, 2003, after again threatening to launch a new party, Jamat-i-Islami of Indian-controlled Jammu and Kashmir completely expelled Syed Ali Shah Geelani. Nazir Ahmed Kashani, who had been elected the amir of Jamat-I-Islami on July 28, said, "We have relieved Geelani as the head of Jamat-i-Islami's political wing and from all other duties." Kashani said that Geelani would continue to be a member of Jamat-i-Islami but would not hold any office.[42]

Geelani was furious, and he did indeed break away to found his own group. On September 7, 2003, he held a meeting at his residence in Srinagar that was attended by the thirteen groups that broke away to join his faction. At the meeting, he expressed his lack of confidence in Abbass Ansari, and he announced the formation of a new Hurryyat Conference, of which he would be chairman.[43] Pakistan immediately recognized Geeelani's faction of the Hurryyat Conference. On September 9, 2003, Jamat-i-Islami of Azad Kashmir announced its support as well.[44]

The separation of the two Hurryyat factions was permanent, and Geelani was a major defection from Hurryyat and the peace process. Though he initially failed to attract important political groups or politicians, his breakaway faction of Hurryyat slowly gained momentum, and his loss was significant enough that the ISI tried to court the new organization and reunite it with the original Hurryyat. Geelani, however, was no longer interested in working alongside Ansari's group: He wanted instead to take control of Jamat-i-Islami of Indian-controlled Kashmir.

At the end of July 2004, Geelani constituted the "Save Jamat Committee," the one-point agenda of which was to divide Jamat-i-Islami of Indian-controlled Kashmir if it refused to support him. Geelani leaned on Nazir Ahmed Kashani, Jamat-i-Islami's amir, asking that he recognize his breakaway group as the political wing of the party.[45] Geelani put significant pressure on the group's leadership—and they threatened to remove Kashani if he refused to comply.

Geelani's men also sent death threats to most of Jamat-i-Islami's leaders.

On August 1, 2004, Jamat-i-Islami decided to revoke its decision to retire Geelani and reappointed him as its chairman. Geelani launched his own party, Tehreek-i-Hurryat Jammu and Kashmir, on August 7, 2004. He vowed to work to achieve the right of self-determination for the people of Jammu and Kashmir. According to Geelani's organization, they would work for the implementation of the UN resolutions in Kashmir, though he would also consider the possibility of an independent Kashmir, if such a resolution could be reached in tripartite talks.[46] Salahuddin strongly supported Geelani's new party.

The Hurryyat Conference and the Indian government again started moving towards talk soon after Hurryyat elected Abbass Ansari chairman.

Though Hurryyat had long been refusing to meet representatives of New Delhi, the Indian government continued to try to make contact. On October 22, 2003, India's powerful security cabinet designated Deputy Prime Minister Advani to hold talks with Hurryyat, a proposal that Hurryyat accepted, although it called for the talks to be without precondition. In November, Indian Minister of State for Home Affairs I.D. Swami announced publicly that talks between the Indian government and Hurryyat had been arranged. Swami said, "we have been making it clear umpteen times that we have only one condition that the opposite party should abjure violence, which they have done."[47]

On November 21, 2003, the last Friday of Ramadan, a gathering of nearly 200,000 Muslims at the Jama Masjid mosque in Srinagar passed a resolution by a show of hands supporting a political solution to the Kashmir problem and confirming their support for Hurryyat. The resolution read:

> We ask the leaders of all the various parties of Jammu and Kashmir that we transcend our various differences and pressure India and Pakistan to find an acceptable dignified and durable solution to the Kashmir problem. We ask that towards this end, India and Pakistan should pay deep and special attention to this resolution that is being put forward by the APHC.

Yet again the jihadis threatened the process. Tehreekul Mujahideen warned the Hurryyat Conference that mujahdeen would take action against their leaders if they did not change their anti-jihad policies.[48] Ghazi Barood Khan, divisional commander of Tehreekul Mujahideen, said that the sacrifices of 100,000 people could not be forgotten. But days before the talks, Hurryyat Conference chairman Ansari responded, saying "Kashmir is burning, people are dying daily...one of our main efforts will be to press India for a cease-fire [against militants]. I am extremely hopeful India will agree to it. This will push the peace process forward." Ansari also said that Hurryyat would attempt to finally persuade India to allow them to visit Pakistan and confer with the jihadis: "Maybe if India allows us to visit Pakistan we can persuade mujahideen leaders also to call for a cease-fire, which will pave the way for a suitable atmosphere."[49]

On January 22, 2004, the meeting between the Hurryyat Conference and Indian Deputy Prime Minister L.K. Advani finally took place. However, it turned out to be a largely symbolic affair. The joint statement issued at the end of the meeting said,

> The APHC delegation stressed that an honorable and durable solution should be found through dialogue. It was agreed that the only way forward is to ensure that all forms of violence at all levels should come to an end. The deputy prime minister endorsed the APHC's view that the role for the gun should be replaced by the sound of politics.

The Hurryyat Conference's demand for permission to go to Pakistan was, however, rejected. Significantly, however, Hurryyat leaders did get an opportunity to meet directly with Indian Prime Minister Vajpayee. On January 23, 2004 the delegation, in the words of Mirwaiz Umar Farooq, "paid a courtesy call" on the prime minister. Supporting Vajpayee's bid to resolve the Kashmir dispute and make peace with Pakistan, the Mirwaiz said, "We believe that Vajpayee's leadership will play a big role and that a new beginning will be made that India, Pakistan, and the people of Kashmir will live in peace and the solution will involve everyone."[50] After these meetings, the Hurryyat leaders, particularly the Mirwaiz, made several appeals to militants to observe a cease-fire.

But the Hurryyat Conference was visibly disappointed with its meetings with Deputy Prime Minister Advani and Prime Minister Vajpayee. It responded by trying to move closer to the ISI and by attempting a limited rapprochement with some elements of the rival Hurryyat faction. As violence escalated, including a high-profile assassination by Indian forces, the Hurryyat delegation started backing away from the peace process. On February 15, 2004, Mirwaiz Umar Farooq threatened to quit the peace process entirely: He said, "Repression does not breed rapprochement," and added that dialogue could not go forward with the ongoing Indian violence. He cited recent carnage in the northern township Bandipora, calling it "the worst kind of war crime perpetuated by Indian forces." Other Kashmiri groups also stepped back from talks. On February 18, 2004, Fazlul Haq Qureshi of the Peoples Political Front withdrew from talks with the Indian government, saying, "The government of India is not serious about talks. Despite assurances, no perceptible change has taken place on the ground." Qureshi added that the Indian government had failed to create an atmosphere of security in the region and that troops continued to violate and abuse the human rights of civilians.[51] On February 25, 2004, Ansari added his name to the chorus, threatening to pull out of talks. He told a news conference in Srinagar that "the behavior of the Indian security forces is unforgivable. If the terror they are spreading in the countryside does not stop, we will have to rethink our decision to continue peace talks."

In spite of the rhetoric, the Hurryyat Conference continued its dialogue with the Indian government. On March 27, 2004, it held a second round of talks with Deputy Prime Minister Advani, and the two sides agreed to hold a further round of talks in June. Advani said he had demanded that the security forces "have a human face" while discharging their duties in the valley and "try to see that ordinary citizens are not subjected to harassment."

Another roadblock, however, finally closed the talks: In March, the Bharatia Janata Party lost the Indian Union elections, and a Congress Party–led government took the reins of power in New Delhi. This gave the Hurryyat Conference an excuse to discontinue the dialogue with the Indian government, and it did.

But the second round of talks between Hurryyat and the Indian government had severely angered the jihadis. In May 2004, the Valley of Kashmir was abuzz with rumors that Mirwaiz Umar Farooq, Ghulam Mohammad Bhat, and Abbass Ansari would be targeted. In late May, Ghulam Mohammad Bhat said he had information regarding a plot and added that he knew the individuals charged with carrying it out. Bhat also claimed that Pakistan had been backing their dialogue process with New Delhi all along. Bhat said, "We talked to Pakistan for five hours and with India for two and a half hours. But, we are still being accused of a sellout. We want to know what kind of sellout we have indulged in."[52]

On May 29, 2004, suspected guerrillas shot and fatally wounded Maulvi Mushtaq Ahmed, the uncle and close confidante of Mirwaiz Umar Farooq, as he exited a mosque. A few hours later, apparently the same guerrilla group hurled a grenade at Farooq's home. However, no one was injured. The little-known Save Kashmir Movement claimed responsibility for these attacks. Its spokesman, Shaikh Tajamul, said that the group wanted to stop the sellout of Kashmir by moderates such as Farooq.[53] On June 8, Maulvi Mushtaq Ahmed died of his wounds, and on July 5, 2004, Mirwaiz Umar Farooq was again targeted: Militants set fire to the school he headed, the Islamia High Secondary School, Kashmir's oldest and most prominent and influential school. The 115-year-old school, built of brick and wood, was completely destroyed. The school had housed one of the oldest libraries on Islam, with some 30,000 books, including one of the rarest manuscripts of the Quran, handwritten by Usman bin Affann, the third caliph of Islam. Farooq claimed that the incident was the handiwork of the same group that had assassinated his uncle.

This long campaign of violence and intimidation finally proved effective. On July 7, 2004, Abbass Ansari resigned as the chairman of the Hurryyat Conference and nominated Farooq as his acting successor. Farooq, sensing the chaos that had developed since the split in the Conference, attempted to use the opportunity to reunite his group with Geelani's faction. But Geelani again refused, pointing to the Peoples Conference participation in the 2002 elections. The ISI involved itself again in the dispute, sending assassins who killed a close confidant of Geelani's, Hussamud Deen. Deen appears to have known the assassins, who came by appointment. The killing had been ordered to push Geelani to settle his rift with Farooq. But Geelani proved to be a hard nut to crack; he refused to bow down.

On September 24, Mirwaiz Umar Farooq met with General Musharraf in Amsterdam for three hours in an effort at reconciliation. Musharraf was returning from the United States after attending the UN General Assembly and holding talks with Indian Prime Minister Manmohan Singh; Farooq was traveling from Jeddah to London via Amsterdam to meet his family. In Jeddah, Farooq had met Sardar Qayyum and ISI officials, including Lieutenant General Ehsnul Haq, who arranged the meeting with Mushar-raf. In the one-to-one meeting, they were believed to have discussed issues such as the split in the Hurryyat Confer-ence and Pakistan's recognition of Geelani's group. Farooq claimed they discussed the question of involving Kashmiris in the ongoing India-Pakistan talks.[54] But the meeting final-ly put an end to the long process of talks between Hurryyat and the Indian government. On October 31, 2004, Farooq announced that the Hurryyat leaders would not hold any more talks with the Indian government unless they were allowed to visit Pakistan. He said, "In Pakistan we would like to talk to the people and politicians there to discuss how the issue can be resolved."[55]

During the first week of June 2005, four and a half years after they first expressed their wish to visit, the Hurryyat Conference leaders finally arrived in Pakistan. By this time, Pakistan had come around to recognizing them as the only legitimate political representatives of Jammu and Kashmir. Geelani was described as an elderly politician who had failed to deliver. Pakistani officials, including ISI officers who had kept their distance for nearly five years, welcomed the delegation. It was a symbolic victory for the original Hurryyat members.

Though they had long hoped to successfully appeal to the jihadi leadership, they were disappointed. While they were able to meet privately with a number of jihadi leaders and appeal to them to end the militancy, the jihadis refused.

Since June 2005, violence in Kashmir has declined dra-matically, though the Indians reported nearly 700 violent incidents in 2008. There has also been a further string of terrorist attacks inside India. In October 2005, militants carried out a series of coordinated bombings, killing more than sixty. And in July 2006, three passenger trains were bombed, killing more than 200.

Though the political process of negotiating has slowed in recent years, Syed Ali Shah Geelani's Tehreek-i-Hurryyat has once again reemerged at center stage in Kashmir. The future of further talks remains uncertain.

In the spring of 2007, the ISI arranged several meetings between a group of Pakistani and Kashmiri jihadis and the Afghan Taliban. The most prominent among the Kashmiri jihadis to participate in these meetings were Syed Salahuddin and his senior commanders. These meetings were aimed at creating coordination between the two jihads, in Afghanistan and in Kashmir. Though the ISI had pulled the two groups apart in the aftermath of September 11, and pushed the Kashmiris to keep a low profile, there is now reliable evidence that the ISI has a renewed interest in joining the groups.

As a result of these meetings, some Pakistani jihadi groups joined their Afghan comrades in the tribal areas of Pakistan and also inside Afghanistan. However, most importantly, more jihadis were pushed to cross the Line of Control or use other routes to reach India and Indian-controlled Kashmir during a 2007 "launching" season. In a new strategy, most of them were ordered to establish sleeper cells. Among the most important goals of the meetings between the Taliban and the Kashmiri jihadis was reducing Indian support of Afghanistan's Karazai government, and the regional jihadis meetings likely led to the bombing of the Indian embassy in Kabul in July 2008, perhaps the deadliest terrorist attack in Kabul since September 11, killing fifty-eight people.

The November 2007 appointment of former ISI chief General Ashfaq Pervez Kayani to the post of chief of the army staff was also a significant development, signalling a continued strengthening of Pakistani support for jihadi groups. In 2008, many of these groups began re-opening their offices and running training camps more openly. They also again started holding public rallies and advertising them. Hizbul Mujahideen held its first open public rally since September 11 in Muzaffarabad during the second week of March 2008. An al-Qaeda affiliate, Jaish-i-Mohammad, started operating a training camp in the middle of the city of Bahawalpur in southern Punjab. In the words of a Hizbul Mujahideen commander, the jihadis "never had it so good since 1999."

These events, taken together with the continued rise of Muslim extremists in the North-West Frontier Province of Pakistan, signal a coming consolidation of militant movements in the region. What's commonly called the Pakistani Taliban has established a quasi-state within the Valley of Swat in the North-West Frontier Province of Pakistan, from where they are continuing to extend their control to the adjoining areas.

If the jihadis continue spreading their influence, which is the most likely emerging scenario, they will ultimately extend their control to the borders of Jammu and Kashmir in the East and of Afghanistan in the West, connecting the two. If the territory between Jammu and Kashmir and Afghanistan comes under the control of jihadis, they would be able to freely move between Kashmir and Afghanistan. Since they would also gain access to the Himalayas, they are likely to establish sanctuaries there. All of this increases the likelihood that the jihad in Kashmir continues, extends deeper into India and Afghanistan, and throughout the rest of the world, and with more impunity.

NOTES

CHAPTER ONE

1. Prem Nath Bazaz, *Inside Kashmir*, Verinag Publishers, Mirpur, 1987, p. 8.

2. Victoria Schofield, *Kashmir in Conflict*, I B Taurus & Co Ltd, London, 1996, p. 33.

3. Prem Nath Bazaz, *Inside Kashmir*, Verinag Publishers, Mirpur, 1987, p. 34.

4. As quoted in Victoria Schofield, p. 63.

5. I have largely depended on the account given in Prem Nath Bazaz, *Inside Kashmir*, pp. 70–166. This is the best account of the Revolt of 1931.

6. Some of the present day jihadi parties in Pakistan, affiliated with al-Qaeda, take inspiration from this party or consider themselves its successors.

7. The Punjabi Muslims formed a Kashmir Committee to help the Muslims in Kashmir soon after the Revolt of July 13, 1931. The Ahmadia community nominated Mirza Bashir Ahmed as its representative. The other important member was philosopher/poet Sir Mohammad Iqbal.

8. There are two 'Id festivals in a lunar calendar. The first falls on the first day of the tenth month and the other on the tenth day of the twelfth month.

9. Prem Nath Bazaz, *Inside Kashmir*, p. 160.

10. Joseph Korbel, *Danger in Kashmir*, Oxford University Press, Karachi, 2002, p. 18.

11. Prem Nath Bazaz, *Inside Kashmir*, p. 183.

12. Alastair Lamb, *Kashmir: A Disputed Legacy 1947–1990*, Oxford

University Press, Karachi, p. 4. I have largely depended on this book for this section.

13. Joseph Korbel says there were 584 princely states which covered 45.3 percent of the British Indian territory. The confusion arises because different people define princely states differently and there were no well-defined borders for these states.

14. Alastair Lamb, *Kashmir: A Disputed Legacy 1947–1990*, p. 5.

15. M.J. Akbar in *Kashmir—Behind the Vale*, Roli Books, New Delhi, 2002, p. 97.

16. Quoted in M. J. Akbar in *Kashmir—Behind the Vale*, Roli Books, New Delhi, 2002, p. 89.

17. To read detailed neutral discussion on the Radcliffe award, see Alastair Lamb, *Kashmir: A Disputed Legacy 1947-1990*, Oxford University Press, Karachi, p. 101-117. Prem Shankar *Jha Kashmir 1947*, Oxford University Press, New Delhi, 1998, gives a rival and Indian point of view.

18. See Major General Akbar Khan, *Raiders in Kashmir*, Jang Publishers, Lahore, 1992. The name "General Tariq" is taken from Muslim conqueror of Andalusia (Spain).

19. The narrative of Akbar Khan's book shows that there were several plans to create a revolt in the erstwhile state of Jammu and Kashmir, which were implemented at the same time.

20. As quoted in M. J. Akbar, p. 108.

21. Michael Brecher in *The Struggle for Kashmir*, Oxford, 1953, as quoted in M.J. Akbar p. 108.

22. M.J. Akbar in *Kashmir—Behind the Vale*, p. 103.

23. Joseph Korbel, *Danger in Kashmir*, p. 76.

24. As quoted in M.J. Akbar, p. 110.

25. Maurice Cohen. *Thunder Over Kashmir*, Orient Longman Limited, Hyderabad [India] 1995, p. 36.

26. Other members of the committee were Sardar Ibrahim, Kha-

waja Rahim, the finance minister Ghulam Mohammad, and Major Yusuf of the political department, who was to deal with the tribesmen.
27. Major General Akbar Khan, *Raiders in Kashmir*, p. 82.

CHAPTER TWO

1. Joseph Korbel, *Danger in Kashmir*, Oxford University Press, Karachi, 2002, pp. 87–129. I have depended largely Joseph Korbel's account of the UN's role.
2. Ibid., p. 91.
3. Ibid., p. 91.
4. Ibid., p. 91.
5. Ibid., p. 98.
6. Ibid., p. 98.
7. Ibid., p. 105.
8. Ibid., pp. 113–114.
9. Ibid., p. 121.
10. Ibid., p. 129.
11. M. J. Akbar in *Kashmir—Behind the Vale,* Roli Books, New Delhi, 2002, p. 135.
12. Quoted in in Victoria Schofield, *Kashmir in Conflict*, p. 74
13. See Victoria Schofield, *Kashmir in Conflict*, pp. 74–75.
14. Major General Akbar Khan, *Raiders in Kashmir*, Jang Publishers, Lahore, 1992, p. 125–126.
15. Sati Sahni, *Kashmir Underground*, Har-Anand Publications PVT LTD, New Delhi, 1999, p. 19.
16. Altaf Gauhar, *Ayub Khan*, Sang-e-Meel Publications, Lahore, 1993. This is the only first-hand and largely accurate account

of Operation Gibraltar and Grand Slam. All other accounts are a mix of this account and speculation. All references in this section are from that book unless otherwise stated. Altaf Gauhar was the information secretary at the time Operation Gibraltar was launched. Note that Gibraltar is the anglicised form of the Arabic expression for the mountain of Tariq bin Ziyad. Tariq bin Ziyad was the conqueror of Andalusia. Also note that Colonel Akbar Khan also used the pseudonym "Tariq" while leading the Pakistani tribesmen in 1947.

17. Ibid., p. 321.

18. The names are significant. Most of them were Muslim conquerors.

19. Brig Z. A. Khan, *The Way It Was*, Dynavis (Pvt) Ltd., Karachi, 1998, p. 155.

20. Altaf Gauhar, "1965 War: 'Operation Gibraltar,'" *The Nation*, October 3, 1999.

21. M. J. Akbar in *Kashmir—Behind the Vale*, Roli Books, New Delhi, 2002, p. 169.

22. Altaf Gauhar, "1965 War: 'Operation Gibraltar,'" *The Nation*, October 3, 1999.

23. Altaf Gauhar, *Ayub Khan,* Sang-e-Meel Publications, Lahore, 1993, pp. 315–317.

24. As quoted in Altaf Gauhar, p. 330.

25. Jagmohan, *My Frozen Turbulence in Kashmir*, Allied Publishers Pvt Limited, New Delhi, 2002, p. 159: Though evidence of the groups' activities has not survived, the level of ISI's involvement can be gauged from the fact that the police in Jammu and Kashmir recovered 281 (.303) rifles, 309 guns, 8 stenguns, 4 light machineguns, 44 revolvers, 431 hand-grenades, 66 mortar shell, 5 automatic rifles, 65 bayonets, 117 detonator, 30 bombs, 2 rocket–launchers, 3 wireless sets, and 1,600 lbs of

explosives, items that were most likely supplied by the ISI.

26. The group takes its name from the Palestinian guerrilla group. The Kashmiri al-Fatah fighters included Syed Sarwar, Fazlul Haq Qureshi, and Nazir Ahmed Wani.

27. Interview with Fazlul Haq Qureshi, June 12, 2005, Islamabad.

28. Sati Sahni, *Kashmir Underground*, Har-Anand Publications PVT LTD, New Delhi, 1999, p. 22.

29. The Plebiscite Front (for Azad Kashmir and Pakistan) was independent of the political party with the same name in the Indian-controlled Jammu and Kashmir. However, the Plebiscite Front in Indian Jammu and Kashmir appears to have influenced the thinking of the Plebiscite Front (for Azad Kashmir and Pakistan).

30. Amanullah Khan, *Johd-e-Musalsal*, apparently published by the author, Rawalpindi, 1992, pp. 98–99.

31. Ibid., p. 112.

32. Subedar Kala Khan, Aurangzeb, and Subedar Habibullah Butt accompanied them.

33. Amanullah Khan, *Johd-e-Musalsal*, pp. 113–114: Ghulam Mohammad Dar was working for both the Pakistani and Indian secret agencies and had also somehow joined the NLF group.

34. Interview with Dr. Farooq Haider, October 16, 2003, Rawalpindi.

35. Hashim Qureshi, *Nar Haai Kashmir*, Jidojohd Publications, Lahore.

36. Ibid.

37. M. J. Akbar in *Kashmir-Behind the Vale*, Roli Books, New Delhi, 2002, p. 186.

38. Interview with Amanullah Khan, July 10, 2004, Rawalpindi.

39. Interview with Dr. Farooq Haider, October 16, 2003, Rawalpindi.

40. They included late Chaudhary Abdul Hameed, Nazeer Nazish, Comrade Yunas, Mohammad Bashir, Mirza Bashir, Mirza Siddique, and Arif Ansari.
41. Taken from *20 years (1977-1997) of JKLF.*

CHAPTER THREE

1. Interview with Maulana Abdul Bari, April 16, 2002, Muzaffarabad.
2. Maulana Abdul Bari had become a member of the Rabita Alam Islami, Saudi Arabia, in 1974, one year after the foundation of the Jamat-i-Islami of Azad Kashmir.
3. In-house fortnightly *Jihad-i-Kashmir*, April 15, 2004, Rawalpindi.
4. Interview with Ghulam Mohammad Safi, September 3, 2001, Islamabad.
5. Interviews with Altaf Ahmed Bhat alias Commander Tufail Butt and Almas, January 2003.
6. In-house fortnightly *Jihad-i-Kashmir*, April 15, 2004, Rawalpindi, p. 30.
7. Sati Sahni, *Kashmir Underground*, Har-Anand Publications PVT LTD, New Delhi, 1999, p. 24: Many of these fighters, such as Mushtaqul Islam of Hizbullah, played key roles in the early days of militancy. There were also Islami Jamiat Tulaba members in the crowd.
8. Sati Sahni, *Kashmir Underground*, Har-Anand Publications PVT LTD, New Delhi, 1999, p. 25.
9. Ibid., p. 24: Those arrested included Iqbal Qureshi and Altaf Qureshi, two brothers of Hashim Qureshi.
10. Ibid., p. 25.

11. Ibid., p. 25.

12. Interview with Yusuf Nasim, January 4, 2004, Rawalpindi.

13. Interview with Innnayat Ullahh Andrabi, January 7, 2003, Islamabad.

14. It was not necessary to be a student to become its member.

15. The founding members of the Islamic Students League included, among others, Aslam Wani, Yasin Malik, Javed Ahmed Mir, Shaikh Hameed, Abdullah Bangaroo, Maqbool Alai, Mehmood Ahmed Saghar, Shakat Ahmed Bakhshi, Mushtaqul Islam, Nayeem Ahmed Khan, Yunus Ahmed Taak, Zahoor Ahmed Shaikh, and Altaf Mattoo.

16. Interview with Mehmood Ahmed Saghar, June 12, 2002, Rawalpindi.

17. Interview with Rafiq Dar, January 5, 2004, Rawalpindi.

18. Interview with Ghulam Rasool Shah, March 9, 2002, Islamabad.

19. Most authors give importance to the role of MUF, though it played little role in determining the course of history. There is no evidence of Pakistan or ISI supporting the formation of MUF. Pakistan would not support any political alliance led by a Shia leader, as we see in the following chapters.

20. Interview with Mehmood Ahmed Saghar, June 12, 2002, Rawalpindi.

21. Interview with Ghulam Mohammad Safi, September 3, 2001, Islamabad.

22. These Kashmiri militants included Raja Abdul Qayyum, Jehangir Mirza, and Majeed Ansari. They were all Kashmiri expatriates living in European countries. *Johd-e-Musalsal*, pp. 280–281.

23. Interview with Dr. Farooq Haider, October 16, 2003, Rawalpindi.

24. Interview with Dr. Farooq Haider, November 29, 2003,

Rawalpindi.

25. Interview with Hanif Haidery, April 16, 2003, Rawalpindi.

26. According to an article by Hashim Qureshi in weekly *Chattan*, Dr. Farooq Haider, Hashim Qureshi, Z H Ansari, and Rashid Hasrat took part in the initial negotiations with the ISI. Quoted in *Manoj Joshi*, p. 18.

27. Khan no longer remembers the name of the Brigadier.

28. Interview with Amannullah Khan, July 10, 2004, Rawalpindi.

29. Ibid.

30. Interview with a senior official in the Zia-ul-Haq regime, Rawalpindi.

31. *Johd-e-Musalsal*, Vol. 2, p. 202.

32. Those who actively recruited Kashmiri fighters on both sides of the Line of Control included Ghulam Nabi Bhat (the brother of Maqbool Bhat), S.M. Afzal from Kupwara, Malik anwar, Bilaal Ahmed Siddiqui from Srinagar, Nazimud Deen from Kupwara, Ghulam Mohammad Wani, and Bashir Ahmed Pir.

33. Interview with Dr. Farooq Haider, October 16, 2003, Rawalpindi.

34. They included Abdul Hamid Shaikh, Hilal Ahmed Baig, Waheed Ahmed, Pir Ali Mohammad, Ghulam Mohamma Gojri, Captain Abdur Rashid, Manzoor Ahmed Khan, and Javed Mir from Indian Jammu and Kashmir, annd Ghulam Nabi Shania, Mama, and Bahahuddin from Athmaqam in Azad Kashmir. *Juhd-I-Musalsal*, Vol. 2., p. 48.

35. Interview with Mehmood Ahmed Saghar, June 12, 2002, Rawalpindi.

36. Interview with Dr. Farooq Haider, October 16, 2003, Rawalpindi.

37. *Juhd-I-Musalsal*, Vol. 2, p. 148.

38. Interview with Dr. Farooq Haider, October 16, 2003,

Rawalpindi.

39. Interview with Hanif Haidery, April 16, 2002, Rawalpindi.
40. Those who carried out these explosions included Humayun Azad, Javed Jehangir, Shabbir Ahmed Guru, Arshad Kaul, Ghulam Qadir Rathar, and Mohammad Rafiq. Bilal Ahmed Siddiqui was supposed to lead the group that day, but he did not turn up. Interestingly, Jamat-i-Islami considers September 1989, the day the Hizbul Mujahideen was founded, as the beginning of the insurgency.

CHAPTER FOUR

1. A large number of these actions were carried out by die-hard Islamists, who had joined the movement at the behest of the ISI.
2. The planning for the kidnapping was carried out by Ali Mohammad Mir, Yasin Malik, Ashfaq Majid Wani, Iqbal Gandroo, and Salim Mir, at the house of Mushtaq Ahmed Lone in Chanpora.
3. See M. J. Akbar in *Kashmir—Behind the Vale*, Roli Books, New Delhi, 2002, p. 216. They were Abdul Hamid Shaikh, Javed Ahmed Zargar, Noor Mohammad Kalwal, and Altaf Butt Ghulam Nabi Butt.
4. Manoj Joshi, *The Lost Rebellion*, Penguin Books India, 1999, p. 33.
5. Interview with Amanullah Khan, July 10, 2004, Rawalpindi: Khan mistakenly said Mushirul Haq had been killed.
6. Ved Marwah, *Uncivil Wars*, HarperCollins Publishers India, New Delhi, 1997, p. 109.
7. Interview with Rafiq Dar, September 22, 2004, Rawalpindi.
8. Interview with Ghulam Mohammad Safi, September 3, 2001, Islamabad.

9. Interview with Master Ahsan Dar, August 28, 2004, Rawalpindi.

10. Hizbul Ansar was named after the Ansaars (Helpers) of Madina, who helped fleeing Muslims from Mecca in the early period of the Islamic history. Other key al-Hamza leaders included Ijaz Ahmed Dar, Mohammad Abdullah Bangro, and Shaikh Abdul Hameed.

11. Interview with Ahsan Dar, September 10, 2001, Muzaffarabad.

12. Interview with Masood Sarfraz, October 17, 2000, Rawalpindi.

13. Masood Sarfraz believes that it was just a coincidence and Hilal Ahmed Mir had thought of the same name. Interview with Masood Sarfraz, October 17, 2000, Rawalpindi.

14. Interview with Masood Sarfraz, October 17, 2000, Rawalpindi. Shamsul Haq gives a similar explanation in his Urdu booklet *Hizbul Mujahideen–Tarikh, Qiam, and jiddojuhd*.

15. Interview with Masood Sarfraz, October 17, 2000, Rawalpindi.

16. Prominent among those who joined them were Shaikh Abdul Aziz, Abdul Majeed Dar, Ghulam Mohammad Naiko, Abdul Majeed Pathan, and Fazlul Haq Qureshi.

17. Telephone interview with Abdul Majeed Dar in Srinagar: They included, among others, Muzaffar Shah alias Umar Amir, Mussadiq Adil, Abdul Majeed Pathan, Shaikh Abdul Aziz, belonged to the People's League. Malik Naeem, Malik Abdullah, and Ghulam Mohammad Mir alias Abu Nasir belonged to the Jamat-i-Islami. Almas Rizwan belonged to the Islami Jamiat-i-Tulaba. Javed Jehangir belonged to ISL. Almas Rizwan was put in charge of Kupwara, Abu Nasir of Baramula, Abdul Majeed Pathan of Srinagar, Raoof of Islamabad, Malik Naeem of Pulwama, Shaheen of Butgam.

18. Urdu booklet *Hizbul Mujahideen–Tarikh, Qiam, and jiddojuhd* by Shamsul Haq, Markaz Matbooaat Kashmir, Rawalpindi, 1994.

19. The delegation included Master Ahsan Dar, Ashraf Dar, Maqbool Alai, Shaikh Abdul Waheed, Farooq Qureshi, and Altaf Ahmed Shah. Interview with Master Ahsan Dar, August 28, 2004, Rawalpindi.

20. According to Dr. Ghulam Nabi Fai, the son-in-law of Syed Ali Shah Geelani, Altaf Ahmed Shah, played an important role in brining Syed Ali Shah Geelani to Kathmandu. However, he did not take direct part in the meeting.

21. This included Hakeem Ghulam Nabi of the Jamat-i-Islami of Indian-controlled Jammu and Kashmir, Abdur Rashid Turabi of the Jamat-i-Islami of Pakistan-controlled Kashmir, Professor Khursheed Ahmed of the Jamat-i-Islami of Pakistan, Dr. Ghulam Nabi Fai, and Dr. Ayub Thakur of the former Islami Jamiat Tulaba.

22. Interview with Masood Sarfraz, June 25, 2001, Kotli; and interview with Ayub Thakur, August 20, 2002, Islamabad; and interview with Ghulam Nabi Fai, June 7, 2005, Islamabad. All three participants in this meeting claimed credit for arranging it. However, Fai said that Altaf, the son-in-law of Syed Ali shah Geelani, extended valuable help.

23. Interview with Masood Sarfraz, June 25, 2001, Kotli and interview with Ayub Thakur, August 20, 2002, Islamabad, and interview with Ghulam Nabi Fai, June 7, 2005, Islamabad.

24. Aditya Sinha, *Death of Dreams*, HarperCollins Publishers India, New Deli, 2000, p. 43.

25. The idea to make the Hizbul Mujahideen the armed wing of Islam has not completely died. I saw graffiti on a wall in Peshawar that said "Hizbul Mujahideen is the armed wing of Islam" in April 2003.

26. In several interviews with me, Dar insisted that he had made the announcement on his own "only to draw the Jamat-i-Isla-

mi into the armed struggle."

27. The Budgam and Srinagar units of the TJI refused to accept the merger and instead merged with the MJF. Aditya Sinha, *Death of Dreams*, HarperCollins Publishers India, New Deli, 2000, p. xxiv.

28. Urdu booklet *Hizbul Mujahideen–Tarikh, Qiam, and jiddojuhd* by Shamsul Haq, 1994, p. 17.

29. The JKLF was particularly lacking in funds to continue the training of militants. According to Amanullah Khan, the cost of training one militant came to between 50,000 and 60,000 rupees at that time.

30. Shaikh Rashid was the parliamentary secretary general of the Islamic Jamhoori Ittehad (IJI), an alliance of right-wing political parties that opposed Benazir Bhutto's government in the center. The IJI was in power in the province of Punjab, including Rawalpindi. The then President Ghulam Ishaq Khan was closer to the IJI government in Punjab. The Bhutto-led federal government could not take action against the camp on its own.

31. The cabinet of minister included Abdul Ghani Lone (Jammu and Kashmir Peoples Conference), Abdul Hameed Shaikh (JKLF), Aasiya Andrabi (Dukhtaran-i-Millat), Agha al-Moosvi al-Safavi (Shia leader), Sardar Avtaar Singh (Sikh leader), Azam Inquilabi (Operation Balakot), Bashir Ahmed Bhat (Mahaz-i-Azaadi), Pandit Bhushan Bzaz (Hindu politician), Dr. Farooq Haider (JKLF), Dr. Karan Singh (son of the last Dogra Maharaja and former Sadre Riyasat), Ghulam Nabi Bhat (brother of Maqbul Bhat), Pandit Haday Nath Wanchoo (Hindu trade union leader), Hilal Ahmed Beg (Kashmir Students Liberation Front), Javed Ahmed Mir (JKLF), Mian Abdul Qayyum (President of Srinagar Bar Associaiton), Mirwaiz Umar Farooq (Muslim leader), Mohammad Yasin Malik

(JKLF), Muzaffar Ali Khan (JKLF), Professor Abdul Ghani Bhat (Muslim Conference), Raja Mohammad Muzaffar Khan (JKLF), Shabbir Ahmed Shah (Peoples League), Shakeel Bakhshi (Islamic Students League) and Syed Ali Shah Geelani (Jamat-i-Islami of Indian-controlled Jammu and Kashmir). Amannallah Khan also appointed a fifteen-member panel to project the freedom movement at the international level under the guidance of the provisional government. They included Afzal Jatalvi, Ali Mohammad Khawajwal, Ashraf Sahaf, Azmat Khan, Ayub Thakur, Dr. P. Mir, Ghulam Nabi Fai, Iftikhar Chaudhary, Mohammad Haleem Khan, Mohammad Ajeeb, Shabbir Chaudhary, Raja Zafar Khan, M H Mehboob, Maqsood Ghauri, and Aziz Ashai. He also announced a four-member panel to propagate evidence of human rights violations by the Indian forces. The panel included Farooq Kathwari, Farooq Khan, Rafiq Khan, and M.A. Hussain.

32. Interview with Amanullah Khan, July 10, 2004, Rawalpindi.
33. The following account is based on the interviews with former Hizbul Mujahideen commanders and fighters, unless otherwise stated, who asked not to be named.
34. Abu Sayyaf should not be confused with Ustaz Abdur Rabb Rasool Saayaf.
35. Interview with Masood Sarfraz, June 25, 2001, Kotli.
36. Interview with Advocate Mohammad Abdul Hamid Karimi, July 24, 2001, Muzaffarabad.
37. Interviews with several Hizbul Mujahideen commanders who participated in the meeting.
38. Ghulam Rasool Dar, July 25, 2001, Muzaffarabad.
39. Interview with Ajmal Khan, Rawalpindi. The number appears to be a low estimate, perhaps because the interviewee was still a top Hizbul Mujahideen commander.

40. This is according to Masood Sarfraz.

41. Interview with Rafiq Dar, December 25, 2003, Rawalpindi.

42. Interview with Salim Haroon, January 5, 2004, Rawalpindi.

43. Tavleen Singh, *Kashmir—A Tragedy of Errors*, Penguin Books India, New Delhi, 1996, p. 218.

44. Those murdered included Subhan Shah of Kupwara, Khursheed Islam and Shabbir Ali of Anantnag, Mansur Ahmed of Pattan, and Ghulam Ahmed Rather of Budgam.

45. Aditya Sinha, *Death of Dreams*, HarperCollins Publishers India, New Deli, 2000, p. 92.

46. Interview with Shaikh yakub, June 16, 2003, Rawalpindi.

47. Interview with Masood Sarfraz. June 25, 2001, Kotli.

48. Mirwaiz Farooq was the biggest potential political rival of Syed Ali Shah Geelani. Geelani could not emerge as the sole political leader of the militants while Mirwaiz Farooq was alive. It is commonly thought that Ajmal Khan directed his killers. However, Ajmal Khan not in contact with the Hizbul Mujahideen leaders at that time, so it seems unlikely that he was asked to perform this task.

49. Interview with Shaikh Yaqub, June 16, 2003, Rawalpindi.

50. Interview with Shaikh Yaqub, June 16, 2003, Rawalpindi.

51. Omkar Razdan, *The Trauma of Kashmir: The Untold Story*, Vikas, New Delhi, p. 205.

CHAPTER FIVE

1. The committee consisted of Qazi Hussain Ahmed, Professor Khurshid Ahmed, Pir Syed Salahuddin, Amir Sahib, Ijaz Afzal, Jehangir, Ghulam Nabi Nowshehri, and Mushtaq Gilani. Kha-

lidur Rehman, director of the Institute of Policy in Islamabad, is the secretary of the Jihad-i-Kashmir committee.

2. The Supreme Commander also heads six divisional commanders: Divisional Commander (North), Divisional Commander (South), Divisional Commander (Central), Divisional Commander (Doda), Divisional Commander (Chenab). The North Division includes Kupwara and Baramula, the Central Division includes Budgam and Srinagar, the South Division includes Anantnag and Pulwama. The Divisional Commander (Chenab) includes Doda, Kishtwar, and Udhampur. The Col. Gulab Gard division includes Rajouri and Pooncch. The Jammu Division includes the city of Jammu.

3. Five members of the command council were taken from the Valley of Kashmir, three from the Jammu Division, two from Pakistan, and two from Pakistani-controlled Jammu and Kashmir. In a later re-organisation process, a new structure was implemented, establishing three Deputy Supreme Commanders, one from Indian-controlled Jammu and Kashmir, one from Pakistani-controlled Jammu and Kashmir, and one from Pakistan. In February 1998, the organizational structure of the Hizbul Mujahideen was once again revamped. The supreme commander was designated as amir and the deputy supreme commander as chief organizer.

4. Interview with Nazrul Islam Danish, before March 24, 2001, Islamabad.

5. Interview with Maqbool Pandit, November 21, 2000, Rawalpindi.

6. First, other organizations would also be allowed to join the Hizbul Mujahideen. Second, the name of the Hizbul Mujahideen would be changed at a later date. The Hizbul Mujahideen leadership accepted both conditions at that time

because it needed the TJI commanders but refused to implement either of these conditions later. None of the three Jamat-i-Islamis allowed the merger of any organisation that did not conform to its ideology. They rightly feared that other smaller organisations would weaken their hold and strengthen that of Abdul Majeed Dar.

7. Interview with Masood Sarfraz, June 25, 2001, Kotli.

8. Interview with Amir Hamza, April 19, 2000, Rawalpindi.

9. The author personally witnessed this fighting and interviewed dozens of fighters involved.

10. Interview with Tahir Masood, August 25, 2001, Islamabad. Masood told me that Abbass Ansari had links with the FIU (Field Investigative Units) of the Pakistani Army. The FIU apparently never had the financial resources to operate outside the Pakistani territory. It appears the ISI operatives were identifying themselves as FIU operatives in order to deceive the Indian secret services.

11. When the Taliban took over the camp, it allowed Pakistanis and Kashmiri fighters to leave: According to the Taliban's Khost Syed Abdullah: "We took over the camps and asked the 107 Pakistanis living there to return to their homeland. They were honorably allowed to enter Pakistan at the Pakistan-Afghanistan border near the camp." When it was closed, Governor Abdullah also recognized that the camp had been jointly operated by Hizebe Islami and Jamat-i-Islami.

12. Interview with Masood Sarfraz, June 25, 2001, Rawalpindi.

13. In Pakistani-controlled Jammu and Kashmir, communication centers included Shaheen, Communication det Alpha One, and Communication det A-2. Among the camps setup to house fighters are Umar Khan Markaz and Saifullah Khalid camp. There were more than 400 fighters present at Saifullah Khalid

when I visited it in 2001.

14. *Jasarat*, April 30, 2003: The first batch of the Iraq Relief Mission, a joint delegation of Islamist parliamentarians, representatives of the Doctor's Forum, and representatives of the PIMA, left Karachi on April 29, 2003 for Iraq. The delegation included MNA Dr. Firdous Ashiq Awan, Senator Dr. Azizullah Satakzai, Dr. Aneela Nazeer, Dr. Shahid Parveen, Dr. Saqib Ansari, Dr. Mohammad Javed, and two paramedics.

15. An anti-terrorist court sentenced the two doctors to seven years on March 14, 2005, for allegedly having links with the group. Each of them was also to pay a fine of 50,000 rupees ($839). See the AFP dispatch reprinted in *The News*, March 15, 2005.

16. M. L. Kaul, *Kashmir: Wail of a Valley*, Gyan Sagar Publications, 1999, pp. 109-121.

17. Ibid., p. 200.

18. Ibid., p. 221.

19. Major General Arjun Ray, *Kashmir Diary*, Manas Publications, New Delhi, 1997, p. 57. M. L. Kaul also documents the names of seventy temples destroyed across the valley.

20. M. L. Kaul, *Kashmir: Wail of a Valley*, Gyan Sagar Publications, 1999, p. 257.

21. Militants also systematically eliminated the intellectual class in Valley. They aimed at killing the writers, artists, and scholars, and destroying their books and art treasures. Kashmiri Pandits produced many writers and artists. Most of them had to run from the valley leaving their books and art treasures behind. The militants looted or burned what was left behind. The Jamt-i-Islami of the Indian-controlled Jammu and Kashmir and Hizbul Mujahideen militants, who had no knowledge of their value, made bonfires of these books and art treasures

amid rallies. Thus the Valley of Kashmir lost both its intellectual class and history with the onset of jihad. What remains of the looted books and art pieces have been on sale throughout the country. Distinguished artist P.N. Kachru was one of the earliest victims of the armed struggle. He lost nearly 4,000 rare books and a treasure of paintings.

22. Major General Arjun Ray, *Kashmir Diary*, Manas Publications, New Delhi, 1997, p. 55.

23. AFP dispatch quoted in *The News*, September 25, 1999.

24. AFP dispatch quoted in *The News*, September 27, 1999.

25. Ved Marwah, *Uncivil Wars*, HarperCollins Publisher India, 1997.

26. Interview with Ghulam Rasool Dar, August 11, 2002.

27. Interview with Ghulam Rasool Dar, August 11, 2002.

28. *The News International*, December 9, 2001.

29. AFP dispatch quoted in *The News*, August 10, 2001.

30. AFP dispatch quoted in *The News*, August 21, 2001.

31. AFP dispatch quoted in *The News*, August 31, 2001.

32. AFP dispatch quoted in *The News*, September 5, 2001.

33. AFP dispatch quoted in *The News*, March 15, 2002.

34. AFP dispatch quoted in *The News*, December 31, 2002.

35. AFP dispatch quoted in *The News*, December 25, 2002.

CHAPTER SIX

1. Altaf Gauhar, "Four Wars, One Assumption" in *The Nation*, September 5, 1999. This was one of the few objective articles that appeared in the Pakistani press. Throughout this chapter I have made use of Lt-Gen. V.R. Raghavan, *Saichen: Conflict*

Without End, Viking India, New Delhi, 2002. Unless otherwise noted, please see Raghavan's text.

2. Hassan Abbas, *Pakistan's Drift into Extremism: Allah, the Army and America's War on Terror*, Pentagon Press, New Delhi, 2005, p. 170.

3. In an interview with the BBC world service radio program *The World Today.*

4. See the full text of the Lahore Declaration at: www.usip.org/ library/pa/ip/ip_lahore19990221.html

5. M. Ilyas Khan, "Life After Kargil," in *The Herald*, July 2000, pp. 26-27.

6. Kuldip Nayar, "Inquiry Into Failure," *The Nation* July 30, 1999.

7. AFP dispatch, quoted in *The News,* June 18, 1999.

8. M. Ilyas Khan "Life After Kargil," *The Herald,* July 2000, p. 27.

9. *The News,* July 13, 1999.

10. News agencies quoted in *Dawn,* June 3, 1999.

11. The BBC report from July 16, 1999, as quoted in *The News,* July 17, 1999.

12. Nasir Iqbal, "AIR, naval chiefs military leaders did not know of Kargil: Nawaz," *The News,* June 13, 2000.

13. Raja Zulfikar, "PM authorized 'infiltration' across LoC, claims Benazir," *The News,* July 24, 1999.

14. There are too many contradictions in the official statements to support Musharraf's claims. We do not, for instance, have any credible official version as to where the Pakistani soldiers died. And there have been no precise media reports on militant operations during the Kargil conflict. During the Kargil conflict, most commanders told me privately that there were no militants on the Kargil heights, though they had been asked to claim responsibility. In the beginning, only Tehreek-I-Jihad

and al-Badr Mujahideen agreed to claim responsibility, but, later, many other jihadi organizations started claiming their presence in the Kargil. Both Tehreek-i-Jihad and al-Badr Mujahideen were new jihadi organisations and wanted introduction. The Kargil conflict turned them into household names. Tehreek-i-Jihad was a small group of Pakistani ex-servicemen and al-Badr Mujahideen, a group of Pakistani jihadis, had recently been expelled from the Hizbul Mujahideen.

15. M. Ilyas Khan, "Life After Kargil," *The Herald*, July 2000, p. 28.

16. Most Pakistani analysts and officials including General Pervez Musharraf have tried push the myth that it were mujahideen who occupied the Kargil heights. Consequently, these statements appear contradictory. In piecing this account together, I have read "Pakistani soldiers" instead of the "mujahideen," making it somewhat easier to understand official statements.

17. APP dispatch, quoted in *The News*, June 7, 1999.

18. Lt. General Javed Nasir Kargil, "A flashpoint?–I," *The News*, June 26, 1999.

19. *Dawn*, July 10, 1999.

20. Nasir Iqbal "AIR, naval chiefs military leaders did not know of Kargil: Nawaz," *The News*, June 13, 2000.

21. PTI dispatch quoted in *The News*, June 3, 2001.

22. Reuters dispatch, quoted in *The News*, July 5, 1999.

23. *The News*, July 8, 1999.

24. *The News*, July 12, 1999.

25. APP dispatch quoted in *The News*, June 25, 1999.

26. *The News* August 16, 1999.

27. M. Ilyas Khan, "Life After Kargil" in *The Herald*, July 2000, p. 29.

28. APP dispatch in *The News*, September 10, 1999.

29. According to Finance Minister Ishaq Dar, the Kargil operation

cost Pakistan $700 million. Taken from an interview with the BBC, as quoted in *The News*, July 29, 1999.

30. Mariana Babar, "Aitzaz blames Nawaz for 'diplomatic defeat'" in *The News*, August 11, 1999.

31. Lt. General Javed Nasir, "Kargil: sellout or sane decision?" *The News*, July 16, 1999.

32. AFP dispatch, *The News*, June 14, 2003.

33. Pervez Musharraf, *In the Line of Fire*, Simon and Schuster, New York and London, 2006, p. 98.

34. Kamran Khan, "COAS trying to calm 'disquiet' in Army ranks" in *The News*, September 5, 1999.

35. Kamran Khan, "COAS trying to calm 'disquiet' in Army ranks."

36. He was one of the few generals Sharif trusted.

37. From an interview with an SSP leader.

38. Shakil Shaikh, "Taliban to hand over 150 terrorists," *The News*, October 6, 1999.

39. AP dispatch, quoted in *The News*, October 8, 1999.

40. Tariq Butt, "Nawaz seeks UAE influence on Taliban," *The News*, October 12, 1999.

41. See also *The News*, August 06, 2006: The document referred to here is a 2006 white paper prepared by the Pakistan Muslim League-Nawaz (PML-N).

CHAPTER SEVEN

1. AFP dispatch, quoted in *The News*, October 14, 1999.

2. Bill Clinton, "What I hope to Accomplish in South Asia," Global Viewpoint/*Los Angeles Times* Syndicate, exclusive for *The News*, March 20, 2000.

3. *The News,* July 30, 2000.

4. Telephone Interview with Abdul Majid Dar from Srinagar, December 19, 2003.

5. Interview with Khursheed Ahmed, alias Asad Yazdani, April 21, 2004, Rawalpindi: Those in attendance at the press conference were Farooq Mircha, Khursheed Ahmed (alias Dr. Asad Yazdani), Zaffar Akbar Bhat (alias Zaffar Abdul Fath), and Abbass Rahi. Another commander, Jafar Tayyar, had also planned to attend, though he had been unable to reach the press conference.

6. AFP dispatch quoted in *The News,* July 25, 2000.

7. Interview with Khursheed Ahmed, alias Asad Yazdani, April 21, 2004, Rawalpindi.

8. The United Jihad Council restored the membership of the Hizbul Mujahideen and reinstated Salahuddin in the office of chairman on October 23, 2000.

9. Faxed message from Qazi Hussain Ahmed, quoted in *The News,* July 26, 2000.

10. *The News,* July 28, 2000.

11. *The News,* July 28, 2000.

12. PPI dispatch, *The News,* July 31, 2000.

13. AFP dispatch *The News,* July 31, 2000: The team would have included Ghulam Nabi Fai of Kashmir American Council, Mushtaq Gilani of World Kashmir Freedom Movement and the executive director of the Kashmir Canadian Council, and Mohammad Ali Saqib, member of Overseas Kashmir Citizen Committee.

14. Reuters dispatch, *The News,* August 3, 2000.

15. The Indian delegation included Indian Home Secretary Kamal Pande and a special secretary with responsibility for Kashmir, P.R. Kakkar.

16. AP dispatch, *The News*, August 5, 2000.

17. AFP dispatch, *The News*, August 4, 2000.

18. *The News*, August 9, 2000.

19. Reuters dispatch, reprinted in *The News*, August 22, 2000.

20. *The News*, August 25, 2000.

21. Ibid.

22. Interview with Javed Ahmed Bhat, alias Ajmal Khan.

23. The quote is from a South Asian Free Media Association meeting.

24. AP dispatch, *The News*, November 24, 2000.

25. As quoted in *The News*, November 20, 2000.

26. As quoted in *The News*, November 18, 2000.

27. As quoted in *The News*, November 21, 2000.

28. Jawed Naqvi, "Guns fall silent in Siachin," *Dawn*, December 27, 2000.

29. AFP dispatch, *The News*, December 21, 2000.

30. Reuters dispatch, reprinted in *The News*, December 24, 2000. The spokesman was Abu Osama.

31. As quoted in *The News*, May 26, 2001.

32. As quoted in *The News*, May 30, 2001.

33. AFP dispatch, *The News*, June 7, 2001

34. AFP dispatch, *The News*, June 9, 2001.

35. *The News*, August 27, 2001.

36. AFP dispatch, *The News*, August 23, 2001.

37. Kamran Khan, "Centre Orders Halt to Anti-Jihadis Crackdown," *The News*, August 24, 2001.

38. SANA dispatch, *The News*, August 23, 2001.

39. Translation of the address in *The News*, September 20, 2001.

40. Reuters dispatch, *The News*, October 16, 2001.

41. Reuters dispatch, *The News*, October 17, 2001.

42. AFP dispatch, *The News*, October 16, 2001.

43. The hijackers the Indians requested were Ibrahim Athar, Zahoor Ibrahim Mistri, Shahid Akhtar Syed, and Azhar Yusuf.

44. This included seven Indian Muslim terrorists involved in terrorist explosions that took place in Mumbai in 1993, Dawood Ibrahim, Cchota Shakeel, "Tiger" Ibrahim Memon, Ayub Memon, Abdul Razzak, Ishaq Atta Hussain, and Sagir Sabir Ali Shaikh; one Indian Muslim terrorist who carried out blasts in Delhi in 1996, Abdul Karim; and Sikh terrorists from the Indian Punjab, Wadhawan Singh Babbar, Ranjit Singh Neeta, Paramjeet Sign Panjwar, Lakhbeer Singh Rode, and Gajinder Singh.

45. *The News,* January 12, 2002.

46. By this time, the security agencies had already arrested Hafiz Mohammad Saeed for inciting the public against the government's Afghan policy. Maulana Masood Azhar had also been put into police custody for ninety days, though he was later moved to the Mianwali jail.

47. Rana Mubashir, "16 Jihadis Freed for Lack of Evidence," *The News,* January 25, 2002.

48. *The News,* March 15, 2002.

49. Interview with a Hizbul Mujahideen commander, September 13, 2002, Islamabad.

50. The ISI attempted to divide the MJC into six smaller alliances: Kashmir Resistance Forum "One", "Two," and "Three"; and Kashmir Freedom Forum "One", "Two," and "Three." Again, only Hizbul Mujahideen was allowed to use its old name. Kashmir Resistance Forum One comprised Lashkar-i-Taiba, Brigade 313, Lashkar-i-Islam and al-Badr. Kashmir Resistance Forum Two included al-Jihad, al-Fatah, and Muslim Janbaz Force. Kashmir Resistance Forum Three included the Harakat al-Jihad al-Islami (Muzaffar), Jamiat ul Mujahideen, and Ja-

miatul Ansaar. Kashmir Freedom Forum-I comprised Jaish-i-Mohammad, al-Umar Mujahideen; Kashmir Freedom Forum-II comprised Islamic Front, Jamatul Furqan, Tehreek-i-Jihad, al-Burq, and Tehreekul Mujahideen.

51. This was a U.S. State Department memo that named thirty-eight "other terrorist" groups that are not on its primary list of Designated Foreign Terrorist Organizations (FTOs) but which the United States nonetheless believes need to be watched. The new list included Hizbul Mujahideen, Jamiatul Mujahideen, and al-Badr Mujahideen.

52. Reuters dispatch, *The News,* December 19, 2003.

53. Qudsia Akhlaque, "Islamabad Issued Twice as Many Visas as Delhi," *Dawn,* April 26, 2004: There was unprecedented tourist traffic between the two countries. Pakistan issued approximately 19,000 and India approximately 10,000 visas to each other's citizens in the first quarter of 2004. This was the highest number of visas issued since Kargil conflict.

54. AFP dispatch, *The News,* July 15, 2004.

55. Reuters dispatch, *Dawn,* November 2, 2004.

56. AP dispatch, *The News,* November 23, 2004.

57. Jawed Naqvi, "India Sending More Forces to Kashmir," *Dawn,* November 27, 2004.

58. AFP dispatch, *The News,* November 18, 2004.

59. On May 4, 2002, Salahuddin expelled Abdul Majeed Dar, Khursheed Ahmed alias Dr. Asad Yazdani, and Zaffar Akbar Bhat alias Zaffar Abdul Fath from Hizbul Mujahideen, levelling allegations that they worked for the Indian secret service. There were many protesting voices against this decision. Some of the commanders asked for evidence. Salahuddin responded to this by expelling more commanders and fighters including Commanders Zubeirul Islam and Asghar Rehman Dar, who

was later killed by the Indian task force. Divisional Commander North Abu Obaid and many other commanders also sided
with Dar and were expelled. At the same time, the Jamat-i-
Islami of Pakistan and the Hizbul Mujahideen (Syed Salahuddin's faction) ran a smear campaign against Abdul Majeed
Dar. Office Secretary Babar and Raees Mir, the brother-in-law
of Nazeer Shawl, were circulating a letter alleging that Abdul
Majeed Dar was in contact with the RAW and had asked for
amnesty from the Indian government.

In the meanwhile, Abdul Majeed Dar's supporters kept
swelling. In addition to the expelled commanders, the Abdul
Majeed Dar group attracted such commanders as Tufail Altaf
Butt, Almas Rizwan, Nadeem Usmani Dr. Riaz, Javed Ahmed
Kar, Ajmal Khan, Majid Jehangir, Umar Irfani, Umar Muslim,
Naeeem Malik, Manzoor Ahmed Baba, Ziaul Islam, and Mo-
hammad Shafi, who died in November 2002. The commanders
who supported Salahuddin included Khan Sahib of Ashm, Im-
tiaz Alam, Ghulam Rasul Dar, Mehboobul Haq, Amir Sahib,
Tahir Ejaz, Shahidul Islam, Mubarak Shah, and Babar Sahib.
In November 2002 (Ramadan 1), Hizbul Mujahideen also ex-
pelled Tufail Altaf Butt, Almas Rizwan, and Nadeem Usmani.

60. Interview with Khursheed Ahmed, alias Asad Yazdani, April
21, 2004, Rawalpindi.

61. Interview with Khursheed Ahmed, alias Asad Yazdani, April
21, 2004, Rawalpindi. Yazdani told me he paid 40,000 rupees
to an agent in New Delhi for the forged passport.

62. Interview with Khursheed Ahmed, alias Asad Yazdani, April
21, 2004, Rawalpindi: At that time, he was thinking of consulting Kashmiri leaders like Dr. Ayub Thakur, Ghulam Nabi Fai,
Mushtaq Geelani, Nazeer Geelani, Majid Trumbo from Sopur,
Lord Nazir Ahmed, and the Hurryyat Conference leaders.

63. The ISI investigating team included Brig Riaz or Haji Farooq, Brig Shuaib or Brig Mir, Col Zaka or Col Chaudhary, and Col Zubair.

64. They included Asad Yazdai, Almas Rizwan, Nadeem Usmani, Majid Jehangir, Ajmal Khan, Umar Irfani, Malik Naeem, as well as thirty-two midlevel fighters.

65. Interview with Javed Ahmed Bhat alias Ajmal Khan, June 9, 2003.

66. Interview with Ghulam Rasool Dar, August 1, 2003. Ghulam Rasool Dar was a very secretive person. He had revealed little in his previous two interviews with me. He called me for this revealing interview only when, to use his own words, he "was convinced that [he] was going to embrace martyrdom."

67. *Jihad-I-Kashmir,* July 16–31, 2004.

68. *Jihad-I-Kashmir,* June 1–15, 2004.

CHAPTER EIGHT

1. Farooq Rehmani of the Peoples League became its chairman and Azam Inquilabi of the Mahaz-i-Azadi the Secretary General: Ashraf Saraf (later Ghulam Mohammad Safi) represented Jamat-i-Islami, Ghulam Qadir Wani represented Islamic Students League (Shakeel Bakhshi), Ziaud Din Bokhari represented the Muslim League (Mushtaqul Islam), Dr. Mushtaq Ahmed (brother in law of Asiya Andrabi) represented Mahaz-i-Islami (Inayatullah Andrabi).

2. Interview with Ashraf Saraf, August 9, 2001, Islamabad.

3. Ahmed Rashid, "Playing with Fire," *The Herald,* June 1993, p. 62.

4. Hassan Abbas, *Pakistan's Drift into Extremism: Allah, the Army and America's War on Terror*, Pentagon Press, New Delhi, 2005, p. 148.

5. Aamer Ahmed Khan, "Crackdown in Peshawar," *The Herald*, August 1993, p. 55.

6. The alliance was to comprise, in addition to the Tehreek-i-Hurryyat-i-Kashmir components, Awami Action Committee, Jamat-i-Islami of Indian-controlled Jammu and Kashmir, Ittehadul Muslimeen, Peoples Conference, Jamiat Ahle Hadees, Muslim Conference, Anjuman Tableeghul Islam, Jamat-i-Hamadania, Peoples League, Jamiat Ulamae Islam Kashmir, Bazme Tauheed, Anjuman-i-Shari Shian, Anjuman Auqaf Jama Masjid, Umat-i-Islamia, Liberation Council, Muslim Khawateen Markaz, Political Conference, Human Rights Committee, Kashmir Bar Association, Basic Rights Committee, and both factions of the Employees and Workers Confederation.

7. The members of the committee included former Chief Justice Mufti Bahaudin Farooqi, president of the Kashmir Bar Association, Mian Abdul Qayyoom, Nazir Ahmed Rongha, Pir Hafeezullah Makhdoomi, Shahidul Islam, Shabir Siddiqui, and Firdous Asmi. See Sati Sahni.

8. They included the Hizbul Mujahideen, the JKLF, al-Jihad, al-Umar Mujahideen, Ikhwanul Muslimeen, al-Burq, and Operation Balakotee. Later, and separately, the ISL also offered to cooperate.

9. As quoted in Sati Sahni, *Kashmir Underground*, Har-Anand Publications PVT LTD, New Delhi, 1999, p. 68.

10. *The Herald*, April 1995, p. 62.

11. The two travelled together and rarely missed an opportunity to participate in UN events until their deaths. Andrabi was murdered by an unknown gunmen; Bhat died of an illness in

March 2009.

12. Interview with Abdur Rafey, July 11, 2001, Muzaffarabad.

13. Sati Sahni, *Kashmir Underground*, Har-Anand Publications PVT LTD, New Delhi, 1999, p. 76.

14. Praveen Swamy, "An Uncertain Game Plan," *Frontline*, December 24, 1999, p. 50.

15. Praveen Swamy "Attack on Secularism," *Frontline*, April 18, 1997.

16. Sati Sahni, *Kashmir Underground*, Har-Anand Publications PVT LTD, New Delhi, 1999, p. 78.

17. *Indian Express*, November 6, 1999, as quoted in *Frontline*, December 24, 1999.

18. *Hindustan Times*, as quoted in *The News*, May 8, 2000.

19. NNI dispatch, *The News*, November 19, 2000.

20. See Taimur Siddiqui's interview with Abdul Ghani Lone in *Newsline*, January 2001, p. 49.

21. *Greater Kashmir*, as quoted in Reuters dispatch, *The News*, January 6, 2001.

22. AFP dispatch, reprinted in *The News*, April 17, 2001.

23. AFP dispatch, reprinted in *The News*, April 17, 2001.

24. Iftikhar Gilani, "APHC Leaders Want to Reject Indian Offer," *The Nation*, April 25, 2001.

25. Reuters dispatch, *The News*, April 25, 2001.

26. AFP dispatch, *The News*, April 26, 2001.

27. AFP dispatch, *The News*, April 27, 2001.

28. AFP dispatch, *The News*, May 1, 2001.

29. AP dispatch, *The News*, May 17, 2001.

30. AFP dispatch, *The News*, May 29, 2001

31. AFP dispatch, *The News*, November 3, 2001.

32. AFP dispatch, November 13, 2001.

33. AFP dispatch, *The News*, April 25, 2002.

34. AFP dispatch, *The News*, April 28, 2002.
35. NNI dispatch, *The News*, June 17, 2002.
36. The members of the committee included veteran jurist Fali Nariman, former law minister Shanti Bhushan, former secretary in the ministry of external affairs V.K. Grover, *Asian Age* editor M. J. Akbar, *Times of India* editor Dileep Padgaonkar, and Supreme Court lawyer Ashok Bhan. Another member, Javeed Laiq, joined the Kashmir Committee in November 2002.
37. AFP dispatch, *The News*, September 9, 2002.
38. *The News*, February 24, 2003.
39. SANA dispatch, *The News*, August 7, 2002.
40. AFP dispatch, *The News*, July 6, 2003
41. AFP dispatch, *The News*, July 14, 2003.
42. AFP dispatch, *The News*, August 21, 2003.
43. They also formed a five-member committee to elect a new chairman of the group and write the constitution. Musarat Alam was appointed chairman of the committee and other members included Agha Syed Hasan Budgami, Firdous Ahmed Shah, Ghulam Mohammad Hubby, and Ghulam Mohammad Sumji. They also agreed that the best solution to the Kashmir issue was the implementation of the UN resolutions. The group formally nominated Geelani as their chairman on September 15, 2003.
44. Early supporters of Geelani included: Jammu and Kashmir National Front chairman Nayeem Ahmed Khan; the Muslim Conference's Ghulam Mohammad Soomji; Peoples Conference's Ghulam Mohammad Hubby and Ghulam Ahmed Gulzar; Jammu and Kashmir Muslim League's Musarat Alam; Democratic Political Movement acting president Bashir Ahmed Andrabi and chairman Firdous Ahmed Shah; Agha Syed Hasan Budgami headed by Anjuman-i-Sharyi Shian; Jammu and

Kashmir Peoples Freedom League headed by Nazir Ahmed Payami; Itehadul Muslimeen headed by Syed Muzaffar Hussain Rizvi; Peoples Movement Chairman Ghulam Ahmed Mir; Jammu and Kashmir Freedom Movement's Saadullah Tantray; Mass Movement Fareeda Bhenji and Saleem Zargar; and Muslim Khawateen's Markaz Yasmeen Raja.

45. PTI dispatch, July 18; and PTI dispatch, August 2, 2004.
46. PTI dispatch, August 7, 2004.
47. Jawed Naqvi "Delhi Accepts APHC Offer for Dialogue," *Dawn*, November 22, 2003.
48. Drawn from a Sana dispatch.
49. Reuters dispatch, *The News*, January 21, 2004.
50. *The News*, January 24, 2004.
51. AP dispatch, *The News*, February 19, 2004.
52. *The News*, May 21, 2004.
53. AFP dispatch, *The News*, May 31, 2004.
54. *The News*, November 1, 2004.
55. AFP dispatch, *The News*, November 1, 2004.